Baby,
Unplugged

Baby, Unplugged

One Mother's Search for Balance, Reason, and Sanity in the Digital Age

Sophie Brickman

HarperOne
An Imprint of HarperCollinsPublishers

HarperCollins books may be purchased for educational, business, or sales promotional use. For information, please email the Special Markets Department at SPsales@harpercollins.com.

FIRST EDITION

Library of Congress Cataloging-in-Publication Data is available upon request.

ISBN 978-0-06-296648-3

21 22 23 24 25   LSC   10 9 8 7 6 5 4 3 2 1

For Ella and Charlotte

Contents

Contents

Introduction

The room is still dark when I hear Ella's feet padding into our room, so I know well before she announces it herself that the clock has failed. Again. "Mama, the clock isn't green, but I'm not tired anymore!" she crows.

Great.

After a beat, she climbs up on the bed, opens my eyelid with a chubby finger, peers down, and asks something she's clearly been mulling for the previous eleven hours: "When I get older and marry Daddy, will we be twins?" Dave groans, rolls over, and puts a pillow over his head. He's technically within his rights—he did do the 3:00 a.m. bottle with the baby—but tackling Ella's Zen Kōan–esque queries takes the focus afforded by, at minimum, a full ten hours of uninterrupted sleep. On six hours of interrupted shut-eye, it's near impossible.

That damn clock. It's worked with every other child I know. The premise is simple: it turns green when you're allowed to get out of bed. Jonah, Max, Nora—all friends' kids, all different temperaments, all subservient disciples of the clock. Ella? Not so much. Early one morning when I was uncomfortably pregnant with her little sister (now snuffling in the bassinet beside our bed), I couldn't sleep and watched Ella's whole wake-up routine on my phone, which streamed live footage from the high-tech monitor in her room. She sat up, looked at the clock for a few seconds, went over to bang its buttons, then, when it didn't turn green, hurled off her diaper and marched out of the frame and into my room.

I check my phone. Another fifty minutes until the sun rises. So I take a deep breath and tell her what I've told her the previous three days: we'll wait for the clock to turn green *together*. I know this is idiotic. But I'm so tired, and my defenses so low, I can see only two other options that will keep my three-year-old quiet: (1) starting the day before it's light outside, which is soul crushing, or (2) sticking her in front of the television or smartphone, which I've vowed never to do, because every article on my social media feed has told me that screen time will make her unhappy, dumb, emotionally distant, predisposed to heart conditions, and as socially adjusted as Robert Durst.

So back into her room we go, and I lie on the floor in the fetal position, demonstrating how to pray at the altar of the OK to Wake! clock. She putters around making castles out of Magna-Tiles and keeping a close eye on me. I've tried the "I just need to get a glass of water" escape before, so she's on high alert. Anytime I so much as shift positions, my pint-size martinet barks, "The clock is not green!"—she's not that into contractions, which makes her sentences sound particularly formal these days. So we wait. And as we wait, I wonder if there are other parents out there, maybe across town, or on the other side of the country, or around the world, all of us lying on the ground dutifully waiting for the almighty clock to set us free as our children go about their days. I'm sure there are. I wish I'd snuck my phone in with me, so I could scroll through entries on my Facebook group for mothers. Surely one of the other thirty-eight thousand strangers who occasionally give me advice could offer some help or, at the very least, commiserate. But no, my phone is covered in burp cloths on my bedside table, so I'm left with my own vacuous thoughts, which soon revolve around what newborn-specific item I'll need to purchase that day. Baby Charlotte's been scratching herself. At some point, I'm going to have to give the world's tiniest manicure, and before I do, I need to procure the world's tiniest emery board. All hail Amazon.

An eternity later, the clock turns green. The digital display shows a little friendly dance of lines and dots. Elated, I yelp, "Ella, it's green, it's green, look!" But she's busy conducting an intense checkup on Willy-up, her unicorn, the clock now a distant memory. "Mama," she says, throwing a hand behind her, not even making eye contact. "Can you hand me the Benadryl? Willy-up's fever is twenty-twenty-eighteen."

Before Baby Charlotte was born, Dave handled the predawn wake-ups. He'd take Ella downstairs and, after numerous books and Magna-Tile castles and checkups, guiltlessly plop her in front of a few minutes of *Mister Rogers' Neighborhood*. Or let her swipe through some of the thirty thousand photos on his phone, the vast majority of her. It wasn't like he spent the entire morning with her parked in front of a screen. But it was inevitable that when I waddled in, instead of coming upon them molding clay figurines, or mixing the dough for a skillet cornbread, or doing some other wholesome father-daughter bonding activity that could have been lifted from Laura Ingalls Wilder's childhood, I'd find Ella gaping at the television and him scrolling through his phone. Or he'd be gaping at Mr. Rogers and she'd be scrolling. Either combination I hated.

"We just read *Naked Mole Rat Gets Dressed* fifty times," Dave would protest as Fred Rogers buttoned up his cardigan and got out his guitar. "He was a minister, he sings songs, lighten up." It was in these moments that I started to mull the question of just how technology should be integrated into our child's life— where it could help, where it could hurt. And it was a question I was forced to confront every single day, from the moment I woke up to the moment I went to sleep. While I did my best to exist as far on the other side of the tech spectrum as possible, next to the abacus and the loom, I happened to be married to Dave, tech's greatest apologist. And our clashing worldviews came head-to-head the minute Ella arrived.

* * *

A little background on the two of us: Dave and I met the last week of college, where he majored in psychology. "I figured it'd be good for cocktail party conversations," he once told me, though his academic rigor paled in comparison to his extracurriculars, which included singing in a tuxedo-clad a capella group (see: why we met the last week of school). A few months after graduation, he quit his stable job at a huge company and decided to join a start-up that sold men's pants exclusively online. It was the early days of e-commerce. For two years, as the company honed its strategy and fashion sense, he'd come home with rejects, proudly and unironically wearing wide-wale pink corduroy pants with a fly that started at his knee or blindingly yellow chinos with one leg shorter than the other. He often looked like an actual clown. But he believed in the power of the internet to disrupt retail, and years later, the company was acquired by a huge retailer. It kick-started his love of Silicon Valley, cementing his certainty that tech could make all our lives better. He went on to join another start-up before founding his own, and now he works as a venture capitalist, spending his days meeting with and advising young guns who are dying to disrupt anything—the dentist, the parking garage—in the name of progress and convenience.

His day begins tethered to the cloud, as his Apple Watch logs data on how he slept and spits it back to him in the form of charts and graphs. He'll dutifully consult it even after an obviously terrible night, during which Charlotte and Ella trade off wake-ups until the sun rises, then glumly report through squinted eyes, "It says I slept poorly." No shit, Sherlock. Next up: testing some beta-stage product. For months after Charlotte was born, before his feet even hit the floor, he'd huff and puff into a device that uses a CO_2 sensor to determine if your body is burning fat or carbs for fuel (tagline: "Hack your metabolism"). "I'm in ketosis!" he'd gloat, as Charlotte nursed furiously beside him, chowing down on a highly caloric breakfast that went directly to her thighs. On his way to the subway, he'll walk, head bowed to Jobs, as he scrolls through Slack, Twitter, and his email, which contains a medley of futurist newsletters. His workday is a constant juggle of meetings and Twitter and Slack and back again, and he'll often return home with some patent-pending doodad that does something I don't understand, like hold crypto currency in cold storage. A neat freak living in a Manhattan apartment with no space to spare, I throw them out with gleeful abandon, and every time he realizes one of them is missing, he'll protest, "But that's going to be worth something someday!" (After verifying with friends of his in the tech industry, I can report that he's telling the truth approximately one out of every twenty times, a risk I'm willing to take.) And bedtime happens only after that Apple Watch is locked 'n' loaded on his wrist, so he can track just how poorly he's going to sleep.

As for me: try as we might to escape our lot in life, we are fated to become our parents. And when it comes to tech temperament, I am very clearly my mother's daughter. By all accounts, she's a creature from an earlier century, one in which reading and piano playing and high culture were paramount. A former professional ballerina who'd play hooky from school to travel to the library and read on her own, she remains the best-educated person I know—this despite the fact that she went straight into a ballet corps after high school. She has studied Russian for years, to be able to read Pushkin in his original language, and I remember a period in grade school when I'd open cabinet doors to find Cyrillic flash cards taped up for impromptu vocabulary tests. For her, technology is mostly an annoyance to be tolerated, an irritant of the modern world that allows her to email, but not much more. To wit: Her desktop is a mosaic of tiny Word documents, since she can't bother to figure out how to save them anywhere else (in a folder, say), she still has an AOL account, and despite being exceedingly skilled at epistolary writing, she seems unable to translate the act to the digital world—she'll often sign off "Love, Mom" somewhere in the middle of an email, then continue right on going beneath. Occasionally, she'll write me emails SCREAMING IN ALL CAPS, which remind me of telegrams of yore written by a slightly unhinged general: WATER MAIN BREAK NEAR YOUR

APARTMENT. DRINK BOTTLED WATER. LOVE, MOM. OR AM I INSANE? She got a Kindle, then left it on a plane and never replaced it. She once visited a Russian newspaper online to test out her language skills, and now, she claims, half of all her internet searches return results in Cyrillic. This she just ignores. Largely due to her, our family didn't have a working television until I was about ten years old, which I later realized was acutely hypocritical, since for years my father worked in television.

Blessedly, he complemented her and did his best to keep us in this century. He attended Brooklyn Technical High School to appease his father, an immigrant who wanted his son to acquire some marketable skills, like being able to rewire a faulty television set. But as a naturally skilled musician who traveled each weekend from his home in Brooklyn to Washington Square Park to play the banjo and sing folk songs, he didn't exactly fit in. At school, he was such a nerd that the Italian guys in the automobile course, "with grease stains on their lunch bags," as he describes them, used to mess with him by bending his T-square so no two lines were ever parallel in mechanical drawing class. But even though he went on to a career in the arts, he's always been on the cutting edge of tech. A born tinkerer who used to take apart and then reassemble his radio as a kid, he installed a Zack Morris mobile phone in the family car when they first became available, and I was among the first kids in my middle school to have home internet access—we had a 14.4 kilobits/second dial-up modem that connected through our landline, making that mechanical yodel my children will never be able to identify.

So family history seems to be repeating itself with me, my mother's daughter, marrying a more modern version of my father.

Whereas Dave's day begins tethered to the cloud, I do my best not to strap any tech device to my body. A fear of unseen molecules penetrating my skin started back in grade school when I was told that standing too close to the microwave could hurt my ovaries, and I haven't been able to kick it. I can't focus when reading on a screen for longer than a few minutes. I prefer to sit down with the newspaper in my hands and turn actual pages. I subscribe to print versions of magazines and still go to the library for books. After graduating from college and accepting a job at a nonprofit where I spent much of my day emailing colleagues who sat a few feet away, I decided that office life wasn't for me, attended culinary school in the evenings, and ended up quitting my job to join the line at an upscale Manhattan restaurant. I'd wake up before dawn and spend hours chopping vegetables in a windowless kitchen, prepping for the lunch rush, then whipping up plates of lamb ragú and carrot risotto for the business elite. I thrived on the energy, the little choreographed dance we cooks did as plates whipped from our stations to the pass, the physicality of it, the camaraderie; I found the same camaraderie, the same energy, the same pressure, in the newsroom of the *San Francisco Chronicle* and later at a food magazine in New York City. When I was on staff at *Chronicle*'s food desk, the paper still was home to veteran metro reporters who wore suspenders and tasseled loafers to work each day, regaling us young'ns with stories of a pre-iPhone world, when they'd feverishly call in copy to the main desk from a payphone to be written up for the evening edition. I glamorized those days, and still do. In fact, I'm such a reluctant adopter of new forms of technical communication that, at the much more tech-savvy magazine where I was most recently a staffer, I simply ignored the invitation to the Slack channel. Nobody seemed to notice.

Dave often teases me that I was born in the wrong century, that I'd be happier writing with a quill pen by candlelight. And I don't entirely disagree. But for years, the clash over tech didn't result in more than the occasional quibble. Then we had Ella.

Having kids turns up your convictions to an 11—at least initially, before the reality of child-rearing hits and all your belief systems go out the window, because most first-time parents have no clue how to raise a human being and spend their days guessing. And can you really develop a codified parenting philosophy on three hours' sleep? But in the beginning, your convictions fire on all cylinders.

As in: Ever on brand, Dave subscribed to the paleo diet when I was pregnant and told me that he'd die before a graham cracker, that mass-produced, sugar-packed gluten bomb, passed the lips of our untainted yet-to-be-born spawn. He stuck to this until Ella was one year old. She managed to procure a Teddy Graham from a friend at the playground and grinned so widely that he caved immediately. "But look how happy she is!" he said, sheepishly handing her another.

I was fine with her eating crackers. What I didn't want was to have her childhood saturated with the tech that infiltrated my own life, however hypocritical my hesitations and protestations. Clutching my phone in my pocket, I bit my tongue when nursing friends paused between sides to tap on an app that logged information about left boob versus right boob production. I cringed when I saw toddlers blindly swiping phones in the checkout line at the supermarket or striking a pose for photos before they could tie their shoes. I'd read somewhere that Finnish kids run free in the forest amongst the willows until they're seven. That seemed like an appealing baseline. Dave, on the other hand, felt strongly that tech could improve everything, if implemented correctly. Child-rearing was no exception.

The disagreements started immediately. A few days after Ella was born, Dave brought home something called an Owlet Smart Sock. It looked like a tiny neon Grecian sandal, which, affixed to her foot, monitored her heart rate, pinging the phone with data and blaring loudly if her heart rate plummeted. At my protestations—Sensors! Next to her baby skin!—he made the compelling case that we'd never taken care of a child before and didn't want her to die. Well, sure. So one evening before bed, on it went, registering a reassuring blood oxygen level of 98 percent. I drifted off, musing about the missing 2 percent. And then: A few hours later, a digitized version of "Hush Little Baby" blared in our tiny one-bedroom. I assumed we were headed to the emergency room. But no, Ella was breathing fine, her heart chugging along, as hearts do in all but the wildest of circumstances. The thing had just lost connection to our shoddy Wi-Fi and was letting us know in its ear-splitting way. Deep down, I knew that had it worked seamlessly, I would have strapped it onto her little body until she went off to college. The promise, the pull of the data, was too strong to escape. But, twenty new gray hairs later, I called our pediatrician. He confirmed that if her vital signs needed monitoring, he wouldn't have released her from the hospital. I threw the thing into the far depths of a closet.

When we moved into a larger apartment, Dave arrived with a Nest home-security system, which many a helicopter parent has co-opted as a baby monitor. It livestreams crisp HD video to your phone, so you can watch your child sleep and burp and cry wherever you are. (If you're a step more Big Brother than we are, you can choose to record everything, too.) The morning I went back to work, leaving Ella with a nanny who soon became an important part of our family, I kissed Ella goodbye, took the subway to the office, settled in at my desk, then popped open the app and found myself watching hours of her sleeping and burping and crying, lured, against my better interests, into keeping track of her every move. I couldn't escape the pull. But Dave insisted on keeping the Nest up, so I decided to delete the app and use an old-fashioned audio monitor instead, our dual monitoring systems transforming our nursery into baby mission control.

The creeping infiltration of technology began before she was even born, and I allowed it, even embraced it. Someone invited me to a Facebook group of mothers when I was thirty-eight weeks pregnant, and within days, I was checking the group five times a day, sometimes to seek out answers to questions—*To pacifier or not to pacifier?*—but more often just to see what my new non-real friends were up to. This, despite the fact that I could barely keep in touch with my actual friends. The moment Ella arrived, the Internet Marketing Gods knew I'd become a mother. Suddenly, ads for BPA-free straws were marching in lockstep behind me around the internet, which led me to spend hours reading reviews of different BPA-free straws on Amazon. If America is the land where the consumer is king, its capital city is Parentville.

So much data was zinging at me and at Ella, so many opinions, so much information, that I had no idea what my convictions were, or if I'd ever even had any. Why did I equate Laura Ingalls Wilder with wholesomeness? Didn't people keep dying of diphtheria on the range? But on we zinged, from one month to the next, barely having time to react to one form of tech before we were on to the next, until I realized that any intuition I might have held about what was right for my own kid was shot. I yearned, diphtheria aside, to be more like Ma. Not only did she know how to make lard cakes amidst the wildflowers on the prairie, she wasn't nervous if her three little girls spent all day making rag dolls and not learning how to read on an educational app. And bedtime was never a struggle to be hacked, because the girls were so tired after their days trying to catch gophers and prairie dogs that they just said their prayers and went to sleep. Why couldn't I tap into the same sort of reassuring, steadfast maternal instinct I seemed certain my ancestors had in their blood?

I had no real time to ponder why I felt icky about it all, but I knew something was off. As Ella grew into a crawler, then a walker, it didn't *seem* good that she also developed the ability to swipe away a text message that popped up on my phone or that she'd stop what she was doing and crow "Cheese!" when I held the phone up at a particular angle. The digitally enhanced plush dog someone got her, which vowed to teach her the ABCs at one touch of a paw, surely wasn't as enriching as a plain set of wooden blocks . . . or was it? Putting her in front of a screen, some headlines blared, would forever ruin her. Other more touchy-feely articles said that parents were being too hard on themselves, that we should give ourselves a break. But weren't we the generation in which everyone got a part in the school play? Parenting is difficult. Should we be cutting ourselves slack and using technology to ease our parental burdens, or should we toughen up?

* * *

Cut to: Charlotte's birth. My mindless visits to social media start up again. So, too, do the passive data tracking, the hours sunk scrolling Amazon reviews for the perfect swaddle, the impromptu photo shoots of Charlotte's fingernail beds. It all comes to a head one fall day when she's about four months old and I attend the Good Housekeeping Institute's parenting summit (#wearefamily) at Hearst Tower. An editor at another Hearst publication, I am starting to think more critically about the child-related technology I use at home, and on the forty-fourth floor of the tower, overlooking Central Park and the New York City skyline, is a room full of people discussing just that intersection.

I arrive as Dr. Harvey Karp, speaking to a captivated audience, says, "There never was a mother, a father, and a baby. That structure is totally artificial. There were aunts, uncles, grandparents. You're all doing the work that no mothers or fathers had to do in the past."

For this group—largely composed of mothers who are entrepreneurs, a social subset of the world that I learn, cringingly, is referred to as *mompreneurs*—it's a particularly appealing message, met with nods and grunts. And it was something Karp told me, almost verbatim, when I had interviewed him on the phone months ago, seven months pregnant with Charlotte and gearing up for our new strategy of man-to-man defense. He has his shtick down: We're overburdened, it's unnatural, and we need another family member in the house to help with newborns, which is something humans had for millennia. Enter the SNOO, Karp's $1,300 smart bassinet, which adjusts its rocking and white noise to soothe fussy babies, who get straitjacketed into the thing via a swaddle called a Sleepea. The object itself is beautiful, something straight out of Jony Ive's dreams, and actualizes, in furniture form, the lessons from Karp's bestselling book, *The Happiest Baby on the Block*. The book, a favorite of new parents, posits that since human babies leave the womb earlier than other mammal babies—due to the size of their brains and the mother's comparatively narrow birth canal—replicating the environment of the uterus for the first few months of their lives is a simple way to activate their natural sleep reflex. It's loud in there, kind of like being in a washing machine, which is why so many of us were strapped into car seats and driven around the block as infants. The SNOO, essentially, allows you to replicate that without leaving your bed.

"We created a baby bed that's really your older sister," he tells the room, then cites a statistic—which I later am unable to confirm—that in Canada, despite getting up to a year of maternity leave, women report higher postpartum depression rates than in the United States. The implication?

"It's hard to be home alone with a child," he says. Rachel Rothman, Good Housekeeping Institute's chief technologist, who's almost nine months pregnant and has two daughters under three years old at home, snorts in agreement. As for the price point, Karp points out that through the rental program, you can have one in your house for around four dollars per day.

"It's a Starbucks coffee," he quips. But instead of paying for caffeine, you're essentially paying for its opposite.

Karp had sent the SNOO to me for a free trial a few weeks after Charlotte was born, which I accepted under the guise of research. We arrived home one day to find an enormous package on our doorstep. I'd never seen Dave unpack anything as quickly. I blinked and there was Charlotte, strapped in and ready to go. As she began to cry, the slow back-and-forth motion of the bassinet sped up, jiggling her little body faster and faster, like she was about to launch from Cape Canaveral. Stunned, she grew silent and, moments later, fell asleep. I later learned that if the machine's attempts to soothe go rebuffed for long enough, it's programmed to shut off and alert the parents to enter the ring again, most likely because their little one is hungry. ("There's nothing more depressing than the sound of the SNOO powering down," my sleep-deprived, SNOO-evangelist, new-parent friend told me.) But for Charlotte, the machine never shut off. It just . . . worked.

For months, I had a love-hate relationship with the thing. It felt, in a sense, both too *Fifth Element* and too royal to outsource rocking to a machine. Who the hell was I to hand off my child the minute she was in distress? Didn't the snuggling, the rocking, the shushing, come with the territory of being a parent? Weren't all those things steps on a path toward building a loving, caring, trusting relationship with your new human?

"Part of the process of raising a child is to make that child feel emotionally secure. And being there for your baby even when it's not convenient for you is kind of important," Dr. Rachel Moon confirmed when I called her after the SNOO arrived. Our conversation turned into a confession of sorts, in which I came clean about plugging Charlotte in every now and again, and how it made me feel ashamed. A practicing pediatrician for thirty years, Moon is the division head of general pediatrics at the University of Virginia and serves on the American Academy of Pediatrics' task force on SIDS. As for the SNOO and various other tech gadgets? "It diminishes the time you get to bond with your baby, and babies are smarter than we give them credit for."

I'm sure Karp would agree that it's preferable to hand off a child to a person, evolutionarily programmed to snuggle, and not a machine, algorithmically programmed to gently shake. This, sans SNOO, I did for Ella's first four months, which I was lucky enough to spend mostly at my parents' house a few blocks away.

Karp's point is that you often don't live just a few blocks from your parents; you often don't have the village you so desperately need during those critical first few months. There often isn't another human there with you—so why not let a machine step in? But this begs the bigger question, which came into sharp focus that afternoon as various panel speakers took the stage touting the benefits of a diaper that can ping your phone when a child needs a change or a social networking site that connects far-flung mothers: Why on earth isn't there another human there with you?

If we had the parental leaves we deserve, if we had the societal support—not just subsidized day care but also workplaces that sanctify the importance of the first year after birth, and a culture that values childcare as much as it does stock returns—we might not be forced to turn to a machine to do the loving and caretaking that, for centuries, fell to an extended family, to a village of caring individuals. I am privileged enough to have the means to afford a stand-in mother to stay at home with my children when I return to work, but my wonderful nanny has a nine-year-old daughter of her own, whom she rushes home to after the end of a long day caring for and loving someone else's daughters. With my parents a few blocks uptown, ready to pitch in for weekend babysitting and sleepovers, we have one of the better modern villages I've seen. But it's also monstrously complicated. I look, with envy, at my friend who moved to France and has a state-sponsored crèche a few blocks from her house, where she started dropping off Baby George when he was only a few months old. There, he was supervised by trained professionals, often septuagenarians who were grandmothers themselves, while my friend was able to spend a few guilt- and worry-free hours on herself. Sans crèche, we are encouraged to outsource large parts of our village to the cloud.

And of course, the tech market has us parents by the jugular—not only the tech that bills itself as a stand-in support system but the tech that purports to make our children smarter, more success-ful, more resilient. *Forbes* marked the 2019 US babytech market to be worth almost $46 billion; since 2013, investors have thrown half a billion dollars into funding companies in a space that, just ten years ago, was virtually nonexistent. From childhood, we've been spoon-fed the notion that we can buy our way toward a bet-ter life, be that by purchasing the right lipstick color or upgrading our iPhones to the latest model. If we can swing it, why not buy our way to a better child? There are enriching apps, enriching toys, enriching Playmobils, all playing into a widespread parental anxiety that children might be falling behind. And the truth of our increasingly unequal society is that the vast majority of par-ents are facing the very real prospect that their kids were *born* behind. Promised a way to level the playing field, what parent wouldn't sit up and start paying attention?

During a break between panels, as people swarm Karp for photo ops, I wonder if there's real innovation in what Silicon Valley is pumping out or just a lot of high-tech wrapping around questionable products. While the majority of this technology is marketed and available only to parents who have $1,300 to spare on a bassinet, much of what is expensive now—sensors, cameras—will become smaller and cheaper in time, eventually making these technological enhancements available to nearly any parent who wants them. When the doodads and trackers be-come affordable to most of us, should we avail ourselves of them, or run kicking and screaming away from that dystopian night toward the safe, analog space that feels, instinctually, more in line with being a loving and caring parent? The stakes couldn't be higher: on the line is not just parental sanity and billions of dollars but the future success of the next generation. It seems like forces from on high are putting on a vast smoke-and-mirrors show for us—*Look over here, at this shiny new gadget, and worry about whether or not you should use it on your kid, and don't look over there, where the American social safety net has been lit on fire and left to smolder.*

I take the elevator forty-three floors down, using the spare minute to pop into my Amazon app and reorder the size 2 diapers I know Charlotte needs. When implemented correctly, I know there is value in introducing some technology into the nursery—I am just not sure what the parameters should be. Tech can be helpful, even magical. The SNOO, love it or hate it, worked with Charlotte. I got a few more hours of rest, a few more slots in the day with my hands free. E-commerce means I don't have to spend my time schlepping an infant and a three-year-old to multiple stores. One of technology's greatest promises is that it can shoulder annoying, routinized tasks—in the realm of babies, monitoring them, tracking their weight, or rocking them—and make life a little more convenient and efficient. But how much convenience and efficiency is too much? How much friction do parents need in their lives to ensure that their relationships with their children are rich, full, and loving but not tedious and monotonous? The image we have in our minds of parenting young children—of holding them and rocking them to sleep, of tending to boo-boos and tucking them into bed at night—none of it involves a flashing, beeping, pulsing piece of technology that purports to simplify your life. To borrow a word from Silicon Valley, can you *disrupt* your nursery and everything in it—including the baby itself? And if you can, should you?

* * *

Dinnertime has become like the Oslo Accords, so that night, as Charlotte jiggles away in her SNOO, Ella watches an episode of preschool TV in exchange for eating her broccoli while Dave Slacks with a work colleague. Our apartment is so far from a Scandinavian forest, a willow would spontaneously combust the minute it stepped into the lobby.

After Ella goes to bed, I declare a state of emergency. Parenting rights and wrongs are often fickle, changing every generation, sometimes multiple times within each generation. My mother had been given formula; I nursed. I'd been put on my tummy to sleep; Ella and Charlotte, on their backs. Maybe their kids will sleep in zero gravity pods in a space station and eat keto pellets. But with a second unblemished kid living in our house now, it feels urgent that we determine a value system for how to raise kids in a tech-saturated modern world.

And we have to do it quickly, not just so I can regain whatever sense of maternal instinct I feel sure is deep down inside me being battered by gadgets and data. We have to do it for the girls. In an insomnia-driven research session, I'd recently found myself up at 3:00 a.m. trying to figure out what was happening in Ella's brain that allowed her to hear "I'm calling the shots in this house" (uttered by me one time after she demanded a ninth book before bed) and, three days later, announce, "Mama, tonight, *I'm* calling the shots!" They are sponges, but *why?* I learn that just as political wonks, thanks to FDR, track a president's first hundred days, early child researchers talk about the first thousand days of a child's neural development, which starts in utero and during which time the brain grows from 333 grams, on average, to 999 grams. As it expands, the brain forms myriad connections, called synapses, between its neurons. We're born with 2,500 for each neuron; by our third birthday, this number has exploded to 15,000. These first few years are critical to a kid's development, and with the increasing ubiquity of tech in our household, I don't want Baby Charlotte's synapses to be short-circuited. Ella's just three—her synapses seem fine to me, but if I've mistakenly screwed them up, we still have a slim window of opportunity to repair them.

So, once Charlotte falls asleep, I get out a pen and paper and make a list of all the technology that I have mindlessly let saturate my life for Ella's first three years—the tech that leaves me feeling unsure of my maternal instinct, the tech that I know, having done this with Ella, is coming down the pike again. In her first year, I'll have to grapple with:

- the intense nursery monitoring systems and the overwhelming amounts of data they spew to my phone, complete with charts and graphs that rival MSNBC's on election night;
- the inevitable hours spent on social media mothers' groups, scrolling in rhythm while my breast pump wheezes beside me, grappling with the questionable support I get from a virtual village while I all but ignore my actual friends;
- the endless baby photographs that clog up my phone, starting from the hospital, and then the questions of whether and how to share them; and
- the middle-of-the-night e-commerce binges that deliver hyperspecific newborn items to my doorstep the next day, carbon emissions guilt notwithstanding.

And once Charlotte is able to behave less like a burrito and more like a baby, I'll be faced with all the tech that will target her, not me—the stuff I'm just starting to get a handle on with Ella:

- the numerous toys that chirp and yip and promise to get her into an Ivy League college; and then,
- that modern-day parental minefield: screens—the programs watched on them, the apps played on them, the books read on them.

I'm not a tech expert, but I've been a reporter for years and know how to find the people who know more than I do about a given topic. I'm naturally curious and much prefer to be asking the questions than answering them, which is why a career in journalism was such a good fit. When I started at the food desk in San Francisco, I delighted in spending my days calling up chefs to get ideas of what to do with the fourteen million radishes that arrived with my CSA order or researching deep in the *Chronicle*'s cookbook library, up a rickety set of stairs and packed with books with copyright dates in the 1940s. Maybe if I could take this meta-expertise, I reasoned—the expertise to get to the experts—I could separate the signal from the noise, figure out what tech was really wonderful and what was junk. And in doing so, maybe I could save my fellow parents unnecessary angst, answer burning questions, help them find their gut in the midst of all the swirling information—or, at the very least, give them ammunition with which to tell their tech-loving spouses that strapping Owlet Smart Socks on their children is as nurturing as ditching vitamin D drops, slathering their babies in coconut oil, and setting them outside to broil in the sun.

The first few years are when parents are most vulnerable,

most sleep deprived, and most unsure of themselves, and the world of babytech is vast and amorphous. So I decide to focus only on the parent- and child-related technology that targets the preschool set, meaning birth to about four years old. Another book could be written about the myriad apps and technologies trying to help women conceive, but those don't fall in my bucket. Neither do technologies that existed, in various forms, five or so years ago. Ella's OK to Wake! clock is, yes, technically tech. But it isn't smart, it doesn't utilize the cloud, it doesn't use metrics to help me algorithmically program Ella to fall asleep at a certain time. So that is set aside. In my crosshairs is the technology that is taking advantage of our new, always-connected-to-the-cloud world, where data is paramount and the promise of simplicity just one click away.

I know that specific technology will change, likely even as I'm reporting on it, but the trends aren't going anywhere. In a world where tech pummels you with data you aren't sure you need, where more is always better, and where you can outsource parenting to robots—*Have this machine rock your kid for you; have that screen teach your kid for you*—when is the data actually useful? When is outsourcing acceptable? Does the dictum "everything in moderation" pertain to technology, or, as I suspect, are there science-backed discoveries that can help shape my household's tech parameters?

As I am writing this list, sitting on my desk is the book *The Gardener and the Carpenter*, written by lauded developmental psychologist Alison Gopnik. At her lab in Berkeley, she conducts studies to determine what goes on inside babies' minds and how they "create intuitive theories about the world, other people, and themselves," as her website states. It's heady stuff—

read her books and you'll find yourself wrestling with concepts like Bayesian inference, free will, and theory of mind, all in relation to a tiny individual whose preferred pastime is gumming a rattle—but that's to be expected when you learn that Gopnik is the older sister of Adam (of *The New Yorker*) and Blake (art critic for the *New York Times*) and three other equally impressive Gopniks. I had picked up her book after hearing her on a number of podcasts; she is reassuring, whip smart, and the perfect companion on maternity-leave walks in the park.

"It is very difficult to find any reliable, empirical relation between the small variations in what parents do—the variations that are the focus of parenting—and the resulting adult traits of their children," she writes. "There is very little evidence that conscious decisions about co-sleeping or not, letting your children 'cry it out' or holding them till they fall asleep, or forcing them to do extra homework or letting them play have reliable and predictable long-term effects on who those children become. From an empirical perspective, parenting is a mug's game."

The book's central thesis is that many modern-day parents view their role as a shaper of children, à la carpentry—you carve away here and there and then boom, you present the world with your perfect specimen. The way to let a kid flourish, she says, is to act like a gardener and create the right environment in which they can explore and use their eminently moldable and sponge-like brains.

That sure sounds comforting—these minute decisions of day-to-day parenting essentially don't matter as much as we think they do. But in the moment, faced with those minute decisions, Gopnik's message is often impossible to internalize. And practically speaking, if we're going to carry the gardening and carpentry metaphor forward, it's not like I want to use AI-controlled lasers to carve my children into slick, smooth, Adonis-esque specimens worthy of the sculpture gallery at the Met. But should my garden have a sprinkler in it? Or just dirt and the occasional worm?

I look over at Charlotte, grunting in her sleep. I know that being a parent to a second child will be wildly different from being a first-time one—at the very least, I am an old hand at nursing and pumping, and I am no longer overwhelmed by choices like which swaddling blanket is the best, since Charlotte will just use Ella's hand-me-downs. But the newest babytech gadgets keep hitting the market, Dave keeps bringing them home, and my news feeds continue to be overrun with articles about all the tools at my disposal which might enable me to shape a most perfect child, should I avail myself of them, or forever doom her. I pet her little head, instinctively feeling the soft indentation on top, a physical representation of how moldable she still is. I silently vow that by the time she is old enough to defy the dictates of the OK to Wake! clock, our family will have a Unified Theory of Tech. And ideally, it won't involve my lying in a fetal position on the floor of the nursery as the sun just begins to peep over the horizon, waiting for a clock to turn green.

Postscript

Four days after I finished dotting my i's and crossing my t's on a draft of this manuscript, New York governor Andrew Cuomo issued a mandatory, statewide stay-at-home order. As COVID-19 started spreading around the globe, the world heaved on its axis, the sky fell, stock markets roller-coastered, and Dave and I were faced with the prospect of months of living in lockdown in our New York City apartment with two people under the age of four while attempting to continue our day jobs, not get divorced, and procure Lysol from the outside world.

The simplest solution, as so many Facebook posts and emails amongst friends told me, was to stick the kids in front of the computer or television and cut ourselves some collective slack when it came to screen time. *Ramblin' Dan is livestreaming at 10 a.m. tomorrow!* one friend texted. *American Ballet Theatre is offering free classes at 11 a.m. on Thursdays!* my mother emailed. *Mo Willems is doing lunchtime doodles!* a third wrote in our WhatsApp chain, next to a photo of her five-year-old's surprisingly well-drawn Willems pigeon. I appreciated the resources but careened from task to task so deliriously, only stopping every now and again to check my phone for the next dose of apocalyptic news, that I could barely find time to set Ella up in front of a computer. Time seemed to constrict, anxiety formed a basis for my every day, and vacuuming became my therapy.

In the one hour each evening between when the girls fell asleep and I went to bed, after I'd exhausted myself on the news and the worry and the endless to-dos, and in an attempt to maintain a semblance of my pre-COVID self, I'd plaintively open up my book manuscript and wonder if the year-plus of reporting I'd completed just a few weeks ago would now have to be taken out to the trash, doused in a chemical that killed 99 percent of all bacteria and viruses, and lit on fire.

With the birth of my children, I'd been drawn to answer one question: When it came to technology and little kids—specifically newborns to preschoolers—what was helpful and what was harmful? Would my virtual village of far-flung Facebook friends ever come close to replicating an actual village of parents going through similar trials? The thousands of photos we took of our little ones each day—did they take us out of the moment, or help us preserve the moment? Did the baby data-tracking monitors Dave brought home from his job as a venture capitalist relieve anxiety, or provoke it? Was our addiction to e-commerce helpful and efficient, or overwhelming and inefficient? Would buying the right toys enrich our children for the better, or should they be playing make believe? And finally, was screen time—setting our kids up in front of a computer, app, or e-book—terrible no matter what, or could these digital resources be used in moderation to help us keep our sanity as parents while raising smart, successful offspring?

I selfishly feared that in addition to upending the very world, the pandemic would also upend the work I'd done. On the list of worries that parents faced, being nervous about how many photos they took of their kids likely sat way down in the fourteen gajillions, somewhere after "stop Lysoling the bananas." And parents often had no choice but to set their children up in front of the computer or television so they could get their jobs done, assuming they still had them.

But as the pandemic and stay-at-home orders dragged on, it became clear that the conclusions I'd drawn—informed by scientifically backed research about how best to utilize screens, the importance of being bored, how children develop, and how best to grow as parents alongside them—proved to be perhaps even more true in a post-COVID world than it had been in the Before Times. Everyone was forced to reevaluate his or her reliance on technology, parents particularly acutely. It wasn't just that those of us with preschool or school-age children were growing weary of juggling Zoom school schedules, of keeping little butts in seats, of cringing when our children started talking about unmuting themselves. It wasn't just that Kara Swisher, technology reporter for the *New York Times* and longtime proponent of the benefits of technology, wrote an ode to the analog world and the beauty of seeing her older sons, who were free from their phones for the first time in forever, happily making silly faces so that their new baby sister would laugh. COVID had forced us to ramp up our reliance on technology, whether to educate our kids or procure toilet paper, and as we ramped it up, we all, collectively, began to tire of it.

"I just got home from picking up Nora's laptop for kindergarten," a friend wrote on our shared WhatsApp chain a few weeks before the fall 2020 school year. "Just let that sink in." "Ughhhhhhh," one of us responded. "Sigh," wrote another.

We yearned not just for schools and in-person playdates but also for the luxury of walking outside and into a store, of seeing more than half of people's faces, of eye contact and real connection. We were starved for it. And when articles popped up saying as much, when friends started emailing with the same sentiment, it echoed something that came up in my research time and time again—children need in-person connection to thrive. And technology interrupts that. But, in our commercially driven society, technology sells.

I spent months entrenched in the disciplines of neurobiology, pediatrics, venture capital, and psychology, and it is clear to me more than ever before that there are specific, research-backed ways to thoughtfully incorporate technology into our daily lives and to evaluate the new tech that continues to rapidly hit the market. I believe my findings will give other parents, similarly confused about how best to navigate this fast-changing terrain, comfort, context, and practical advice for how to do right by our children. But after my research, I am quite a bit more skeptical of the messages that Silicon Valley and the media spew at vulnerable parents, many of which relay some version of "Let's upgrade your baby!" *Disruption* is an appealing term. It implies becoming more efficient, making things better and faster and simpler, giving something we always took for granted a second look and realizing that, at long last, it can in fact be improved. The catch is, while technology can indeed make certain parts of parenting simpler, you can't hack child-rearing, however much you may try. And, perhaps more to the point, it's not something we, as individuals and as a society, should strive to do.

My research provided me with a science-based framework to understand what I felt intuitively, before technology weaseled its way into the equation: having a child might not be efficient, might not be easily reduced to a series of inputs and outputs—*Show your child this television program, and you'll make them smarter, or more patient, or more resilient.* But what makes children thrive is simple and straightforward: love. And, as the Beatles (kinda) said, you can't buy that.

August 2020

Part One

Parentech

1

The Quantified Child

Do We Really Need This Much Baby Data?

Two days after we brought Ella home from the hospital, I found myself barreling up Amsterdam Avenue to a store in my neighborhood called Upper Breast Side. Its motto: "You bring your breasts, we've got the rest!" It was my first solo expedition outside the house, and it hadn't even occurred to me to use the spare hour to see a friend, or get a coffee, or lie on a park bench. I was like a homing pigeon, drawn toward this mammary mecca, which I'd been told would solve my most pressing problem.

Those first few days had been subsumed with working out the kinks of nursing, and in my sleepless state, everything in my apartment had started to resemble a breast—the chandelier, the cabinet pulls, the lamp finials. When I opened the store's door in search of something called Mother's Milk Tea, I entered a world where everything was breast-like by design: the bras hanging off racks, the nipple covers called Bamboobies that stacked the shelves, the sleeves of lactation cookies at the register.

Nursing had proven to be a bit of a challenge. Whenever Ella caught sight of my breast, she'd shriek, then cry inconsolably, then fall asleep, having nursed not one drop. She'd been born in the twelfth percentile for weight, a teensy little birdlike thing, and my one body part made specifically to nurture her had morphed into a wrecking ball. Whenever it was time to enter the lactose-filled battlefield, I pinned her body into position, looked down at my breast, which was a good three times the size of her head, and thought, *Oh Jesus, I better not drop that thing on you.* A few days in, my neck developed a crick from adjusting her during feeds. The lactation consultant suggested a new nursing position, wherein I'd lie on my side on the bed facing her. New problem: my lower nipple settled a good three inches above her mouth. We'd have needed some sort of pulley system to get her anywhere near proper latch position. (That some women could lie on their sides and nurse babies from their top breast seemed like sorcery.) She was losing weight, and though she'd drink from a bottle, I could never pump enough to give her a full feed. My *production*, as I now knew to call it, was abysmally low. I gave her formula—my pediatrician recommended it and I was blissfully unaware that large swaths of the population believed this was a failure that would set up Ella for all sorts of medical and emotional problems and doom our relationship from the start—but I figured that, as millennia of babies and mothers had before me, Ella and I could crack this whole nursing thing with a little help.

Which is how I ended up bringing my breasts to Upper Breast Side and telling my woes to a middle-aged earth mother behind the counter who, I knew after a glance at her ample bosom, could effortlessly feed the entire nursery ward at Mount Sinai hospital should she desire.

"I like analogies," she told me, absentmindedly squeezing a plastic stress ball shaped like a breast. "That pump you have? Yours is a Corolla. What you need is a Corvette. They both get to sixty miles per hour, but one is a whole lot smoother of a ride."

Having grown up in New York City, I know as much about cars as I do about riflery, but I understood she wanted me to shell out money for yet another pump that my insurance company wouldn't cover. I protested as much. She stared me down, squeezing the breast stress ball, uttering not a word. That night, $33-a-week down, I sat with my breasts hooked up to a rented hospital-grade model the size of a four-slice toaster and pumped a full bottle for Ella in a quarter of the time it would have taken with my Corolla. I fell asleep awash in the glow of maternal achievement. I would nourish my baby, and I would do so from my very own body.

And yet, like many women before me, I grew to despise my pump. Yes, it enabled me to spend more than four hours at a time away from my child, to go back to my job as an editor at a food magazine while knowing my kid was still getting the nutrients the American Academy of Pediatrics told me were critical in the first few months of life. But it made me feel like a cow. I hated cleaning its parts. I hated the wheezing, dying-animal sound it made when it milked me. I hated the verb form of *milk*. I hated how I had to basically get undressed to use it, and how exposed I felt as my nipples rhythmically poked through my hands-free nursing bra. When I returned to work, my boss graciously offered me his office for pump time. It was the one space, other than the bathroom or the utility closet, with a door. But milking—ugh—

with my shirt off next to the small batch whiskey he displayed for post-work drinks felt untoward. I opted, instead, to perch on the toilet twice a day.

Thankfully, I lived in the era of disruption. I started seeing articles about newfangled breast pumps, backed by (mostly) male Silicon Valley investors who'd finally come around to throwing money at ladies' problems. They saw an opportunity in reimagining the entire pumping experience, which hadn't changed significantly since the first self-operating pumps, modeled after bovine milking machines, hit the market in the 1920s. These pumps would be lighter, more discreet, quieter. Some would fit inside your bra, so you could, at least in theory, pump while giving a presentation to the board. I was intrigued, until I realized that, in these early days at least, they cost a pretty penny—hundreds of dollars in certain cases. So, tapping into the innate grifter's instinct shared by many a journalist, I pitched a story to an editor about this disruption, got an assignment, then procured a few of the new models for research purposes.

Some were, indeed, quieter. I guess I'd have felt slightly more comfortable pumping in my boss's office with the machinery nestled into my bra, though I started to resemble Wonder Woman. But the thing that struck me most about each of them was their smart features—that they were connected to apps that tracked how much milk you'd pumped and the volume produced by each side. With my old-school, insurance-subsidized pump, I'd pump for ten minutes a session. I could technically do the same with these new pumps and just use the timer, but now that the info was there, I was intrigued. Why did my left breast produce slightly less than my right, for instance? Over the course of reporting the article—during which I learned, among other things, that women founders had to jump through hoops to get funding from male VCs, who, at the time, comprised more than 90 percent of partners—I became unduly concerned with my left breast. Did I neglect her in some way, during puberty perhaps? The more I thought about it, the more I realized it was a tidbit of information I'd rather not take up space in my brain, like the lyrics to Salt-N-Pepa's "Shoop," which have been in there since third grade. And so I decided to stick with my wheezing, 1990s-style pump, which worked fine and kept my brain free of lactose-related numbers.

Then: Charlotte arrives. (She registers, I am thrilled to learn, in the ninetieth percentile for weight.) I still have my wheezing, 1990s-style pump, but learn there are many other pump 2.0 options available to mothers with means, and all of them link up to an app that milks your milk for data.

"It's a stereotypically male approach to breastfeeding," Dr. Amy Bentley, author of *Inventing Baby Food*, tells me when I reach her office at NYU a few weeks after Charlotte comes home from the hospital, and I'm in the thick of nursing conundrums. "'Let's quantify breastfeeding.' It's technically proficient, it's technically efficient, but what it is devoid of is emotion, love, cuddling, bonding, all those things we know are so important for infants to thrive." She pauses. "It's like Soylent: You're missing this broader, social, cultural, celebratory, human aspect of eating."

Her book examines, among other things, how and why breastfeeding has fallen and risen in favor over the years, and she likens today's scientific, technocratic take on nursing to the 1920s, when chemistry started to take off as a discipline. Scientists, newly able to isolate nutrients in food, turned their sights to breast milk. The upshot: formula, a literal formula of protein and calcium and fat that they developed, then kept a secret, so mothers had to come to their (mostly male) pediatricians if they wanted it.

"Previous knowledge was female centered—midwives, mothers, communities," Bentley tells me. "All of that knowledge and power gets transferred to the medical professional who happens to be male, and who has the secret formula for formula. What's going on in Silicon Valley may feel like an eleven, but a similar thing happened in the early twentieth century."

Numbers and nurturing seem like they should exist at opposite ends of the spectrum. But parent- and child-related data are pouring out of Silicon Valley at such a speedy clip that it's a wonder people don't jockey for position according to their kid's daily poop count.

My left breast's output at the 11:00 a.m. feed is just one example of the mass of Baby Charlotte–related data that I could collect every day, should I so desire. The Owlet Smart Sock could track her heart rate. The Hatch changing table could track her weight and the amount of milk she ingests each feed. Various next-level monitors could use night vision to track her sleeping patterns. They're all expensive, all cater to a particularly wealthy subset of the world, but they indicate a general trend toward data gathering that has saturated parenthood. (I once attended a panel in which a spokesperson for Pampers said that "80 percent of parents in the US track their babies, and 50 percent do it on pen and paper, but don't always know why they're doing it. They just track!") My instinct is to dismiss all of these tracking devices out of hand, mainly because I now spend at least part of each day considering my left breast's milk output, which I'm certain is using up multiple units of my very limited brain capacity. My friend who's a doctor and mother of two doesn't track a thing.

"I figure if there's something I need to track, my pediatrician will tell me to, and after the first few weeks, there's . . . nothing to track," she tells me.

But not all of us have that gumption, and it sure is hard to look away.

At Charlotte's two-month visit, when I ask our pediatrician, Dr. Yaker, if there's any real reason to track her weight gain between checkups or how much milk I'm producing each time she eats, he gives me a look. "If it makes *you* feel better, fine," he says. "I have a lot of anxious parents coming into my office. But medically? For a healthy kid, absolutely not."

As Charlotte does slow bicycles on the examining table, unaware of the onslaught of shots she's about to get, he tells me how this influx of available information and data tracking has changed his practice.

"Look, thirty years ago you'd go into the pediatrician's office and you wouldn't have known anything!" he says, plunging a syringe into Charlotte's kielbasa-like thigh and slapping on a sparkly Band-Aid half the size of her leg. Charlotte responds by opening her mouth wide and bleating out an insistent alarm. Her face turns the color of a stop sign. "Today, parents come in *with the diagnosis*. Thanks, Dr. Google!" In quick succession, Yaker dispatches the other two syringes, one in her other thigh, the third in her left tricep. "If you need to be tracking things like weight, we really wouldn't discharge the child from the hospital." He hands me Charlotte, who now looks like a demented rave-goer coming off a bad trip: half-naked, howling, covered in sparkles. "My general outlook is, you love them, you nurture them, they'll grow, they'll be happy," he says, bidding us adieu. We're supposed to see him in four weeks, for a weigh-in, but we'll be out of town. "Is there a grocery store where you're going?" he asks. "Just take her to the produce section and throw her on the scale." No app required.

* * *

Sixteen years ago, Ann Crady Weiss, founder of Hatch Baby, was a new mother. Like me, she had trouble nursing her daughter, Maya. And, like me, as her daughter lost weight, her pediatrician recommended she supplement with formula. Unlike me, she borrowed a scale and weighed her daughter before and after feedings, determined that her body was working just fine, and resolved that there was, as Hatch Baby's website puts it, "a role for technology to help make the lives of new parents easier." Her company—which she founded after a stint at Yahoo! and after building Maya's Mom, a social networking site helping mothers connect online—specializes in smart nursery products. In addition to a night light/monitor/white-noise-machine hybrid (known as the Rest), the company makes a smart changing pad (known as the Grow), which weighs your child every time you change him and kicks that info to your phone.

"For me, the most important thing as a parent is to figure out how to know yourself well enough, and have enough confidence in yourself, to infuse that into your kids," Weiss tells me on the phone. "If you're parenting by data, you're robbing yourself of training that intuition."

And yet, her changing pad is metrics driven, no?

"Grow is a device to help people understand that their bodies are doing what they're designed to do, to provide reassurance," she says, referencing a stat, which she can't cite and I can't verify, that 90 percent of women report anxiety about nursing. Ease that anxiety, and more women might nurse for longer. "We don't recommend checking weight every day, but frankly there are some people who do that, and if it makes them feel more comfortable, then great."

This "to each his own" argument keeps popping up around data gathering and analysis—it's what Yaker told me and what I hear when I interview not just founders, who understandably have to parrot back the company line, but friends, too. One is married to a data scientist. Since their son was born, they've been tracking his pees, poops, sleeping schedule, and daily activity in a big book, manually. He is now a toddler.

"So, you're saying you can tell me what he ate any day last week?" I ask her.

"Absolutely!" she replies, and later sends me a photo of the log, which indicates that the previous Friday, her son ate a buttered English muffin with honey for breakfast and lunch and had a robust dinner of pasta, chicken, tomato, and fish. "No wonder he took a poop," Dave says, peeking over my shoulder.

You'd imagine that a data scientist, of all people, would be well aware of the pros and cons of obsessive tracking. I'm not sure what anyone could do with the knowledge that three months and four days ago, their kid peed twice in the morning. But, my friend tells me, it brings her and her husband peace of mind.

When I consider these conversations, I'm left wondering the same thing: whether tracking, via app or pen and paper, is simply furthering a false promise that we can control a situation that is, by definition, beyond our control. The implication is that if you know how many ounces of milk your child is drinking, and that he's napping precisely two hours every day, and that his heart rate is strong, you just might find yourself living with a perfect specimen. Bonus points if you can make sure he poops at the same hour each morning.

It's not that I don't understand the pull. When Ella was born, I was one of the trackers. In my spare waking hours, I pulled up Microsoft Word and made a chart, complete with Kid Pix–level icons, to track left- and right-boob nursing times, poops, pees, and naps, meticulously jotting everything down and bringing it to my first few pediatrician appointments so I could get a gold star. (Dr. Yaker responded with a kind but unimpressed smile when I walked him through my system. I recognize the reaction in myself, years later, when I ask three-year-old Ella to put her shoes away neatly and she arranges them in a pattern that stretches down the hall: one of her shoes, one of my shoes, one of her shoes, one of mine, and on and on.) This initial need to track, this primal impulse to become data statisticians—is any of it grounded in necessity? Or just neurotic?

* * *

The precursor to left-breast output measurement is anthropometry—the study of measuring the human body. We owe the growth chart to Count Philibert de Montbeillard, who, in the late eighteenth century, plotted his son's height every six months from birth until he turned eighteen. Ezra Stiles, the New England minister and seventh president of Yale College, was a little more OCD: he reportedly weighed his kids before breakfast and then again after dinner. Poke around too deeply in its history, and you're bound to come across studies that use these metrics in pursuit of eugenics. But as pediatrics started to formalize and people began to realize that lower than average weight might lead to infant death, doctors starting jotting down the measurements that would later become the basics of sound pediatric practice. For example, by the 1890s, primers like *Practical Midwifery* counseled that "nothing is more important in the routine care of infancy than the daily weighing of the child."

But even way back when, mothers chafed against the notion that parenting was, somehow, quantifiable.

Take *Weighing the Baby*, a poem published in 1867 by Civil War poet Ethel Lynn Beers, which begins,

> *"How many pounds does the baby weigh—*
> *Baby who came but a month ago?*
> *How many pounds from the crowning curl*
> *To the rosy point of the restless toe?"*

Then, a few stanzas down, after the girl is pronounced "only eight," her mother leans over and murmurs softly: "Little one, / Grandfather did not weigh you fair." Why not?

> *Nobody weighed the baby's smile*
> *Or the love that came with the helpless one;*
> *Nobody weighed the threads of care*
> *From which a woman's life is spun.*

These days, when it comes to healthy children, pediatricians care about three measurements, and three measurements alone: height, weight, and head circumference.

"Looking at growth charts is the bread and butter of the pediatrician's world," Dr. Yaker tells me when I call him one summer

Sunday evening. "Clearly these measurements are very important, because one of the ways you know that a child is healthy is if they're gaining and growing properly."

I'm certain that Charlotte is gaining and growing, but whether she's doing that properly I can't say. At three months old, she is enormous, so adorably dumpling-esque that I have to make sure to powder her chin rolls and take a cool cloth to her back knee fat every day, something I imagine was done to King Henry VIII when his gout started to act up. (If I don't do this, sweat and milk accumulate and she starts to smell like a ripe Camembert.) I am now operating with two very loose data points with regard to her weight: she's comfortably wearing clothes Ella wore at nine months, and she maxed out the produce scale at the grocery store (yes, I actually did that). What if she is literally off the charts? Yaker is unfazed.

"For a healthy child, you absolutely do not need to be tracking weight gain more frequently than we do at the well-child visits," he tells me. Most pediatric practices in the States follow the schedule set forth by the American Academy of Pediatrics' *Bright Futures Guidelines*, which has children in and out of the pediatrician's office every few weeks.

Why track these three calculations at all? Two types of abnormal readings might arise, either of which acts as a red flag for pediatricians. Either all metrics are lower or higher than expected (symmetric), or some are (asymmetric), and each scenario can indicate any number of underlying medical issues. Usually the first number to register as wonky in some way is weight. And there is, indeed, something known as "tracking I's and O's"— input and output: what the child eats and what he excretes—on a daily basis. But that is generally for sick children in the hospital, Yaker says.

"In the first year of life, we see babies quite frequently and that's because we need those growth parameters documented. Not daily, but that's really objective information we can use to make sure a child is thriving. But in general, children are healthy," he tells me, reassuringly. "And in standard healthy-child world, after that first couple of weeks, when people have settled in, I'm not really so sure what needs to be tracked at this level of detail."

* * *

But there's one area where parents might rightly protest and say that there's a legit value-driven proposition in data, and that area is: bedtime. Next to feeding, there's likely no more anxiety-prone part of the day than getting children to sleep—the fear that they're not on a schedule, or that once they've gotten on one, it might be the wrong one, or that once they're actually asleep, they might never wake up.

When Ella was little, I'd often see various products on my Facebook feed, or floating around elsewhere on the internet, that purported to calm parents who were anxious about sleep using data, but I would dismiss them out of hand—we were sharing a room with her, and I was aware of her every snort and snuffle. Dave would have slept through all of them if I hadn't kicked him to ensure, in the name of spousal equality, that I wasn't the only one awake, logging snorts and snuffles. It made for a fun first five months of her life. Of course, in retrospect it seems obvious that we could have had her sleeping through the night a little earlier—if we'd only settled on a sleep training method.

Whichever one you pick slots you into a neat little parental taxonomy. Are you an adherent of Dr. Richard Ferber's method, known as Ferberizing and popularized in the 1980s, which encourages that you let your child "cry it out" until you're popping Xanax like popcorn and wearing construction-grade earmuffs to bed? Perhaps you're a disciple of *Twelve Hours' Sleep by Twelve Weeks Old*, which guarantees as much, so long as you're willing to meticulously track how much she's consuming and occasionally force-feed her, gavage-style, like a foie gras goose. Or maybe you purchased a California King the day you found out you were pregnant, and now you all sleep together, your breasts exposed to the night air so Junior can sidle up and have a sip whenever he'd like, as your husband's penis shrivels into a raisin.

I couldn't let Ella cry for a few seconds without picking her up, was not organized enough for *Twelve Hours' Sleep by Twelve Weeks Old*, and already managed to commandeer an 80 percent stake of the bed most nights, often waking to find Dave clinging to the edge of the mattress like a free soloist. So when we decided it was time for Ella to drop one of her night feeds, I wasn't exactly sure where to turn. Then I learned that some mothers will just straight up leave and let their husbands handle sleep training, a small reciprocal payment in exchange for carrying the child for nine months. This, I could do. So Dave, ever the saint, bid me adieu and off I went to my parents' house for three nights, during which time I stayed awake the entire time, hearing phantom baby screams. When I returned, Ella had fully dropped the 11:00 p.m. feed, and Dave looked like a raccoon. But it worked. Now we just had to kick the 3:00 a.m. feed.

Most parents will always remember the first time their child slept through the night. Ours was the day we moved into our new two-bedroom apartment, when we fell asleep for the first night with Ella in her own room, surrounded by cardboard boxes, the paint still drying in the living room. When I blinked open my eyes to find light already streaming through the windows, my maternal instinct told me that one of three things happened: Ella hated the new digs so much she packed a suitcase of onesies and pacifiers and skipped town in the middle of the night; she'd actually slept through the night on her own; or we had become an unthinkable statistic. Of course, conditioned by a sleep industry that has its crosshairs on my back, I assumed the latter.

My pediatrician had assured me that if I breastfed, put Ella on her back, and didn't smoke, risk of SIDS—the unknown, panic-inducing acronym that kills approximately thirteen hundred children in the US each year—would plummet. Sleeping in the same room, for at least six months and preferably a year, was believed to be another key prevention factor. We were one month short. *Have we jumped the gun?* I wondered as I ran around the corner to her room. As the dust settled behind me, I braced for the worst, but there was Ella, asleep on her back, happily snuffling away. I tiptoed back into our room, the large lump on the other side of the bed still rising and falling evenly, blissfully unaware of the minefield I'd just walked through, solo. I poked it with a toe and got a grunt back.

"Dave," I whisper-hissed. "She slept through the night." The lump offered up a slightly more enthusiastic grunt. "But the AAP says she should sleep with us until six months at least, so maybe we should move the crib in here. Just for another few weeks." The lump contracted, turned into a compact ball, and rolled away from me, like a hedgehog who'd been sucker punched in the gut. If we'd strapped some sort of sleep tracker on her, would I have felt more comfortable letting her be?

It would have been an easy sell to Dave. Ever since I've known him, he's tracked his own sleep. Every few months, it seems, he returns home with a new device, each resembling a sleek prisoner's ankle bracelet designed by Le Corbusier, each claiming to tell him how deeply he's slept, or how long it took him to fall asleep, or how much he worked out during the day and how that affected that night's sleep. One study, conducted by the National Sleep Foundation and the Consumer Electronics Association, found that one in five people owns or uses some sort of sleep technology, so he's not alone.

But by the time Charlotte was born, the market was full of sleep trackers made specifically for baby, and she is alive not two days before Dave starts sending me links. Now that we have, in addition to a newborn, a toddler in the next room throwing Scarface-level tantrums at bedtime, I'm generally too tired to register more than the featured picture, which unfailingly shows two well-rested parents of different ethnicities beaming at a sleeping child.

One, though, I click on, mostly because it seems to have taken monitoring to *Onion* headline–level extremes. The Nanit is an award-winning camera that uses night vision and machine learning to track your child's movements and then spits out a sleep score in the morning. The number factors in how long it took the child to fall asleep, how many times the parent came in, and how deep the sleep was.

When I tell a friend with five children (three older sons, tried for a girl, got twins) about it, she snorts.

"As if I need data to know how well my children sleep," she replies. "Either I feel like hell in the morning, or I feel like hell warmed over."

But this time around we may be in need of a real sleep training strategy—not just for Charlotte but for Ella, too. The tantrums start at bath time (*"But I need to squeeze this entire bottle of hair conditioning into the bowl or else my soup won't taste good!"*), stretch on for hours (*"Only mama can put on my diaper! NOOOOOOO I need Dada!"*), and usually end with one of us lying on the floor of her room until she announces that she is ready for us to leave (*"I won't be ready for another eighty minutes, okay? Onnnnne, twooooo, threeeee, . . ."*). Sometimes she'll force us to listen to her rendition of Raffi's "Down by the Bay," wherein she substitutes the word *bonk* in at random, then laughs uproariously. (On limited sleep, I'll admit it's a decent joke.) Now that I am mostly tied to Charlotte for feedings, Dave has become a solo operator, and I decide to do a solid for the family and learn a bit more about the inner workings of this Nanit.

"I've seen Excel spreadsheets that are color coded, and the colors change over time, and each color corresponds to something different," Assaf Glazer, Nanit's founder, tells me of the manual tracking systems he saw users rely on pre-Nanit, when we meet at the midtown WeWork where he houses part of the company. Inspirational quotes cover the walls, and there's free pineapple-infused water for the taking. "It'll just go on forever and ever and as you look at it you become more and more pale because it is so labor intensive. But I see the value."

Glazer—bald, clean-shaven, formerly of the Israel Defense Forces—completed his PhD at the Technion in Haifa, specializing in machine learning and computer vision, and later worked on solutions for missile defense systems. When he became a parent, he found himself working late at night, checking in on his son, Udi, and wondering something only a former Israeli air force man who worked for missile defense systems would ever wonder: *Can*

I apply process control to a baby? Glazer knew that if the answer turned out to be yes, he had an audience. On average, parents lose forty-four days of sleep during the first year of a baby's life. For Glazer, love isn't a battlefield. Bedtime is.

"Putting a child to sleep is one of the first problems you're dealing with as a new parent," he tells me. "The Nanit helps you formalize a strategy."

The camera Glazer developed uses smart sensors to transmit real-time sound and motion notifications to your phone and, by tracking sleep patterns over time—specifically with your child, but also by bundling the data of thousands of babies and millions of nights of sleep—offers up sleep tips to groggy parents. Imagine a child, Glazer tells me, who has just thrown his pacifier out of the crib for the fourteenth time and is wailing. If you know that it'll take him only two more minutes of crying to put himself back to bed, but you'll prolong that by twenty minutes if you go in to fetch the pacifier, won't you stay outside a little longer? I don't have to imagine. When Ella was younger, we'd load up her crib with seven different glow-in-the-dark pacifiers at bedtime. A few hours later, Dave and I would inevitably find ourselves on our bellies like worms, inching around the floor of her nursery and straining to detect a faint glow as Ella stood and pouted in her crib, a mini overlord of a glowing kingdom.

Glazer's alleged goal is not to capture the irrelevant but cocktail party–worthy data he's generated—though he'll gladly serve that up: babies in Denver tend to wake up one more time per night than other babies; parents put their babies to sleep earlier on Thanksgiving—but to expand the field of human monitoring.

When I ask Glazer about the necessity of this level of detail for the lay consumer, he brings up the concept of progressive disclosure. "You don't want to overwhelm people who are looking for simplicity," he says. So if you're the kind of parent who simply wants to see how long their child slept last night, fine. If you'd prefer charts and graphs about nap habits over time that rival the metrical intricacies of a spaceship launch, the Nanit can give you that, too. And the NASA-level data on Junior sure is sexy. For the right clientele, it occurs to me, marketing this product is the equivalent of shooting fish in a barrel: your audience is sleep addled, desperate, and susceptible.

Beyond the astronomical price tag, way down in the website's fine print lies the real issue for me.

Nanit is not a medical device. Nanit is a connected product designed and intended to continuously learn from the data it collects to help you understand your baby's sleep patterns. It is not intended to diagnose, treat or cure any disease or other condition, including but not limited to, Sudden Infant Death Syndrome (SIDS). False positive or false negative readings about your baby's breathing patterns are a potential risk of Nanit. Nanit should not substitute for the care and oversight of an adult or consultation with medical professionals.

Well, sure. But the first thing you see on the website is the tagline: "Peaceful Nights. Peace of Mind." The implication being, you go to bed without the Nanit, you lie awake at night either because your child is shrieking in the next room or she's not and you're afraid she's not breathing. (I later learned that Nanit changed its tagline to "Peaceful Nights. Lasting Memories." Quite a bit tamer.)

"They are very clever in how they advertise on their websites," Dr. Rachel Moon tells me about these baby sleep tech devices, when I reach her at the University of Virginia, where she is the division head of general pediatrics. She also serves on the AAP's task force on SIDS and has been a practicing pediatrician for more than thirty years. "They never say that this will prevent SIDS, but they come pretty close. They get right up to the line so they don't have to be regulated by the FDA, which I think is irresponsible. The vast majority of parents believe the FDA is regulating all these products, so if they're sold that means somebody has blessed them and that they are safe. We know that's not true."

Moon has built her career on studying factors affecting SIDS and sees myriad problems with much of the consumer-marketed sleep-related technology out there.

"It gives you this false sense of complacency—*Oh, since I have this device on, it gives me permission to do what I know I'm not supposed to do,*" she tells me. So, you know your baby should be on a hard, firm mattress in a crib, but you want to cuddle at night? As long as the device is on, the reasoning might go, I can snuggle away. "They use one behavior to compensate for another behavior, which is potentially magnified with technology."

As for whether or not advanced technology can help prevent SIDS, she refers me to studies that were done years ago, involving sending high-risk babies home with hospital-grade monitors.

"These were the gold standards of monitors, and they didn't prevent SIDS. What's out there now, none of it is hospital grade." She pauses. "If we already know the hospital-grade monitors don't work, there's no reason to say these will."

Back at WeWork, as we wrap up our conversation, I tell Glazer that Ella used to be a perfect sleeper, but when she turned three she started staying awake for hours, turning every step of bedtime into a negotiation. He looks at me, unblinking.

"Is there anything we should be doing?" I prod after a beat, trying to dampen the obvious hysteria in my voice. I don't dare tell him about the contract that I recently wrote up with Ella one morning after a horrific night's sleep and then forced her to sign in an octopus-like scrawl, clinging desperately to the power of the written word. It's full of contingencies, due to Ella's negotiating prowess. ("Mama, when you say 'no whining,' what if it's just a *quiet* whine, like"—whispers—"whine?" "Okay fine." Writes in "Quiet whines allowed." Outfoxed, yet again, by a three-foot Erin Brockovich.)

He squints slightly.

"Look, babies do not have a background," he tells me. They are, in a sense, pure, more interchangeable than older children. "You can impact a baby's future in a really simple way. But when you are talking about a three-year-old, there are a lot of environmental conditions and psychological aspects you cannot capture with a camera. They are much more complicated."

I start thinking of Ella as less like a toddler and more like a vet returning from her second tour in Nam. And I am unsurprised when, a few months later, I learn that Glazer is being replaced with another CEO, Sarah Dorsett, a bubbly mom of three who can convey, a bit more effortlessly, maternal concern.

* * *

The thing is, however much I want to ignore the influx of information, sleep related or otherwise, I somehow can't look away, and I want to know why: Why can't I just ignore the data, put my phone away, internalize all the research I've done? Why must I know whether Charlotte's heart rate is up to snuff? If she poops as much as the average baby? Whether my left boob is slowly evening out its milk production with my right? All signs point to the fact that this information is irrelevant—Charlotte is breathing and gaining weight. But any hint of available data, and I want it.

I am somewhat reassured when I learn this impulse—to ingest data and process it—lives deep within our fish brains, embedded there after generations and generations of evolution.

"We are the only species that has this biological imperative built in to the degree we do," Daniel J. Levitin tells me. A neuroscientist who taught for years at Stanford, he is now professor emeritus of Psychology and Neuroscience at McGill University. He's the author of a few books, including *The Organized Mind: Thinking Straight in the Age of Information Overload*, which explains both how the brain processes information and how we can work within its confines to handle the constant barrage of modern-day life. As Levitin explains, when we left the cover of trees as primates and went out onto the savannah, we became prey. In order to survive, our brain evolved to acquire and process information about the environment, other primates, and that lion over there behind the rock. Those of us with good information-gathering skills were the ones who didn't just sit there, in the wide open, twiddling our opposable thumbs and waiting for said lion to come over and turn us into a midmorning snack.

"To the extent that information gathering helped preserve the species," Levitin tells me, "those are the ones we have around."

Each new hit of information we got, back then, and get, today, triggers a release of dopamine, the same chemical the brain releases after you take a hit of ecstasy or get an iPhone notification.

The problem, as Levitin compellingly paints in the book, is

that, in the last five years alone, we've created more information as a species than in all of human history before it.

"Five thousand years ago, you'd learn about where the new fruit tree was and that was the big event of the week," Levitin tells me over the phone. "Maybe the month." Today, should you so desire, one click of a button will pull up Street Tree Map, which identifies any tree in the entirety of New York City. And tells you the diameter of its trunk, to boot. At this very moment, I have one mote of my brain's processing power taken up with the information that outside my apartment building there is a Japanese pagoda tree with a trunk that measures fifteen inches in diameter. This means that I'll have slightly less attentional capacity to access when Ella inevitably catapults herself into the room after she wakes up in a few minutes to ask if she can start her day with an ice cream sundae. "There's evolutionary lag," Levitin tells me of this information overload, "and it takes about ten thousand years for our brains to catch up." We're using brains that were evolved to suit the precomputerized era, with a few thousand years to go before they're up to speed.

At issue is our *attentional filter*, or the set of neurons that zing about in our brains, constantly trying to ensure that we are paying attention to the right things—the lion lurking behind the rock, not how the blade of grass you passed ten minutes ago looks similar to other blades of grass you've seen before. "Attention is the most essential mental resource for any organism," Levitin writes. In the modern era, with so much information bombarding us, the filter becomes clogged and stops working properly.

Mihaly Csikszentmihalyi, the psychiatrist most famous for coining and studying *flow*, that state of überconcentration that feels less like work and more like play, estimates the processing capacity of the conscious mind to be 120 bits per second. (This was later confirmed by Robert Lucky at Bell Labs.) We use 60 bits of information per second to understand one person talking to us. So we can just barely understand when two people speak to us at the same time, let alone when five apps are pinging us with notifications and updates.

What's to be done?

Levitin offers up various solutions in his book, from hiring personal assistants to organizing tasks on three-by-five cards. But when I hang up the phone, my crucial takeaway is that I have quite enough information being flung at me simply by living in the modern world. While my inability to look in the other direction is understandable at an evolutionary level, if I can opt out of poop data, particularly since I now know it's meaningless, I should. All it really does is clog up my neural pathways with gunk.

Perhaps the more important question is: Even if I were able to process all the data, to what end? My doctor has assured me that tracking, after a certain point, is medically unnecessary. As to whatever part of me might hope to use this data to program my child to behave in a certain way—to sleep at a certain time, to gain a certain amount of weight—well, any more seasoned parent will easily tell me: You can control a child as much as you can force her to nap on command.

* * *

Perhaps the easiest way to internalize that conclusion is to have a second child. At the very least, it worked for me. How far I've come from my tracking days becomes abundantly clear after Charlotte gets her two-month shots and I head to Brooklyn to visit a friend who gave birth to her first son five days after Charlotte was born.

We're standing in the middle of the room doing the patented mom sway, one foot to the other and back again, chatting about the last eight weeks.

"I just spend all day being like, *What if he doesn't fall asleep, is he asleep now, shouldn't he be asleep longer, how long does he have to go without sleeping to spontaneously combust?*" my friend says.

She's had to cut dairy out of her diet because he's intolerant to milk protein, which I imagine is contributing to her anxiety. No one wants a baby to spit up on them after every feed; no one wants soy cream cheese on a bagel. But I recognize in her a fear that I've found in many mothers (and that I harbored as a first-time parent): if the metrics they're tracking—in this case, the length and time of a nap—do not adhere to some Platonic ideal, they're not only doing something wrong but also causing their baby to suffer. Try as she might, my friend can't force the baby to sleep at regular intervals, and it's driving her nuts.

"But look at him," her husband says as he comes over, scoops up the baby, and immediately starts bobbing lightly on the balls of his feet, which causes his voice to fluctuate lightly with each bob. "He's clearly happy, and clearly fine! When he's tired, he'll nap." That surely sounds right. The baby gurgles into his fist in affirmation, and my friend shrugs wearily, then returns his gummy smile with a huge one of her own.

A few weeks later, I'm crying alone at a bar as it flash floods outside. I've had a bit of a rough day, full of crying babies and work half-done and a brief period when I unwittingly walked around in public with two wet circular patches on my shirt, à la *Mean Girls*, due to leaking breasts. So the minute Dave comes home, I hand him Charlotte and wordlessly walk out of the apartment, with all the grace of a tantrumming teen. I text my friend that we should meet up sometime soon and commiserate—I've done this once before, but it's still hard as hell. She writes back immediately that she's game. Then, after a brief ellipsis, she asks, not unreasonably, what Charlotte's schedule is.

"We've been putting him to sleep at seven, starting to get him ready at six," she says of her son. I snort. All my tracking has gone out the window. I am pretty sure this is not because I've internalized the data, the talks with my pediatrician, the research I've done. It's much more likely due to the existence of Ella, who encourages me to spend time building Magna-Tile castles with her and making elaborate soups in the bathtub instead of engaging in the numerical minutiae of newborn life. I'm vaguely aware that Charlotte is eating and sleeping and pooping. But beyond that, I have no idea. I tell my friend as much, and then, after the bar bill comes, head to the grocery store to buy a dinner of Doritos. I feel depleted, overwhelmed, full of anxiety, and crushed by the prospect of yet another sleepless night. Plus I'm sweaty and starting to smell like cheese due to all that dried milk and spit-up on a tank top I haven't bothered to change since yesterday. I know that Charlotte will start sleeping through the night soon enough, that I'll be back on some sort of schedule, that my brain will be able to focus eventually—but it just feels so far away.

A few weeks later I am able to take a deep breath and put this all in perspective, with the help of a septuagenarian psychiatrist. We've rented a house outside the city for a few weeks in August, to take advantage of our joint parental leaves. It's charming, with little chipmunks hopping out in the garden each morning and

dragonflies hovering in the dusk. The new setting, the late sunset, the bed in the shape of a truck in Ella's room, the excitement of being able to pee naked in the grass, our newest family member—some factor or combination thereof means both that Ella's sleep schedule immediately goes out the window and that she demands to be slathered in sun lotion right before bed. Lacking reserves, we comply. She slips into bed lubed up and glistening, and I awaken in the wee hours to the smell of Coppertone whooshing into our bedroom as she marches in, announcing she's no longer tired. That month, in between laughable attempts to research and write, I stagger around, mulling questions of control—whether some computer vision technology might be able to help Ella avoid these crazy middle-of-the-night wake-ups; whether I could figure out the exact perfect time to dream-feed Charlotte so that we could get her to sleep past 5:00 a.m. and all get more than three hours of uninterrupted sleep; whether I could somehow program Ella differently so that our household wouldn't be single-handedly keeping the sunscreen industry thriving during off-hours. As is my wont these days, I do some research, pick up the phone, and call an expert to get a handle on my current situation.

"Parents are concerned with feeling in control, but the important part of parenting is to encourage your *children* to feel in control," Dr. Ellen Langer tells me when I reach her in Cambridge. "So when your child wants to wear socks that don't match, what's the difference?" she asks me, then fires off the first of many one-liners she's honed over the years: "Ask yourself, is it a tragedy or an inconvenience?"

I guess it's a tragedy if Ella grows up thinking she needs to protect herself from getting moon burn. But I admit that her bedtime

demands are likely just a coconut-scented inconvenience—and kind of charming, to boot.

One consequence of being sleep addled is that I've lost all sense of inhibition, which is how I ended up cold emailing Langer—one of the leading psychologists in the nation, the first woman to get tenure in Harvard's psychology department, and the so-called mother of mindfulness—without so much as batting an eye.

I'm looking for someone to help situate the ideas I'm wrestling with daily—how quantifying our children relates to control, how technology has affected our ability to be present as parents—in the psychological pantheon. Langer's work, which involves the mind-body connection and how control, decision-making, and the ability to be mindful can positively impact our lives, hits the bull's-eye. If all this tech isn't making our lives easier, or us happier, then what's the point?

A few of her notable and provocative studies:

- She transported elderly men to a retreat that was made to resemble a time twenty years in the past, had them talk about the past as if it were the present, and showed that they actually seemed to grow younger—after one week they sat taller, looked younger, and could even see better.
- She gave one group of nursing home residents a plant to keep alive and told a second that the nursing home staff would take care of their plants for them. A year and a half later, twice as many plant carers were alive than the others, indicating that feeling responsible can have measurable psychosomatic effects.
- She took two groups of women who did heavy physical work all day and told one to view their work as

exercise. Just by changing their mindset, those women lost weight and decreased both their body mass index and their blood pressure.

Langer's work turned on its head the then current academic understanding that mind and body lived on separate tracks. "If the mind is fully in a healthy place," she writes in her book *Mindfulness*, "the body will be healthy as well."

And while Langer is not a parent herself—she has dogs, stepchildren, and step grandchildren, she tells me—her wide-ranging interests mean she's applied her unconventional approach to fields that directly intersect with my daily life as a parent. For Langer, the cure to what ails you lies in becoming more mindful. And that's not the kind of mindfulness that's been co-opted by the meditation app–followers of today. It's a mindfulness that involves actively noticing what is going on and making conscious choices about your actions instead of reflexively responding to environmental cues that cause you to think or feel or act a certain way. It does not rely on technology of any sort.

"What's one plus one?" she asks me, in her signature brassy style, half-academic, half-Borscht Belt comedian. I know the answer, having watched any number of the talks she's given, and having read her work: two . . . unless you're dealing with one wad of chewing gum and another wad of chewing gum. Or one load of laundry and another load of laundry. Put them together and you have just one larger wad, one larger load. Unconventional thinking, not just parroting back what you've been taught, not just mindlessly trusting what someone tells you—all go toward keeping you aware, alive, happy. It's a sense that children are born with, that's rooted out after just a few years on earth. If we can emulate them, find the beauty in changing our underwear five times before breakfast, in slathering ourselves with sun lotion at night, we just might find ourselves feeling more grounded, more present.

"There's the airline commercial, *Put the mask on yourself first, then put it on the child*," Langer tells me. "The first rule of parenting is to take care of yourself."

For me, at least one part of that involves excising as much extraneous baby-related data as possible from my brain. After the first few weeks of life, there's scientifically no reason to track anything beyond what your pediatrician tracks for you at each visit, and doing so makes me nervous, twitchy, focused on the wrong things—on whether Charlotte, a healthy, thriving child, is gaining enough weight at the right clip instead of on how happy she clearly is right before a nursing session, how she giggles with delight and shoots her four limbs out in all directions, like a frog midleap, when she sees her personal, mobile, short-order cook approaching. Loving a human, as anyone knows who has a mother of his or her own, is a messy business—no amount of metrics and data can clean it up. So, I figure, maybe we should stop trying.

2

It Takes a Virtual Village

Can Online Parenting Groups Replace IRL?

On a lunch break shortly before Charlotte was born, I created a profile on Peanut, which is basically a "dating" app for moms—swipe right and you connect; swipe left and a fellow mother gets the axe. I was eager to rethink my membership in multiple "Mommas" Facebook groups—a cutesy, internet-only moniker for what I now am—that I'd mindlessly joined before Ella arrived. This app, targeted at millennial mothers, was one example of tech trying to foster real-life community through the virtual ones that have sucked us all online. If my first maternity leave was any indication, I would likely spend my second pushing a sweaty baby around the park alone, listening to podcasts and feeling myself up to figure out which boob to offer next. I didn't really need any more friends, but none of the ones I already had were free at 11:00 a.m. on a Tuesday, plus I couldn't shake the feeling that this life stage, perhaps above any else, warranted real interactions with real people who were going through similar experiences. So, I figured, let's give it a whirl.

I puzzled over which "packs" to add to my profile, cutesy logos that reduced me to an instantly recognizable type of person. I knew I wasn't CRAFTY (indicated by an origami crane) or a DANCE MACHINE (disco ball). But was I a HOT MESS (chili pepper)? Sometimes. ROUTINE QUEEN (calendar)? Well, yes, but given three slots, who wants to broadcast that they're anal retentive? I settled on BOOKWORM (shelf of books), BUT FIRST, FOOD (hamburger), and CITY GAL (buildings), which seemed like an honest, if boring, way to let people know who I was. I wished the packs allowed for a little more nuance—TRIED TO WATCH THE PRESIDENTIAL DEBATES WHILE PUMPING AND DRINKING A BOURBON, GOT TOO TIRED AND FELL ASLEEP (rocks glass, NBC logo, pump flange, sleepy face)—but that would have to do.

Over the course of a full month, I connected with one person, a seemingly nice enough lady named Devorah who lived nearby and had a two-year-old. We both swiped right, waved at each other, then exchanged chats back and forth for a while, trying to find a time to get together and meet in real life, by the swings at a nearby playground. But our chat history devolved into every single other text message chain I have in my phone—*Let's meet up now, oops, I'm the worst, let's reschedule.* And when I speak to Michelle Kennedy, the founder, after Charlotte's birth, I learn that while the original concept of Peanut was to connect moms in real life—it's often referred to as "Tinder for moms"—the company's mission evolved, and quite quickly, once it hit market.

"Within months, people were saying, *I want to be in a group,* or *Is there a way to speak to everyone across the platform?*" Kennedy tells me when I reach her on the phone a few weeks after she's given birth to her second child. "It meant we really had to change the approach."

The course correction—to encourage women to use online services to get off-line—essentially failed. But the company didn't. The platform now has over a million users who avail themselves of various online chatboards, and when I meet Kennedy a few months later during a whirlwind trip she's making to the States from her home in London, she's just raised $5 million and is promoting her latest virtual village. Called Trying To Conceive, or TTC for short, it is targeted at aspiring mothers, whether those going through in vitro, trying to adopt, and everything in between, and offers up a virtual community of online chat rooms that can get very specific. Think: just for women on their fifth round of IVF.

"If you're sitting around the table with seven girlfriends, one of you will have fertility issues," she tells me, offering up a colloquial version of an oft-cited NHS statistic that about one in seven couples will experience difficulty conceiving. "If two have babies, and three are pregnant, you become the odd one out. If you're at that table, and they haven't been through it, how do you find your community?"

I wonder aloud if you'd rather be sitting at a different table, then. Surely close friends are the people you'd *want* to include in your difficult moments, no? Why seek connection in a void of far-flung strangers, who may or may not have your same values? Is sharing a single characteristic enough to truly bond you to another person? But Kennedy, who strikes me as the kind of upbeat, type A person who'd be chipper during a summer blackout in Death Valley—*Let's just change into our bathing suits and go find a sprinkler to splash about in!*—remains unfazed.

"The opportunity of the virtual village is that these are taboo conversations that women are not having, about IVF and the like, until they have a babe in arms. With TTC, they can have them!"

I leave the meeting certain that even if the logic isn't entirely broken, it's somehow warped—humans are social beings, they need that hug, that arm squeeze, that look in the eye. Later that evening, though, I eat my own words. (What is parenting except for an exercise in eating your own words, again and again and again?) I'm texting a few friends about how to ward off Ella's bedtime tantrums while scrolling through relevant Facebook posts, and I realize how much of my own maternal support system exists online. And how different that is from generations past.

On one end of the spectrum, to the left even of Trying To Conceive, are websites populated by anonymous users who want information and support—but only the support afforded by anonymity. Then there's Facebook, that great morass where mothers can group together based on location or specific need. According to a 2015 Pew Research Center study, 75 percent of online parents use the platform. Somewhere in the middle are apps, like Peanut's first iteration, which are trying to wrench mothers off their phones and into the real world. One, which connects neighbors for babysitting help, hand-me-down giveaways, playdates, and the like, bills itself as "a real social network" that aims to do away with the "awkward" task of connecting with neighbors. And far on the other end of the spectrum are analog groups—though when I ask my pediatrician, Dr. Yaker, if he ever refers women to them these days, he responds, "Not nearly as many in-person groups as there were earlier in my career. I used to speak to them way back when I had hair on my head!"

When she was pregnant with my sister and then with me, my

mother studied with Elisabeth Bing, known as "the mother of Lamaze." She'd go to Bing's Upper West Side apartment with my father and five other couples, sit on the floor, practice breathing exercises, and chat about how to prepare for birth. It was just what people in her cohort did.

"She told us what to put in the backpack and have ready before you go, like—a rotisserie chicken!" my mom responds when I email asking about her experience as an analog mother in the 1980s.

It's not like she forged some immutable bond with her fellow Lamaze-goers. She remained friends with precisely none of the other couples she met during that class, and her lasting Lamaze memory has to do with poultry. But her note leaves me wondering if I should be more thoughtful about the way I navigate my digitally mediated motherhood journey, since I have a choice—I can, should I so choose, log off entirely. Has tech diluted our support networks during a life stage when we arguably need them more than ever? Provided a Band-Aid that makes interacting with neighbors, which used to just be "life," less "awkward"? Should we be fleeing the virtual village for the real one, only using apps to help us when necessary? Or, if we're going to participate in the virtual village of online mothers—and statistically, we know we are—are there loose kinds of best practices we Dance Machines, Routine Queens, and Hot Messes should use?

* * *

I was invited to join the grand virtual motherhood village even before Ella was born, by a friend's friend who sent along a link to her Facebook group. She'd warned me that this particular group of Mommas was "a little intense, but can be valuable for crowd-sourcing." I barely knew her. How different could it be to filter info from 37,999 other people I also barely knew?

Um, just a smidge.

My first few days as a member, I sunk hours scrolling through posts that ran the gamut from asking for tips on sleep training to mini diatribes about nightmare mothers-in-law. Everything was broadcast to a virtual land of strangers that rivaled the population of Liechtenstein. I marveled when, within fourteen minutes of someone asking for opinions on the best stroller configuration for two kids—side-by-side or stadium-style—forty-four members weighed in, pros and cons thought through, positions firmly guarded. I couldn't muster as much conviction about the presidential primary.

If a lawyer offered to give me a pap smear, I'd decline in even the most dire of circumstances. If someone sidled up to me at a party and, unprompted, began to vent about a nightmarish cross-country flight during which her toddler projectile vomited all over the flight attendant, I'd flash the same smile I give to the guy who roller-dances in Central Park with a cat on his head, and back away. And if a complete stranger started weighing in on the size and shape of my nipples, I'd likely call the police.

And yet, in the early days of motherhood with Ella, I found myself lapping up anecdotes, medical recommendations, and general parenting advice from my newest community. I never posted, but silently observed, riveted. Post-baby, I was on the Facebook app for one, two hours a day. (Dave wasn't part of any equivalent fathers' group, and when I later informally reached out to twenty of my friends who are fathers asking if they use

Facebook for anything parenting related, not a single one said yes. Although some spouses engage less in multiple aspects of day-to-day parenting, which I find problematic, this is one area that seems not only okay but beneficial to ignore.) After thirty seconds of gazing into Ella's eyes when she nursed, which I'd been told triggered some primeval mother-child dyad connection, I'd reach for my phone and start scrolling, the isolation of this weird, in-between life stage making the appeal of this virtual community particularly hard to resist. She'd gaze at my eyes; I'd gaze at the Mommas. This, despite the fact that gazing into her eyes was probably the simplest, most pleasurable way to spend a few minutes. The phone was just so bright and shiny, so irresistible.

Yes, as my friend's friend said, the group's promise was partially that it could crowdsource information, medical or otherwise. Sometimes I'd pick up the random useful tidbit. Mostly, though, I found that the information was both overwhelming and conflicting—what could I really learn from knowing that fourteen moms weaned their kids at six months, ten waited until eight months, four stopped at three months, and one was still happily nursing her sixteen-month-old? Particularly when my pediatrician had told me to do my best to nurse exclusively until six months, and the American Academy of Pediatrics recommended nursing for a full year. Seventeen people had thoughts on which BPA-free straw was best. As long as they weren't BPA-full, I figured, who cares? But I mindlessly sifted through the conflicting opinions anyway. It felt kind of like drinking from a fire hose of vodka after making it through the desert—yes, I was thirsty and it sort of did the trick, but the liquid was coming too fast, too frequent, and with horrific aftereffects. But my days were cut up into twenty-minute chunks and I couldn't focus long enough to read a full article or book chapter—nurse here, change a diaper there, try to scarf down some cereal, rinse and repeat. What else was I going to do all day?

When Baby Charlotte arrives and I later find myself pulled ever closer to the Mommas vortex again, I have an opportunity to rethink my mindless behavior.

Intuition tells me that women have gotten together to talk about child-rearing since the most pressing parental issue was how to avoid mastodon attacks. But hitting the history books, I learn that the first official maternal association on record in the United States was formed in 1815 by one Mrs. Payson of Portland, ME, with the stated goal of "combining the practical experience of a community of mothers and adding thereto all the information which they can obtain from reading, as to the best methods of training up children in the way they should go." A proto-Mommas. So we've been at this, officially at least, for two centuries. And my generation isn't the first to be overwhelmed by conflicting advice, which I suppose is comforting.

"Even by the 1920s, there are already tremendous complaints by mothers about having various different perspectives thrown at them, and them going crazy," Dr. Paula Fass tells me when I reach her by phone. She's a professor emerita at the University of California, Berkeley, where she taught for thirty-six years, and the author of numerous books on children's history, including *The End of American Childhood: A History of Parenting from Life on the Frontier to the Managed Child*. The roots of the current advice maelstrom started in earnest nearly a century ago.

"In the twenty-first century, after more than one hundred years of child-rearing advice and harangues, during which mothers (and also fathers) have been given so many, often conflicting, forms of advice regarding their children's proper nurture," she writes, "it is difficult to realize that originally there was a simple goal about which there was no confusion and no conflict. That goal was child survival."

In the early twentieth century, American mortality rates were abysmal, due to a perfect storm of rapid urbanization, increasing population density, and infectious disease. But as children began to survive—pediatrics was formalized as a profession in 1891, and more attention was paid to infant and mother mortality—two camps formed in the land of parental support, which still exist to this day: the experts in white coats on one side, often male, armed with charts and numbers; and the laypeople, often mothers themselves, wielding experience and common sense. Once you've tackled how to keep children alive, parenting becomes part science (infants at this age should be sleeping this number of hours per day) and part art (as anyone can attest who's watched a mother successfully talk a toddler off a tantrum ledge, which can be as beautiful as a Mozart aria). Because there is often no "right way," both sides can, in a sense, be right. The 1920s were a crucible for these conflicting opinions, Fass tells me—the first parenting magazine hit stands in 1926, a Yale psychiatrist named Arnold Gesell got busy developing a theory of child development, and pediatricians established themselves as viable specialists.

"I don't think any middle-class mother since the beginning of the twentieth century has entirely parented by gut," she reiterates. There has always been a chorus of influencers on either shoulder.

But when I press her on whether the internet has amped all this up, she pauses before admitting, "I don't think it could get a lot worse, let's put it that way. One of the problems with online resources is that there is an absence of trust. You have anonymous people who may not have anything in common with you telling you what to do."

And yet, even though we recognize this, only one friend of mine has escaped the pull of the virtual village—and she's always been smarter and more reasonable than everyone else, an impossible example to live up to. The rest of us are all members of at least one group, which I confirm with an email blast to a few close friends.

"It can be a lifeline for 3:00 a.m. feeding tips . . . and also general comparative paranoia spreading," one replies.

"I skim through it for the shock value—like to read the crazy stories of moms and dads who co-sleep in a twin bed (!) with their toddler," another writes, "but sometimes it's super helpful. I found my pediatrician on it."

"All of these groups make me crazy but when I need to ask a specific question or look something up I drop in like a ninja," a third says. She recently moved her family to a new city and was invited to join a local group there, which she says is "notorious for being nasty as all hell," what with mothers guilting other mothers about their child-rearing choices, ganging up on each other, and on and on.

So, it seems, we opt to spend time parsing out the good from the crazy, the useful from the paranoia, the supportive from the shock value, for a single reason: we value the collective wisdom and support of other mothers, even if they drive us batty.

And we're not alone. According to that 2015 Pew study, 75 percent of online parents use Facebook. But that number increases to 81 percent if we're just talking about mothers. And parents are also particularly active users: 75 percent log in daily, and over half log in multiple times a day. One more stat to throw into the mix: according to one study, 44 percent of women increased Facebook use when they became mothers. Isolated with a newborn, we're ravenous for community, even if we know it's diluted; we're ravenous for information, even if we know it's unfiltered. Most of us aren't proud of our behavior—if caught scrolling, we'll sheepishly shrug, as if it's just part of the territory of being a modern mother—but can't look away.

Of course, there are cases when a wide reach can be a godsend. When I speak to Brian Copeland, the founder of the Gay Fathers Facebook group, which at eight thousand members is the largest gay fathers group on the site, he tells me that his members are thrilled to be able to find others like them outside their geographic communities.

"You can't just go out into the middle of the street and yell, 'Hey, I'm gay and I just left my wife and I have a kid!'" he explains. "We're a quick, one-stop way to connect."

And when my friend's daughter is diagnosed with ketotic hypoglycemia, a blood sugar disease, she joins a ketotic hypoglycemia parents group—there are a few—which she describes as "a lot of worried parents worrying each other, but given how rare it is, it was reassuring to have a community."

Of course, no community is perfect.

In Gay Fathers, some of the members are foster fathers, others have adopted, others used a surrogate, and yet others were once married to women.

"You'd think *Oh, big group hug, yay!*" Copeland says before stopping short. "*No.* Not at all. The foster dads criticize the surrogacy dads because they went and created a baby when there were all these children in need. The fathers who were never married criticize the formerly heterosexual fathers who came out."

And in the ketotic hypoglycemia group, "You get thoughtful, personal responses," my friend tells me, "but the people on it are all sort of the ones having the worst time. So it gives a distorted picture. On the small groups it's hard to tell the outliers."

She was told her daughter would outgrow the disease. But if your kids do outgrow it, you're likely not going to spend your time on the group anymore. So if anyone takes a poll asking how many kids outgrew it? "Crickets," she says. "Selection bias is a problem."

So, there's an obvious case for employing a wide reach, so long as you recognize the drawbacks: connecting with outliers.

But for those of us facing more mundane parenting crises, is a social media group a useful, necessary community? Or just noise?

As far as I can tell, we use it for one of three things: to vent, to ask medical questions, and to get general "parenting hacking" advice on how to troubleshoot toddler tantrums or get little Johnny to eat his zucchini.

For those seeking emotional support, social media seems fine if you're searching for camaraderie to complement fulfilling in-person relationships, but problematic if you're in the market for deep, meaningful connections. There is a study for everything, but I find one from Ohio State University that's nuanced enough to stand out: for new mothers, "more frequent visits to Facebook accounts and more frequent content management were each associated with higher levels of parenting stress." In plainer terms: if you're using it too much, if you care too much what other people think of your posts, then you should likely dial it back. This may be the biggest irony of Facebook's mission—that it perpetuates insecurity, anxiety, and competitiveness while claiming to foster community.

There's also the issue of crowd hysteria: how masses of people can both fuel and legitimize anxieties that aren't actually big deals. On a plane to Vegas to attend the Consumer Electronics Show—the last one before COVID arrives and the show goes virtual for the first time in its history—I sit next to a woman who works as a humanitarian advisor to the UN. As we start to chat about the two pumping sessions I'm going to have to do on the flight, she tells me that she was most recently stationed in Poland but is making a brief stop in New York City with her young family before heading to Mexico City, where her husband has a job. She has lived all over the world, worked in Middle East war zones while pregnant, and is charmingly unflustered by the minutiae of parenthood. It's hard to get anxious about first world problems, she tells me, when you've seen how resilient mothers and parents can be in the poorest of places.

"Now I'm part of this New York mothers group on Facebook," she tells me. "There are all these moms on it panicking about taking their kid on a two-hour flight to Miami or whatever. I'm like, call me when you're pumping in the back of a cargo jet on your way to a humanitarian crisis."

For those seeking pediatric advice, can we all agree that crowd-sourcing medical information from someone who hasn't taken the Hippocratic Oath is about as sane an endeavor as asking your cat to pick stocks? It's baffling how many posts I come across that have to do with toddler rashes or banged-up fingers. As Bethany Johnson and Margaret Quinlan write in *You're Doing it Wrong!*, which explores the history of mothering advice through the lens of medical expertise, "Perhaps the most unfortunate impact of social media is the false confidence these platforms provide—a unique combination of some level of anonymity and limitations on post length allows individuals to make confident claims devoid of context and lacking sufficient explanation." It's like that *New Yorker* cartoon: on the internet, nobody knows you're a dog. When I speak to Quinlan, she brings up that there may be very real reasons people seek medical advice from non-practitioners: they can't afford to go to the doctor. But that becomes a minefield, too, she tells me: "Those moms just get torn apart for posting a rash photo at three in the morning—people freak out and say, *Go to the hospital!* Nobody is asking, *Okay, why can't you go to the hospital right now? Can you not afford the co-pay? Do you have other children asleep in the next room?* There's just so much judgment."

(If you're one of the lucky 115,000 to be part of the Physician Moms Group, composed solely of doctors who've been vetted and who list their specialty next to comments, good on you. When I speak to Hala Sabry, the founder, I beg to be admitted to the group, in the interest of research. I am firmly rebuffed.)

The best case for crowdsourcing seems to be for relatively anodyne parenting questions, that third bucket, but Dr. Daniel Levitin—the neuroscientist I approached to help me get a handle on my baby-related data compiling and author of *The Organized Mind: Thinking Straight in the Age of Information Overload*—tells me to take online advice with a handful of salt.

"Crowdsourcing works for some things," he tells me after we set up a time to talk, "like guessing the number of jelly beans in a jar at a fair." If you have enough people guessing, the average guess will be astonishingly close to the correct number. "But it doesn't seem to work so well for how to raise a kid."

One portion of his book focuses on the power, and drawbacks, of crowdsourcing. Combine our natural proclivity to be social with our inability to master many topics and the internet-dog problem, and you've got what Levitin deems "a recipe for disaster."

But the scientist pinpoints another pragmatic reason not to crowdsource certain types of parenting decisions, one that's an obvious concern for someone used to running randomized controlled studies that then get peer-reviewed.

"People who are raising other kids don't have a very large sample size," he tells me. "What's the largest sample size they could have, ten?"

Even then, they're raising them in a particular environment, with a particular partner. What applies to one child will not necessarily apply to another.

"Parenting involves so many thousands of decisions," Levitin says. To coddle or not coddle when Ella scrapes her knee? To force her to join in the conga line at a friend's birthday party if she's feeling shy? To give her an extra graham cracker if she has behaved, or try to instill a sense of pride in simply having behaved well?

"You're not dealing with interchangeable auto parts," Levitin tells me. "No matter what the advice is, you have to apply some common sense and empathy." And, of course, technology doesn't do common sense and empathy the way a human does. You can absorb all the advice you want, but if you don't know the advice givers that well, and they don't know you, no amount of filtering will spit out the perfect solution to your particular kid's problem.

Whenever I complain to my mother about being constantly inundated with information, she tells me to try what she did: call my pediatrician. On the phone.

"I'd call at any hour of the day," she tells me. "Three a.m., six a.m. I called him when your sister wouldn't take her medicine, and he'd pick up and say okay, do this and call me back in fifteen minutes. I called him when you wouldn't change out of those yellow leggings for a year. He told me to sneak into your room and wash them at night." Pediatricians these days may not answer their phones at 3:00 a.m., but I take her point: pick a rabbi, and get the information directly. But that's just not something that my generation is as comfortable doing. Having grown up in the internet age, we always associate more input with more value. Why have one rabbi when you can have 38,000?

* * *

One afternoon I find myself in the land of MI6-style parenting, complete with black-ops-level anonymity: Reddit. The discussion website, brought to us by pre-Serena Alexis Ohanian, is one of the most visited websites in the United States, frequented by millions of people who identify themselves by username alone. Before I learned about r/Parenting, a subreddit—essentially a small online social world, generally populated by like-minded individuals— with 3.2 million members, I thought of the site as a black hole of male testosterone, where programmers who survive on Soylent discuss conspiracy theories about George R. R. Martin.

But after I log in, I find myself drawn into posts that run the gamut from "My kindergartener threatened a classmate and I don't know how to respond" to "How did you adjust to being a single mom after being with your partner?" to "Motherhood is lonely" to "Baby won't nap. Tried every training method. Looking for sympathy and reassurance, not advice." I find myself deep down a thread of thoughtful responses to the horrifying question "How do you explain school shootings to your kids for the first time?" and then down another, titled "I need help," in which a parent writes that while she's never hit her child, "sometimes I get so overwhelmed with emotion I'm afraid I'm going to. I was yelled at constantly as a child so I'm committed to not yelling . . . but this has an unintended side effect—I have no way of releasing any emotion." The responses are both caring (*I feel ya!*), pragmatic (*try tickling; have you thought about smoking some weed?*), and validating (*this is normal*). In fact, on the whole, I'm surprised to find the Reddit parenting community to be pretty . . . great. Even though I personally know some women on my own Mommas Facebook group, it doesn't feel nearly as judgment-free as this, though the user base is more than eighty times larger. There is safety, I realize, in numbers. And real safety in anonymity.

For users who want to crank that anonymity way up, there's a further phenomenon: the throwaway account—one that is not associated with your main, more public account, and which is often temporary, created for a specific purpose, likely to discuss something you'd rather not have associated with your main username, and then deleted entirely. A burner username, essentially. The upshot for parents?

"Self-identified throwaway accounts provide a crucial environment for supporting parents with stigmatizing experiences," argues one paper from the University of Michigan's School of Information.

"It's a confessional," Tawfiq Ammari, an assistant professor at Rutgers University and the lead author on the paper, explains when I reach him by phone.

Ammari conducts what is called sociotechnical research—looking at the affordances of technology not purely from a computer science perspective, or a sociological one, but the melding of the two. For this particular study, he and his coauthors drew on ten years of Reddit boards and found that these throwaway accounts—be they created to discuss postpartum depression, infertility, disability, abuse, LGBTQ children, pregnancy loss, or, in the case of some fathers, the realization that the child you thought was biologically yours is, in fact, not—are immensely powerful tools. Ammari found that burner users not only have a forum for engaging in taboo subjects but also receive a greater number of longer, more supportive responses than non-throwaway accounts. Toward the end of the paper, Ammari argues that Facebook and other social media sites could learn from Reddit, providing a service that allows users to move between different levels of anonymity, which might go a long way toward providing a more supportive online experience.

Like Facebook, Reddit uses volunteers from within each community to enforce community norms—deleting posts and comments that might be hurtful or questionable. The politics of posting as a parent on Reddit are nuanced and fascinating. As Ammari explains in a follow-up email, "Moderators might deem some posts offensive on a particular subreddit, while they might be the norm in another. For example, explicit sexism is not the norm on r/Daddit. So, some fathers who might want to engage in sexist/misogynist attitudes (usually after a divorce), might move to r/MRA (men's rights) to post about it."

In other words, there is likely a subreddit out there for you, however kind and wonderful or sexist and heinous you are, but the very existence of subreddits comes with enormous strings. Ammari brings up the anti-vaccination movement as one exam-

ple of anonymity gone wrong in the parenting space, though he tells me that anti-vaxxers are not welcome on these parenting subreddits—they're policed out by the moderators. Reddit has garnered many a headline due to its toxic subreddits, be those catering to incels (r/braincels) or misogynists (r/beating_women) or racists (there are many, all of them unprintable). But, by and large, he tells me, parenting subreddits tend to be pretty supportive. If you find yourself in the right group, it might just be the difference between burying your biggest secret and unburdening yourself of it.

Toward the end of our conversation, Ammari brings up something that not only gets to the root of my ambivalence about virtual villages but also shines a bright spot on their potential.

"There are lots of questions that might be better answered by people in your network, maybe family, or your partner," he allows. "But your initial discussion with a throwaway account might give you just enough scaffolding to gain the strength, and the grit to go talk to them." In other words, you see that multiple other women have also had trouble getting pregnant and, in time, find yourself ready to bring it up with your mother, who might come back and say, *Oh, sweetie, I went through that, too.*

The fear, of course, is that redditors will never come offline—the stakes are so low. As part of a social diet, a little MI6 anonymity might be fine, but aren't there serious ramifications to relying too heavily on that anonymity?

* * *

To wit: One day when Charlotte is almost four months old and my maternity leave is coming to an end, I head to the playground, where I encounter the same six other parents I've seen every

weekend prior, and I realize I don't know a single one of their actual names. I privately identify them according to whom their children resemble—Golda Meir's dad, Bernie Sanders's mom—but we've never actually spoken. And it's not like they're exhibiting particularly intimidating behaviors. Golda's dad likes to make rhythmic farting sounds to accompany his swing pushing. The sight of a squirrel often sends Bernie's mom, clearly trying to amp up her kid's interest in wildlife, into fits of ecstasy.

I'm not sure that the simple fact of having had unprotected sex at the same time means we should fall into each other's arms and start singing "Kumbaya," but having immersed myself in the literature of virtual versus real motherhood communities, I'm aware that the only other people in New York interested in swinging or blowing bubbles at this ungodly early hour are coming off of Molly. Surely we could muster up *something* to talk about with each other—the awesomeness of late-in-life Marlon Brando's bubble blower at the very least. And yet, we choose to parallel play, occasionally glancing at our phones for a hit of connection. It freaks me out. I don't entirely blame Facebook, but I don't *not* entirely blame it, either.

"Go on, say hi," I urge Ella whenever we're at the playground. Why the hell can't I do the same?

Back at home, like a chain-smoker watching lung cancer documentaries to set himself straight, I start binge-reading Sherry Turkle. An MIT professor and a leading researcher on the topic of people's relationship to technology, Turkle has written extensively about the detriments of tech on human relationships. Her TED Talk, "Connected, but alone?" has been viewed more than six million times, no doubt by people like me who are wrestling with this question of community, relationships, and how those

play out online. I know my inability to say hi isn't *good*, but is it *bad*?

Turkle sure thinks so.

"Without conversation, studies show that we are less empathic, less connected, less creative and fulfilled," Turkle writes in *Reclaiming Conversation*. "We are diminished, in retreat."

So, what's to be done? Well, there's an app for that. And it's grounded in evolutionary theory.

"On one end of the spectrum you have moms' groups, which is very traditional, very low tech, but very high friction," Catherine Hrdy, a graduate of the elite Y Combinator seed accelerator program, tells me. "Sometimes the time doesn't work, or it's across town. There's less friction with digital communities—the best example are Facebook groups—but they get massive really fast, and you lose a lot of that more traditional, small mom meetup vibe."

Her solution: Allo, an app that connects people in the same neighborhood and offers them a platform to ask for help—be that for dog walking, unloading hand-me-downs, babysitting, or simply connecting. When I point out that asking a stranger, even if he or she lives nearby, to babysit your most prized possession is a little different from having a TaskRabbit come over to fix the drawer, she tells me, "The idea is people will use it first to meet up, use it more socially, develop more of a real village, and then use it more transactionally." It's a variant on Peanut, but with an innovation she thinks is critical.

"Spurring that initial conversation without a call to action is really tough," she says. I think back to my unsuccessful time trying to meet up with Devorah. We both swiped right, chatted idly, and then never followed through. If I'd needed a onesie or wanted a partner to go for a walk right at that very minute, and she'd answered, perhaps she would now be part of my extended village.

Something that will likely be lost on most users: the name isn't just a chirpy, Eliza Doolittle–esque way of saying hello. It refers to *allo*, as in *alloparenting*, the term for parental care provided by those other than the mother. (*Allo* is the Greek root for *other*.) The concept is the foundation for some of the most groundbreaking work of her mother-in-law, famed anthropologist and primatologist Sarah Blaffer Hrdy.

Since she started her career, Hrdy senior, heiress to an oil fortune in Texas who left the high life behind to study the Hanuman langur and get her PhD at Harvard, has challenged many of the sexist notions put forth by male evolutionary theorists. She's authored a number of influential books about women's role in evolution, including *Mother Nature* and *Mothers and Others*, both of which discuss the critical role of alloparents to human evolution, and is a National Academy of Sciences member, which an academic described to me as "as good as it gets for scientific status." Our hominid ancestors wouldn't have survived unless they were "cooperative breeders" who relied on each other for help, Hrdy argues. Think about chimps, who have children about every five to eight years. Our human ancestors, conversely, got pregnant every few years. And even after their babies were weaned, they didn't become nutritionally independent for quite some time. So how was a nursing mother with a dependent toddler supposed to continue foraging enough calories to keep nursing, enough calories to feed her children (it takes thirteen million to raise a child to self-sufficiency), and enough calories to be healthy enough to procreate again? Enter: aunts, grandmothers, cousins, even nonkin.

Among the myriad implications for this theory, I home in on a particularly calming one, which partly explains the stressors of the modern mother. We love our children, adore them, can't wait to hold them, and then are also grateful when we can hand them off to someone else.

"If, instead of evolving like chimpanzees where mothers are turning themselves over in a totally dedicated, single-minded way to their infants, we had evolved as cooperative breeders," Hrdy said in an interview with *Scientific American*, "it makes sense that I would feel the need for more social support and more help rearing these children than an American woman living in Cambridge in the 1970s was likely to get as a postdoc." My reliance on my husband, my mother, and my nanny has to do with the demands of the modern world—and my full-time job, yes—but it also has an evolutionary underpinning that existed long before the phrase "have it all."

Building on this, in an article published in *Natural History* magazine in 2001, Hrdy lays out the issue with assuming a thriving child is one that is securely attached to his mother, and his mother alone, which developmental psychologists have long considered an important indicator of success. The family unit of today is, largely, viewed to be a nuclear one, and not an extended, interconnected one—which Hrdy points out was *not* the case in days of yore.

"In terms of developmental outcomes," she writes, "the most relevant factor might not be how securely or insecurely attached to the mother the baby is—the variable that developmental psychologists are trained to measure—but rather how secure the baby is in relation to all the people caring for him or her."

In other words, secure infants may be secure because their

mothers—and in turn, they themselves—have a robust support network. Hrdy's theory removes from the mother the burden of unquestionably adopting the role of the selfless, ever-present caregiver. (NB: Unlike evolutionary psychology, an approach to studying human behavior that has come under a lot of fire for, among other things, promoting genetic determinism, I confirm that Hrdy's work is grounded in behavioral ecology, a rigorous discipline.)

Within minutes of getting on the phone with Sarah Hrdy, we're talking infanticide.

"If some mothers don't get social support postpartum, they bail out," she tells me, speaking, it should be made clear, of monkey mothers. I've reached her at her walnut farm in Northern California, which she runs when not writing. "They either abandon their baby, push it off, or actually kill it. It's such a fraught topic and we forget. If you're human, you come from ancestors with that in their history."

A little reminder that the right social network goes a long way. It's no surprise that Hrdy is an ardent advocate for women's rights and affordable childcare. Great day care, staffed by loving and experienced caregivers, is a simple solution that would serve up extra, loving helpers to myriad mothers in need, particularly those who live far from extended family, work multiple jobs, or just need a social safety net (read: almost all of us).

"If I were a graduate student now and couldn't rely on my family's resources as a parasite," she tells me, "I'd either live in France where I'd have access to *école maternelle*, or else I'd live in a housing situation where I could live with another couple with small children. But all our models are about privacy— your own house, your own ridiculous yard! What we need is a house with joint living arrangements and big fenced-in yards."

She admits that, barring an upheaval in our societal ideas about real estate, apps—her own familial bias aside—can provide an opportunity to help people connect, but she is adamant that mothers need to actually see each other, face-to-face.

"Our relationships are multisensorial," she says. "You're responding to facial expression, smell, touch." It's rooted in our great ape brains.

* * *

The problem, as far as I can tell, is that friction factor Catherine Hrdy spoke of. However much I want to meet up in person with mothers who are going through the same things, I just can't seem to make any time. I find a few local groups, but most meet during the middle of the afternoon, when I'm at work. And the weekends are sacred.

"People crave connection," Tovah Klein tells me the afternoon I meet her at her Barnard College office, where she's the director of the Center for Toddler Development. She has long run in-person groups, and is a friend of my pediatrician, so I offer to take her to coffee. "You need to laugh, have humor, know you're not alone. I don't think anything changes us as much as having a child, and there is no replacement for human interaction. But even people who *ask* me to do private groups, they just don't materialize. It's hard to get people together."

Klein, who joined the psychology faculty in 1995, is the author of *How Toddlers Thrive*, a book that seeks to help parents approach their roles with compassion, to see the world through a toddler's eyes. This she does daily at the center, and, as is obvious to anyone who works to support children, supporting parents is step number one. Klein runs numerous groups for parents, some of which have been meeting at regular intervals for eight years.

"We see our center here as having a park bench model," she tells me. A framed black-and-white photo of herself, extremely pregnant with her third son, hangs behind her on the wall, and a plaque sits on her cluttered bookshelf that reads DANCE LIKE A TODDLER, THEY DON'T EVEN CARE IF THERE IS MUSIC. "Traditionally, parents met other parents, whether it was on the porch or in the backyard or at the playground." Barring that, if you live in New York City, come to the toddler center and get a hit of community.

She recounts one stand-out moment from a group years ago, just when iPhones were coming into vogue. One mother told the group that her young son liked putting on her bras. Her husband was worried and wanted to get help. Within moments, the other mothers in the group were whipping out their phones and calling up photos. *Here's my son in my nightie! Here's mine in my underwear!* And on and on. That's one of the biggest benefits of the group, she tells me. Whatever topic is on your mind, you show up thinking that whatever you're going through is unique and extreme. You leave thinking, *I'm definitely not alone.*

But beyond the anecdotal evidence that women often feel more supported, more calm, and more in control after meeting with fellow mothers, there are noted medical benefits to gathering together. To get the extreme other-end-of-the-spectrum approach to communities, I find my way to a pioneer in the field of group pre- and postnatal care.

"Pregnancy and the early postpartum period is a time of affiliation," Sharon Rising tells me. "Supposedly this is a normal process, except it really doesn't feel that way at all! The literature is contradictory, different people are doing different things, so who are you really going to believe? Going on the internet and having this bombardment from a lot of other women who are just as frantic as you are—you pick up that level of worry and stress right away. I don't think that's terribly helpful. So get off of it."

Rising now serves as president emerita of the group care non-profit she founded, Centering Healthcare, born of a germ of an idea she had back in 1993, when she was working as a midwife in Connecticut and found herself repeating the same pieces of information over and over again to her patients.

"I felt like I was becoming a tape machine," she remembers. "At that stage in their lives, I realized, women are really dealing with similar issues."

So, with an eye toward efficiency and an innate sense that group care would benefit new moms, she gathered ten to twelve women with babies of similar gestational age into one of her hospital's conference rooms to meet and chat about pregnancy as they received their normal blood pressure and belly checks. Though the meetings were two hours, far longer than the usual in-and-out visits that dominated the rest of Rising's day, all the participants—both the pregnant women and the nurse/midwife practitioners leading the group—appeared to be doing something rare in the hospital setting: enjoying themselves. It was years before Rising was able to document a medical upside, but even after the first few meetings, she knew, in her gut, that group care was desperately needed during that relatively short but particularly critical few years of a woman's life when she's pregnant and then the mother of young children.

Rising now has concrete data to back up that initial gut instinct. Centering Healthcare and its two wings—CenteringPregnancy, which focuses on the prenatal period, and CenteringParenting, which focuses on the early postpartum period—today boast almost six hundred participating sites in the States and several more internationally in around a dozen countries. Dozens of studies attest to the positive impact of group prenatal care and of Centering's approach in particular; the American College of Obstetricians and Gynecologists endorsed the practice in 2018. Research shows that group prenatal care reduces preterm births by up to half, decreases emergency room visits in the third trimester, and increases birth weight. The most important finding: the outcomes were shown to be more profound among poor mothers and mothers of color, which means the model has the power to close the health gap.

So, having friends, real live friends who can look you in the eye and tell you to calm the hell down, is actually good for your health. If that's not a compelling reason to lean on real friends during the early days of motherhood, I don't know what is.

Or, as Rising puts it, "There's something about that need to see each other, but even more so to touch—that touch, that hug— that becomes a renewing, and life-giving, force during stages in our life when we might feel particularly needy. Doing that virtually doesn't really cut it."

* * *

Armed with statistics and studies, when Charlotte turns six months old and I reemerge into the real world again, I break my bonds with Facebook—gently. I delete the app from my phone, which means if I need a hit from my virtual village, I have to log on through the clunky mobile website. This, alone, makes my trips to Mommaland far more infrequent. It's there for the occasional crowdsourced question, but it's no longer part and parcel of my everyday search for parenting advice.

I am thankful not to identify with any stigmatized parenting group that might benefit from Reddit, but my hours on the site profoundly changed my view on what anonymity online can afford parents in need. I'm grateful to know it's there, though I visit infrequently.

And while I appreciate the potential benefit of the meet-a-mother-friend apps and the various in-person groups, I can't seem to find enough time in the day, with a toddler and a newborn, to actually follow through. And when COVID upheaved our world, that follow-through became an impossibility.

Oddly, after my research and my pondering, it is a federal agency from the early 1900s that I find myself wishing I could resurrect for all of us millennials who find ourselves awash in advice and unauthorized information. The Children's Bureau—which still exists, but with a much different mandate—is a nice example of how to support overwhelmed and confused mothers with information that is just authoritative enough, just calming enough, and just distant enough to allow for the airing of grievances that you might not want to bring up with even your closest friends. As I see it, a large part of its success was due to presenting that information in a manageable little medium known as: the letter.

Established by President Taft in 1912, the bureau was the outgrowth of a campaign by two women with a mission to help American infants survive. The bureau not only distributed pamphlets to women all over the country about infant and prenatal care—certain estimates state that by 1929, half of all US babies had been helped by the pamphlet's information—but also took the time to personally respond to letters from women, both rich and poor, who sought advice and support on everything from bodily functions to sleep schedules. Imagine: there was a time when women sent in questions about their perinea to the federal government. (All I can think about, when I come upon this tidbit, is writing a letter about my nethers and having it end up in the hands of Mike Pence.)

"These letters are a precursor to the social media stuff you see today," historian Jodi Vandenberg-Daves, author of *Modern Motherhood*, a comprehensive history of American motherhood, tells me when I reach her at her University of Wisconsin–La Crosse office. "You have mothers really laying it all out there. Sometimes they reference things they'd rather not talk to their mothers or neighbors about, taboo subjects. There's an intimacy to them. It's nothing like how we imagine women interacting with the federal government today."

For a few glorious nights, instead of scrolling through Facebook posts on my phone before bed, I read my way through Molly Ladd-Taylor's *Raising a Baby the Government Way*, a collection of bureau correspondence from 1915 to 1932.

Take Mrs. N.W. from Seattle. "Is there not some way that I can do all these scientific and hygienic duties for our babies, keep our house up in proper fashion and still have time to rock and play with my babies?" she writes in on March 4, 1920. "I do not ask time for myself but it would be nice to have a short period during the evening in which to read, as I feel that I am growing narrow with no thoughts other than my household." (Across the space-time continuum, Mrs. N.W., I so feel you.)

The bureau's Mary Mills West, a widower with five children, advises her to get her kids into bed before her own supper. "If you have not tried putting away your children at six o'clock," she responds, "you have no idea what a relief it will be to you. It can be done; I have done it myself with three boys." I take West's advice to heart and, a few weeks before Charlotte is born, start putting Ella to sleep at 6:30 instead of 7. The first few nights are hell, but, I think, if someone with three kids did it, I can handle it with one. I stick it out, and eke out thirty more minutes of adult time. I feel like a warrior.

Some write about nursing problems—their milk supply is too low, the baby won't drink—and others write about marriage problems. One lets drop that her husband is abusing her. The response begins, "You will understand that I am not writing to you now officially but just as one person to another."

And that, I realize, is the key. One person to another.

Three months after Charlotte was born, my closest friend, who suffers from a debilitating autoimmune disease, became a mother. Since she lives in San Francisco, we've kept our friendship alive since college largely by sending long, rambling emails back and forth, a sort of shared journal of our lives as we've grown up through our twenties and thirties, through boyfriends, and jobs, and then husbands, and children. As her baby grows, our emails turn, inevitably, toward the minutiae of newborn life—how to get the little one to sleep through the night, whether or not to take that work trip when the baby is still so young. We've created, in a way, our own little children's bureau. The information I pass along to her is manageable, loving, personalized. I'm obviously not as removed as the federal bureau's responders—we've known each other for almost twenty years—but these emails have always been a safe space for airing even the most taboo subject, likely spurred on by her disease. How scandalous can it be to talk about your postpartum sex life when, for a decade, you've been freely discussing enemas and emptying colostomy bags?

And so, after romping about in the deepest recesses of the virtual village, after trying to make new friends and failing, after attempting and then failing to sit in on an in-person mother's group, I realize that all of that can be trumped by a single loving letter from a single loving friend, who has known you when you've been a Hot Mess, a Book Worm, and even that one time when you were a Dance Machine. With an email from her in my inbox, the rest of the virtual village becomes garnish—which seems, as my innate great ape instincts intuited at the start of this journey, exactly right.

3

Baby Paparazzi

If You're Capturing the Moment, Are You Ever in It?

About a third of the way through an album full of black-and-white photos at my parents' house, neatly labeled "1984" on its spine, is the first-ever photo taken of yours truly. In it, I'm dressed in a white onesie with a Peter Pan collar, I'm sporting a full head of hair, and my eyes are slightly open, gazing just off to the left of the camera lens with the dazed look of someone who, a few days prior, was living in an aqueous environment. My parents didn't bring their camera to the hospital, so any memories they have of my first hours are theirs alone. I was at least two days old, perhaps more, when my mother put me on her bed at home and took a snap with her Nikon.

I tried not to read too deeply into the fact that when Dave and I finally broached the subject of when we should first memorialize our life as a family of three, we had wildly differing opinions. I was, after all, in active labor and literally hours away from delivery—there was no turning back now.

"If there were ever a time to document something, isn't it the first few moments of a person's life?" Dave asked, offering up an arm for me to ravage during one contraction. "It's not like I'll post it to social media or anything. It's just for us to have, to remember."

"IS NOTHING SACRED ANYMORE?!" I wheezed out, when I caught my breath.

We were cutting a stuttering path northwest, from my OB's office past the tulips on Park Avenue, toward the shiny black monolith of Mount Sinai hospital, where, thirty-two years prior, I'd been born. After my doctor confirmed I was "definitely in active labor," Dave shot out of her office and started hailing anything that moved on Lexington Avenue, including a UPS truck. But I told him I'd be walking; he could meet me there. Sure, part of this was that I'm a hardwired New Yorker—who takes a cab ten blocks? And on such a beautiful day? And it wasn't as heroic as it sounds. We were close enough, and my doctor said it might make me feel better to keep moving, so long as we didn't "dawdle." But deep down, there was likely some psychological reason I wanted to delay the inevitable. Once we got to the hospital, I'd become a cog in the hospital machine, spat out at the other end with a baby I didn't yet know or know how to care for. A walk would delay this life inflection point ever so slightly. As the UPS truck trundled down Lex, Dave sighed and took our overnight bag from my arm, and off we went.

And as we walked, we talked—well, we didn't so much talk as I monologued, hopped up on hormones and excitement, while

Dave waited to get a word in edgewise during contractions—about memory, and privacy, and whether or not we were going to be the kind of people who shared baby photos and, if we were, how we'd do it.

"Look, there's the question of how accurate memory really is anyway," Dave said as a contraction started its steady creep. I'd been mid-rant about how certain memories, perhaps, should be accessible only in one's own brain, like my parents' had of me in the delivery room three decades prior. "Like, what is a *true* memory, anyway? That could be a fallacy." He paused then, ever the psych major, said, "You should maybe pick up Daniel Kahneman's latest book."

Enduring mansplaining when rendered mute by pain is the obstetrical equivalent of being lashed to the mast of Odysseus's ship, passing the Sirens. Powerless and writhing, I let him continue, referencing the brilliant psychologist's theory about the two selves—the remembering and the experiencing, which live in conflict—and various other sources and documents I was certain I wouldn't have the mental bandwidth to think about until our child no doubt followed in his father's footsteps and enjoyed an illustrious career in Model UN. (Dave is likely the only high schooler to win the Best Delegate award for representing Azerbaijan. The winning argument turned on a resolution for a two-state solution in the Middle East, brokered by a US-Azerbaijani joint task force.) But as he talked, I silently wondered if maybe he was right. Wouldn't it be nice to revisit the delivery room every once in a while, see how our future child started out his or her life in the world? What if the intensity of the moment turned my brain to mush? What was the harm in, essentially, outsourcing my memory to a mobile device, to be called up as desired?

Baby, Unplugged

Two blocks from the hospital, and no closer to a decision, we found ourselves immobile in a particularly inopportune spot: outside an Italian American elementary school during dismissal. I'd thought we'd be able to overshoot the entrance, but my contractions were coming at a faster clip. As my insides began to roil, little kids, dressed in collared shirts under navy sweater-vests, poured out of the entrance, shrieking and skipping and chattering with each other. Waiting outside to receive them was a posse of stick-thin women, all wearing driving loafers, enormous sunglasses, and the unmistakable air of international sophistication.

As the tightening of my midriff reached its crescendo and started to subside, my eyes refocused. One of the mothers—a Carla Bruni double, with high cheekbones, perfect cascading hair, and a cream-colored pantsuit, probably a PhD in art history—had taken it all in with a single glance: my belly, my hand gripping Dave's, the women's bag slung over his shoulder. I watched as she very gently brought her two hands down on the top of two twirling kids' heads, stilling them. Another mother, picking up on the energy shift, got another two. Silently, the others followed suit, the calm rippling out around us. For a brief moment, all I could hear were chirping birds, punctuated by the squeaking sound of my own clenched teeth. I was certain this moment—this odd, extemporaneous baptism of sorts into the clan of motherhood—would be seared in my memory forever: the sound of the birds, the dirty blond of one of the boys' hair, the little nubbins on the underside of Carla's driving loafers. I might never be able to remember the password to my health insurance provider's website. But this moment? Unforgettable. As I resurfaced and we continued our walk to the hospital, I felt certain Carla was as likely to have had a camera in the delivery room as she was to own a piece of athleisure wear.

"No photos, okay?" I said to Dave as we finally arrived at the hospital. He squeezed my arm and said, "Sweetheart, whatever you want."

Two hours later, during which I briefly considered leaving Dave for the nice young Jewish anesthesiologist who administered my epidural, Ella arrived, blinking and silent and warm, and they placed her in my arms. As we gazed at each other, and Dave leaned over to kiss my forehead, it was perfectly quiet in the room, nothing like the chaos I'd expected. I fixated on her tiny nails, and the fuzz on her upper arms, the light-blue tinge of her fingertips, her wide eyes, all that hair, matted down on the top of her little head. She opened her mouth up a few times like a fish, and I thought, *How could I ever forget this?* In that instant, I vowed to be the kind of mother who slowed down, was present, trusted in her innate ability to filter out the important memories from the junk, and rarely, if ever, inserted a layer of technology between me and a sacred moment with my child. Why invite Steve Jobs into my life's most important moments?

A week later: videos and photos of Ella's tiny hands and toes had nearly maxed out my phone's storage space. I had a whole subgenre of Ella documentation that focused solely on her hiccuping, which she did whenever she was getting tired (read: all the time). Did I really need fourteen photographs of the heft of her cheek, even as the afternoon light streaming in the windows picked up slightly different shadows in each shot? I wasn't sure, but I felt an inexplicable urge to document and then to share them.

I opted out of broadcasting to the masses, for a few reasons, including that I wasn't sure what image I wanted to project. Should I be cut from the same "real mama" cloth later worn by Ali Wong and Amy Schumer, snapshotting raw footage of early parenthood, from nipples poking through pump flanges to poop-splosions gone horribly wrong? Or should I go more "curated earth mother," upgrading my wardrobe from expandable pants to diaphanous caftans, which I'd wear while nursing in a white room with billowing curtains? I was vaguely aware that there were few, perhaps no, legal protections in place for Ella's privacy, should I choose to post a photo that could haunt her years down the line, so I decided to keep things in the family, setting up a private Apple photo stream.

One day, as Ella gazed up at me and I gazed at a photo of her on my phone—I'd taken several in rapid-fire succession to capture a smile that was, I later confirmed, most certainly unintentional and likely caused by gas—I remembered the photo albums my mother painstakingly made of me and my sister, one a year, each bound in a maroon binding that rubbed off on the white shelves under the television set.

"Don't smile. It looks fake."

It's the single directive she used to give us. Inside the albums there are no staged images of the family standing in front of some monument, grins plastered on. Instead, the black-and-white shots elevate the beauty of the everyday: they're equal parts art and documentation. There's one of my sister, age four, gazing pensively at the camera as she sits on the toilet, her little feet dangling in the air. Another of me, stark naked, holding a diaper aloft as I exit the room. A series of the two of us laughing uproariously on my parents' bed.

I guess that was kind of what I was doing, capturing Ella candidly as she hiccupped and burped—but then again, it was also really *not* what I was doing, since my mother had to make real choices, both in the shots she took, then in the ones she developed, and finally, in the ones she pasted into albums. Even now, with a phone in her pocket, she won't take fourteen photos to get the right shot. She'll wait, and wait, and wait, and then—*click*. I felt slightly unsettled realizing that I had to make no choices, ever, when it came to capturing and preserving my child's life, other than how quickly to tap my thumb up and down on the home button. There were simply no limits. Much like economic inflation, it occurred to me, the ease of the digital world served to deflate the value and importance of each snap.

In idle moments, I wondered about that thumb tapping, with questions that fell into two buckets—the act of taking photos in a technological world, and the act of sharing them.

It was obvious that I was less in the moment *avec* camera as *sans*, but what about Ella, who, as she grew up, took increasing delight in going through old photographs of herself on our phones? Was she becoming a little narcissist? I tried to keep Alison Gopnik's mantra in mind—parenting is a mug's game, all these little decisions aren't having as big an impact as I feared—but it didn't seem like the best thing in the world for her to spend time each day cycling through photos of herself. I didn't need studies to tell me that—though, of course, there are studies. Many, in fact. One, conducted by researchers at Swansea University, concluded that the posting of selfies on social media—by people ages eighteen to thirty-four, but still—lead to an increase in narcissism "by an average of 25 percent." Combine that with another study, from the University of Illinois, that suggests preschoolers can form pretty advanced conceptions of body image, and I winced, remembering how cutthroat my middle school was and imagining how horrifyingly ratcheted up that self-consciousness would be when Ella started navigating those waters, buttressed by social media and photo filters and who even knows what else.

On the flip side, was I helping her remember her life story more clearly by having her revisit it so frequently? I can't remember much before I turned four, save for a few images—my father's belt, looped around my tricycle and pulling me down Central Park West; sitting on the cold, smooth marble floor of the American Museum of Natural History and crying, certain I'd been abandoned forever (my babysitter was hiding behind a thick column). Maybe Ella would be able to remember her entire life.

I'd read about the Google effect—the idea that we more readily forget information that is accessible online; furthermore, our brains adapt so that while we might not remember the given fact we're trying to recall, we'll remember how to find that fact. It's an extension of the theory of transactive memory, which posits that groups of people share knowledge. You do not remember alone. You might not know where the turkey baster is, but your husband does, and so you know to turn to him on Thanksgiving morning. In offloading our memories to our phones' photo rolls, I wondered if we were not only engaging in a modern-day extension of transactive memory, wherein the cloud stands in for our friends and family, but also causing our brains to adapt, perhaps freeing up space for other mental tasks or cognitive processes.

A less heady, more pressing problem: What the hell was I planning to do with those fourteen cheek photos? I entertained fantasies of going through each day's haul and editing them down to a choice few—the technological equivalent of my mother going through contact sheets with a red wax pencil—but once Ella fell asleep and I was released from my role as parent paparazzi, I found myself so tired, and so done with the phone, that I'd rather do just about anything else. So there they sat, taking up space, stored in the cloud, which I hoped didn't suddenly spontaneously evaporate and wipe out the record of my child's life.

I was most likely to revisit these random shots when I got a prompt from Apple, asking me to rediscover a certain day, via a slideshow or video the company had made for me. Which led me to a bigger, scarier, more dystopian question: Was I essentially outsourcing my family's memories to an algorithm?

But if I'm being honest, I didn't *actively* ponder these questions. I mostly went about the day hoping I'd get dressed before noon, contemplating whether it was okay to give Ella a pacifier that had rolled under the bed or if it had rubella motes on it. And I continued tapping away.

Then one night, when Ella was about a year old, I realized that I had loads of shots of Dave with the baby on my phone, and he had loads of me with the baby on his phone, but we had none of ourselves. So he shared his Google Photos account with me, allowing me to view anything he'd snapped. The first thing I saw: a series of beautiful earrings.

"What are these?" I asked.

His reply: "Crap." Options for my birthday present.

He fiddled around in the settings and exhaled.

"Okay, I made it so that you can *only* see photos of Ella."

Nine times out of ten, Ella was photographed in a swaddle. How accurately can Google identify an object that looks more hoagie than human?

Very accurately, it turns out.

It was then that I found it: a video Dave took, sneakily, a few moments after Ella was born. She's lying on my chest, and I'm breathing, hard, and looking down at her. The first thing I noticed was the noise. In my memory, the delivery room was unexpectedly peaceful, Zen-like. Here, I could hear the steady beep of a heart monitor, people rushing around off-screen, someone calling for some tests. Her tiny head was outfitted in a hat. A hat? When did that go on? Wasn't there that full head of hair, all matted down? And when did Dave even take the video? I found myself no longer so sure of what my experience had been in the delivery room or when things had happened. I saw the IV line snaking out of my right arm, which instantly made me remember the uncomfortable feeling of the catheter they'd attached during the epidural, something I'd completely blocked out. My rosy picture had, somehow, become tinged in blue. But instead of getting irritated with Dave for taking a video on the sly, of rupturing whatever haloed memory I thought was real, or pure, I found myself watching the fifteen-second video over and over again. It was the first few moments of Ella's life. Even if it was different than I remembered, it was still magnificent.

* * *

It takes until Charlotte arrives for me to put my thumb tapping on the witness stand. Absentmindedly scrolling back through a few days of photos when she's about five months old, I realize I have a ton of selfies of us looking like Greek theater masks: me grinning wildly, her frowning and confused. She's not quite sure what she's looking at, but she doesn't seem to like it. And so, with three and a half years in the books as a card-carrying member of the baby paparazzi, I finally decide to answer the questions that thrum under the surface every time I take out my phone to capture a moment for posterity.

The first thing I do is head to the back corners of Apple's website to read the latest tech brief on their Photos app, dated September 2019. I'm trying to figure out how Big Tech actually curates our photos for us. (The biggies are, of course, Google and Apple, with Apple branding itself as the champion of privacy; Google, the champion of data storage and analysis. If you are scared of Big Tech being able to access your photos and opt for smaller photo-sharing apps, know that your choice is likely six of one, half dozen of another: Tinybeans, a small but beloved app that's all about privacy, uses Amazon's servers.)

In the brief, I read that there are over a trillion photos and videos captured each year with the iPhone. (I later found a crazy statistic that in 2015, more photos were taken than in all previous years combined.) I am reminded of an SNL skit in which Kate McKinnon, playing Elizabeth Warren defending her tax plan, says that "when the numbers are this big, they're just pretend." But the next sentence carries a tinge of the sinister in it.

"As photo libraries have grown larger," I read, "it's become harder for users to organize and rediscover the precious memories of their lives. . . . Using on-device machine learning, Photos curates the entire library to highlight the best images, automatically hiding clutter and similar photos to showcase significant events from the past day, month, or year."

In other words, when we sleep—literally, it's called "overnight processing" and happens when our phones are plugged in and not being used, to conserve power—Apple uses AI to classify, sort, and edit down our photo streams. The result: I never have to see blurry photos or other shots with bad framing and lighting. I think of the ten nearly identical photos I took of Charlotte that morning, as she precariously steadied herself on the bed, tripod-style, to sit unaided for the first time. Many of them were backlit and fuzzy, since my subject was a six-month-old child with the core strength of a jellyfish. "To capture the perfect moment, users often take many pictures of the same thing," the brief reads in a section that explains how it curates photos by the day (as opposed to the month or year). Well, duh. But then: "The Days view identifies similar photos, picks the user's best shot, and intelligently hides the others."

Best? I kind of like the one when Charlotte is midfall, which is how I envision her these days, always teetering, like a bobblehead doll. Would that be classified as best or, more likely, worst by an algorithm trained to demote fuzzy pictures in favor of clear ones? That used to be a decision for Mom or Dad to make as they sifted through snaps from the year and pasted them into an album—a medium we're likely witnessing at the end of its hundred-year history.

(Brief aside on that hundred-year history: The oldest family albums in the Library of Congress date to the 1850s, but albums really started to hit their stride after 1900, when the Eastman Kodak Company released the Brownie camera, a one-dollar square box that brought snapshot photography to the masses. Marketed toward women and children, and building on the Victorian tradition of scrapbooking, the Kodak company's slogan—"You press the button, we'll do the rest"—made the art form accessible to just about anyone who was interested in capturing their own lives. And what self-interested human wasn't? Armed with the cheap little machine, you could take your own photos, send your camera to Kodak's Rochester factory, and, a few weeks later, receive your prints. By 1915, amateur photographers had taken an estimated 1.5 million annual photographs, and album making had become a bit of a phenomenon. It was just a hop, skip, and a jump to today's photo frenzy.)

Unsurprisingly, Dave likes the AI functionality in Google Photos, his preferred storage service.

"The other day, Ella told me she hated clams," he tells me, digging deep in an effort to convince me that there's a legitimate value-add to all of Google's tagging and metadata analysis. "I searched for 'Ella + clam chowder' and Google Photos surfaced that video we took of her last summer eating clam chowder on the beach, face first. And I showed it to her."

"Did she admit that she likes clams?" I ask.

"That's not the point," he grouses.

* * *

The evening of Charlotte's six-month birthday, I check: I've taken 11,402 photos on my phone. Of those, I've "favorited" 1,042—my meager attempt to sift through the swaths of photos I capture each week—and posted 1,661 to a photo stream entitled "Babies E and C!" It's accessible only by my immediate family and filled with photos that capture the minutiae I hope blood relatives are genetically programmed to find adorable: Ella with her morning hair, looking like Christopher Lloyd from *Back to the Future*, a close-up of Charlotte's thigh rolls.

But I understand, innately, that having them live on my phone, and only on my phone, is problematic. There's something inherently dulling about viewing them on a device that also serves as my alarm clock. And there's something inherently amorphous about the scroll, the never-ending roll of memories spanning backward and forward, the lack of limits.

That night, when I plug in my phone and turn out the light, I imagine a tiny little creature, with the head of the Apple logo, humming to himself as he busily sorts through that day's photos, labeling and discarding, Frisbeeing some into the shredder, stamping a precious few with the words "memory worth keeping." The next morning, my phone, quiet and immobile, surely looks the same as when I fell asleep. *Lies!* I think as I tiptoe over to Charlotte's bassinet and find her grinning up at me while furiously sucking half her fist. *You've been burning the midnight oil and restructuring my life story!*

"You have a fantasy of editing, but nobody edits," says Barbara Levine, who served as the exhibitions director at the San Francisco Museum of Modern Art and currently co-runs Project B, which deals in found artwork. "Editing is a skill, and if you're going to be seduced by companies that promise to do the work for you, then you're putting your family memories—what you saw and how you saw it—in the hands of somebody else. So it raises all kinds of questions about what memories you want to pass on."

As for why the vast majority of people don't take the time to edit themselves?

"Who wants to spend more time on the computer?" she asks, rhetorically. "There's a very real aspect of screen fatigue."

At Project B, Levine, together with her cofounder, uses an extensive collection of vernacular photography—the term for photos taken of the everyday—to create exhibitions, publications, and the like. She's rarely more happy than when she's at a flea market, paging through a discarded family photo album from years ago. Her 2006 book and resulting exhibition, both titled *Snapshot Chronicles: Inventing the American Photo Album*, treats old photo albums as pieces of art. Levine grew up surrounded by magazines and sat for myriad shows on her father's slide projector, with the carousel clickity-clacking away, and has serious reservations about how the family album has evolved in the digital age.

"Even though we're making more pictures than ever, they're not material," she says. Although I'm not sure if she means *material* like *physical* or *material* like *significant*, both meanings apply.

In the promises of Big Tech's AI algorithms to create photo albums that you can view with a single click and print into books of preordained tableaus, she sees echoes of Eastman Kodak's brilliant marketing message.

"That's the same thing that's happening now in terms of making it so that it seems like magic," she says. "But what's really different today is that digital promises this idea of creativity, but is really pushing you into these templates. And so what happens is that there's a homogeneity. Some of the charm, of the surprise, definitely the authentic voice, the intimacy—that is all compromised."

Erik Kessels is bucking that homogeneity in a very small, very personal way. I learn about him during the few weeks I spend in the underworld of vernacular photography collectors, a musty, comforting place shielded, a bit, from the shine of fast-paced tech. He estimates he's collected over fifteen thousand family albums, which he then repurposes and republishes in books made at his publishing house. He's a bit of a polymath, having made films and curated exhibitions while also serving as the creative director of KesselsKramer, a renowned advertising agency based in Amsterdam. But his obsession lies in discarded photos, found at flea markets, online, and in junk shops, which he tells me can likely be traced to when he was eleven and his nine-year-old sister was hit by a car that ran a red light.

"My parents were always looking for her last image," he tells me on the phone, "and they reappropriated a very random family snap, cropped her out of it, made it black-and-white, enlarged it, and it became kind of a memorial image."

In the course of his collecting life, Kessels discovered something curious.

"On average, people—all people—make seven or eight family albums in their lifetime, which is quite remarkable," he says. And, regardless of the family, the seven albums tend to follow the same narrative. The first is two people going on holiday, "and the photographing is really close-up—they are in love, and it's pictures of each other, constantly." The second: marriage. The third and fourth: the first baby. Then a couple more with other babies and holidays sprinkled in. And the final one: when the children are out of the house, and parents go on holiday alone and finally start taking pictures of each other again. Take any family at random, and you'll get those same seven albums.

"That is not a lot," Kessels says, "and that used to be your entire photographic life."

Back in the day, then, I'd likely have created just three, maybe four albums by this point in my life. Right now, I have the material for a hundred times that, easily. No wonder we all happily relinquish the sifting to an algorithm—it's overwhelming otherwise.

Today, with the weight of photography obviously diminished due to the sheer ease and thoughtlessness of snapping away, Kes-

sels has spent a good part of his professional life bringing a second life to discarded photo albums, where he finds beauty in the
mistakes amateur photographers have made—a closed eye, some
blur.

"It's almost criminal in terms of creativity," he says, when I
ask him about Google's and Apple's algorithms. "It's creating me-
diocrity and middle-of-the-road, where everything is the same."

He reminds me that whatever performative aspect of family
photography is enabled and promoted by Big Tech and social
media is not new, by any stretch of the imagination.

"Family photography is very much propaganda," he says. "It's
almost advertising—there's a beautiful life, look how happy we
are." Social media may take this to an extreme, but from the first
daguerreotypes taken of dressed-up royalty to the Sears por-
traits in a family's Sunday best, the goal is the same: performing
a happy life.

He is the third person that week—all vernacular photography
subworld dwellers—to tell me that it's just a matter of time before our photographs disappear, either because our storage gets
wiped or because the way we try to view them, on a CD-ROM or
jump drive, has become a defunct technology.

"Phones and computers are consumer products and have
built-in obsolescence," Maggie Schreiner confirms when I reach
her office at Brooklyn Historical Society, where she works as the
manager of archives and special collections. She teaches a class,
Personal Archiving 101: Preserving Your Digital Memories, at
different venues throughout the city, where she gives people tips
on how to make sure they don't lose months of photos or digital
documents when there's a computer glitch.

"We like to say the cloud is just someone else's computer,"

she tells me. Meaning, sometimes they crash. She mentions what happened in 2019 when MySpace migrated their servers, losing over a decade's worth of independent music in the process. Permanently. Poof, gone.

I return home that evening and inform Dave that unless we print out or back up our most cherished photos to a physical hard drive, they'll be erased forever, living only in our memories, which are faulty at best. He laughs.

"Do you know that they're storing data in DNA now, like double helixes?" he replies. "A single gram of DNA can store 215 petabytes of data!"

As he scurries around on his computer finding the *Wired* article to share with me, I flash him the same smile I give Charlotte when she's industriously trying to eat a stuffed animal—slightly encouraging, slightly distant—and send a bunch of my latest snaps to the local CVS.

* * *

Is it about time for a science fiction break?

"One could imagine a scenario where you might have a choice between which company's products you want to use based on how much the narrative they construct for you of your life is palatable to you," author Ted Chiang tells me on the phone, the day his collection of short stories, *Exhalation*, is listed as one of the ten best books of the year by the *New York Times*. "You could imagine a scenario where it's like, *You know, I think I like the way Bing creates my memories better than the way Facebook does.*"

I've called the beloved science fiction writer, perhaps best known outside tech and science fiction worlds as the author of a short story that got adapted into the film *Arrival*, because I know that he's wrestled with the implications of a world where our memories are recorded, faithfully, by devices. He's also one of the few authors I know who could pull off writing the following line of dialogue—"So how are you doing with your Heptapod B practice?"—without eliciting snorts from his readers.

In one short story brought up by nearly every Silicon Valley entrepreneur or venture capitalist I interview, "The Truth of Fact, the Truth of Feeling," he explores the idea of living in a society where everyone has perfect recall. In the story, a new technology called Remem has just been released, which allows individuals to continuously and passively record their lives and then access this recording—known as a life log—whenever they like. While Dave and I certainly don't have continuous video recording, we sure are filling in our life logs at a much more frequent clip than our parents were able to fill in theirs. And the story hits on something that Big Tech currently does allow us to do—search for a memory. Just like Dave can immediately find Ella eating clam chowder, I can type "Charlotte + bath" into the search bar, and up pops all bath photos from the previous few months. What is lost in serendipity is gained in accuracy.

"The idea of having a total video and audio record of every moment in your life, that's something I've been thinking about on and off for a long time," Chiang tells me. "I always had this sense that that would have major repercussions for us, but I didn't know what those would be. What I eventually landed on was that it would affect the way we narrativize our past."

Chiang, a deliberate thinker (he pauses after each question and answers in fully formed paragraphs) and a deliberate writer (in three decades, to the chagrin of his rabid fan base, he's published just a few short stories and a handful of novellas, fewer than twenty works in total), sees a big benefit to making sure these narrations are based in truth.

"People are made of stories," he goes on, "and up until now, we've been able to mostly tell the story we wanted to tell. If we find ourselves having much more accurate records of what happened in our past, if ubiquitous video recording becomes an actual thing, I think we will continue to narrativize, to make stories, but the stories will have to shift in order to accommodate these recordings."

Where he gets anxious is when we allow big tech companies into the equation.

"There's a difference between you having a complete life log and Amazon having a complete life log of you," he says. "This conversation is inextricably linked with questions about privacy."

I hang up with a renewed urgency to wrap my head around two pressing issues: First, does the taking and viewing of photos actually help our memories—either our children's or ours? And second, what happens when we decide to share our photos with others, be that our nearest and dearest or Jeff Bezos?

* * *

A little before her second birthday, Ella became particularly en-amored of one video I'd captured of her at ten months, saying her first word: "Bamba."

It's the name of the Israeli Cheetos-like peanut snack that I started stockpiling and force-feeding her after reading an article in the *New York Times* about how Israeli children likely don't have as many peanut allergies as Americans, due to aggressive

Bamba consumption. (I later heard the article sparked a run on Bamba on the Upper West Side.) She likes to tell people that she remembers saying that first word, that she was sitting in a high chair, that she reached for the Bamba after it flipped into her bib. When she does, I entertain the possibility that recalling images of her recent past has somehow seared early memories into her brain. How cool would it be if Ella could actually remember the first time she stood up? Ate banana? Spoke?

But Dr. Nora Newcombe, who studies children's developing memory, among other things, at the lab she co-runs at Temple University, quickly disabuses me of the notion that Ella has any memory whatsoever of that Bamba-filled afternoon.

"The really early events are probably not there anymore," she tells me. "What you're doing is basically telling a story, and what she'll remember is the story."

Broadly speaking, she explains to me, there are two types of memory: implicit, which demarcates things you just know, like how to ride a bike or how to read this sentence, and explicit, which can be consciously recalled. Within explicit memory, there are two further delineations: semantic memory, which refers to general knowledge—what a Frisbee is, say—and episodic, which refers to specific events in our past—that time you were seven years old and learning how to throw a Frisbee with your Dad and, lacking aim, accidentally threw it directly into a baby carriage where a newborn was sleeping, for example (true story; baby was fine). It's this type of memory that photos help recall. This is sometimes called autobiographical memory, and yes, the demarcations are fuzzy and fluid because memory is complicated. The point is that this episodic, or autobiographical, memory is established once your brain can bind disparate pieces of information—what, when, and where something happened—into a cohesive recollection. The ability to do that rests in the hippocampus.

"Only ten years ago, people thought the hippocampus was mature when you were born," Newcombe tells me. "As we've been able to look more at those neural substrates, it's becoming increasingly apparent that it's not at all mature."

One's explicit memory starts to form around eighteen to twenty-four months, she tells me, and continues to be refined from two through six years of age.

The thing is, even when your brain's memory circuitry is fully developed, as is the case with me (and you), it's still, in a sense, faulty.

"It was fashionable for cognitive psychologists to compare memories to computer files that are placed in storage and pulled out when needed," writes Daniel Schacter, a well-known memory expert and head of the Schacter Memory Lab at Harvard, about his early days in the field. As he explains in *Searching for Memory*, one of his books for the general public, we now understand that the brain divvies up different parts of an experience, which "are in turn linked together by a special memory system hidden deep within the inner recesses of our brain." As for how accurate we are in that composition, he writes, "we are usually correct about the general character of our pasts, but are susceptible to various kinds of biases and distortions when we recount specific experiences."

In other words: memories aren't pure. They're shape-shifters. They are stories we tell ourselves about given moments, and those stories don't always hew so closely to how the events actually played out. Under the right circumstances, individuals can even remember things that never happened, creating what are known as false memories. This can be particularly nefarious and problematic in a legal and criminal setting, when individuals are accused of crimes or sent to prison due to the testimony of witnesses who—sometimes prompted by leading questions—remembered things that never happened.

Even Jean Piaget, a pioneer in the field of child development, was victim to one such illusion.

"I have a childhood memory of my own that would be absolutely splendid if it were authentic, because it goes back to an age when one doesn't usually have memories of childhood," he tells Jean-Claude Bringuier in *Conversations with Jean Piaget*. When he was a child, his nurse was taking him on a walk near the Rond-Point in Paris, and someone tried to snatch him out of his stroller. A nearby policeman saved the day. "I can see him now as if it were yesterday," Piaget tells Bringuier. But years later, his family received a letter from the nurse that she'd made it all up. "I don't believe in pure memories," Piaget goes on. "They always presuppose a greater or lesser degree of inference."

Add technology into the mix and things get even murkier. One study conducted in 2002 showed that if people saw a doctored photo of themselves as a child in a hot air balloon, half remembered the event as happening—even though the photo wasn't real.

And while revisiting undoctored photos of days past will reinforce some parts of the memory, this brings up a bigger issue, which is whether the "purpose" of memory is accuracy. Perhaps it's something else altogether.

In a paper from 1988, I find a particularly compelling reason for letting memory do its thing, unaided by photographic prompts.

"Illusion and Well-Being: A Social Psychological Perspective on Mental Health," written by psychologists Shelley E. Taylor and Jonathon Brown, still ranks as one of the most frequently cited psychology papers. In it, the psychologists introduce the notion of *positive illusions*—the idea that people regard themselves or their circumstances in an unrealistically favorable light.

"These illusions are not merely characteristic of human thought," Taylor later wrote, "they appear actually to be adaptive, promoting rather than undermining good mental health."

Researchers have posited that looking at photos that can jog your memory might actually work *against* this adaptive trait. In other words, maybe it's best, for at least some moments, to let your brain do the sifting for you. As one memory researcher told me, "The memory system is designed to forget, and this is a good thing."

For those of us who want to use photography to reinforce memories—and, after speaking to various Silicon Valley elites, I learn that quite a few of them take photos of their children explicitly with this goal in mind—there may be a best practice: consciously photograph something specific instead of trying to capture a general scene.

In one oft-cited study in the field, cognitive psychologist Linda Henkel, of Fairfield University, asked students to observe certain objects in a museum and photograph others. What she discovered was something she calls the *photo-taking impairment effect*: When participants took photos of objects, they remembered fewer details than when they simply observed the objects. But interestingly, those asked to photograph a specific part of the object remembered not just the detail well but the entire object.

"Even though the camera and your visual attention may be

on one part of something," she explains to me, "your brain is capable of visualizing the whole object." This is likely due to that nebulous word *mindfulness*—if you're photographing with a specific purpose in mind, you'll do it more deliberately. But Henkel is quick to reiterate that there's a fallacy not just of a "pure" memory but also the "pure" photograph.

"Memories are nothing like photographs," she tells me when I give her a ring. "Photographs capture one moment in time, and they aren't veridical versions of a moment either! The lighting, the edits can give you very different versions than what really happened."

I think of that morning, when I'd edited a photo of Charlotte. There she sits, beaming up at something off-screen, a little happy string of drool coming down off her chin, her grin stretching nearly the entire length of the photo. That something off-screen: Dave. Her joy was real; the cause of it, erased forever.

* * *

On February 23, 2016, the French national police (@gendarmerie nationale) posted the following warning on Facebook:

> *You can all be proud moms and dads to your magnificent children, but be careful! Posting pictures of your children on Facebook is not without danger! It is important to protect the privacy of minors and their image on social networks. . . . Sometimes good times deserve to be "just" shared in real life!*

Setting aside how far ahead the French seem to be when it comes to all things parenting related—see: how the state pays for mothers to exercise their nethers after birth, to ensure a speedy recovery and a prompt return to a robust sex life—and how unlikely it would be for the NYPD to post something similarly protective, the warning cuts to the heart of the matter of what happens after we've collected all these snaps. Photographs used to be an art form that could be shared with as many people as could gather around an album. "There is no more social form of picture-taking," Christopher Bonanos, in *Instant: The Story of Polaroid*, writes of the older Polaroids, which forced people to wait and chat as the photo developed in that little sandwich.

Now, with the click of a button, the most social form of picture taking is, in fact, broadcasting them.

I email my friend Anna, a Mexican American who lives with her two young children and husband in France, to see if she heard about the police force's Facebook plea, and she emails back no but, looking at the date it was published, admits she was likely up to her ears in diapers and wipes. But she tells me that the entire culture of taking photos of your children in France is different from the States.

"Schools have pretty strict photo policies," she offers as one example. "They even tried to restrict pics and filming at my daughter's school play this spring. This being France, however, rules are rarely enforced or cared about," she adds.

I'm not much of a sharer on social media—I stopped actively participating entirely a few years ago when I logged on to my Twitter feed and realized it was a long string of links to articles I'd written, which I'd posted at the urging of various editors. Taken as a whole, it was narcissistic and boring, and while I'm as narcissistic and boring as the next person, I didn't really want that to be quite so obvious.

Despite being one of the first Facebook members—Zuckerberg was the class ahead of me at Harvard, and I covered him briefly for the school paper, way back when he crashed the servers with a "Hot or Not" application—I never really got into the swing of social media. And thank God for that. Because the minute I start delving into the ramifications of photo sharing to a broad audience, I learn of myriad reasons not just to keep my children off-line but in a cozy off-the-grid windowless bunker in New Zealand. There are very real fears that data brokers are selling children's online information to advertisers and marketers and the constant, looming threat of a data breach. On top of that, I read stories of mothers who've innocently posted naked photos of their toddlers, only to learn later that they were downloaded, altered, and shared on a website for pedophiles. A 2015 University of Michigan study found that 51 percent of parents, unintentionally or not, offer up personal info that could identify a child's location at any given time. And, by certain estimates, by the age of five, children have almost one thousand shared photos of them online. Taken together, it adds up to a terrifying mess that centers on defining just what privacy means in the digital age—a question that takes on particularly nefarious implications when you're discussing the lives of children.

"By the time a young person enters the workforce, there are hundreds—if not thousands—of digital files, containing a multitude of data points related to the young person and her activities, that can be accessed by different organizations or people," John Palfrey and Urs Gasser, two Harvard law professors, write in *Born Digital: How Children Grow Up in a Digital Age*. "There is no way for the young person to know what all these files are or what they contain."

Could a photo of Ella popping a squat behind a tree in Central Park be used against her during her nomination to the Supreme Court in 2072? After a friend from work, a reporter at a different magazine, wrote a story about the pitfalls of posting on Instagram as a mom, she stopped posting photos of her son altogether, not just to quell the fear of what might happen to his photo but also to respect him.

"I just don't like feeling that I'm posting pictures of my son that he's not consenting to," she told me. "Not that he'd necessarily care. But I'd never do that to a friend. So why would I do that to my kid?" But she's well aware that her point of view hinges, in large part, on her being a reporter and having delved into the data herself. Most of us aren't that informed.

In Europe and Argentina, there is a legal precedent establishing the "right to be forgotten"—a data protection standard that gives individuals greater control over how and by whom their data is used, though it's been roundly criticized in the US, where freedom of speech reigns paramount. There is also 2016's General Data Protection Regulation, passed by the EU, which gives individuals greater control over how and by whom their data is used. But none of this has reached the United States.

In a chapter about privacy, Palfrey and Gasser bring up a fictional girl named Natalie, who has epilepsy. Her parents make her wear a wristband that can detect seizures, despite Natalie's protestations that the wristband could be hacked or that someone could feasibly use the band's app to access her medical records.

"The trade-off might well be the right one in this case," the authors write of the parents' decision to make her wear the band and thereby forfeit her right to privacy, "but the overall issue is chronic. Every day, we make individual decisions about privacy.

Often these decisions are made by or for young people without much consideration of the long-term impact of ceding so much control over personal information to other people."

When I reach Palfrey, a known authority on internet law and emerging media—and also the former head of the prep school Phillips Academy, Andover; the former executive director of Harvard's Berkman Klein Center for Internet and Society, a research center that studies cyberspace and internet-related legal issues; the head of the MacArthur Foundation; and, I learn, a great-great-grandson of Teddy Roosevelt—by phone, I'm curious if he's heartened by the EU regulations. They're ahead of us in so many things—is theirs the right solution? But he's lukewarm.

"The problem is, one, it only obviously affects some people of the globe and these issues are by definition global, so that's a complicating factor," he says. But implementing any sort of regulation misses the mark for him. "The right answer, I think, is ultimately to give as much decision-making as possible to the individual. And from a market perspective, what I imagine will happen is that privacy will become more of a luxury good." You want your data protected, you'll pay. As COVID tracing becomes the norm over the globe, a large proportion of the population may be willing to have their phones tracked and forgo privacy for a greater good—but even in a pandemic, I'm not sure people will so easily relinquish their hold on it. And the notion that only the wealthy among us will be able to opt into protecting their data, photos, and geolocation brings up damning, doomsday scenarios rife with class warfare.

As for fake Natalie and her epilepsy, I'm curious whether there are any legal correctives in place to protect her when she grows up and starts applying to jobs. Absent them, couldn't a company head ignore her resume simply because he knows, from online data, that she is ill and will make the company's health care contributions increase?

"I don't think there's a constitutional bar to such a thing happening," Palfrey allows. "You can imagine a protected class, as there is with race. It *could* happen. It's just not plain to me that the data protection is there to protect someone like Natalie."

In his house, he instituted a simple rule—not to post a photo of his children until they could consent to it, which came around age fourteen. He's about to publish a follow-up to *Born Digital* that is full of advice for parents, and he tells me the prescription of the book boils down to one thing: "Stay connected and have a trusting relationship with your kids. Do no harm. And don't record their entire life."

* * *

But what about those who make it their mission to record their children's entire lives?

The day before Thanksgiving, I find myself in the conference room of Lux Capital—all glass walls and flat screens—waiting to speak to one of the venture capital firm's cofounders, Josh Wolfe. Everything I've been wrestling with, about documenting, and sharing, and memory, and how the future of tech will resolve or evolve them, made an appearance in a sixteen-part, URGENTLY PUNCTUATED WITH CAPITAL LETTERS tweetstorm Wolfe sent out to his more than fifty thousand followers on July 19, 2018, precisely at noon.

"On MOMENTS + MEMORY + MEANING (A thread with a few tangents)," it began. There are those who urge you to be "in the moment," and others who want to capture everything, Wolfe writes in the thread. "I argue (mostly to the eye-rolling skepticism of my wife @LTwolfe) that capturing everything is actually ADDING salience to the MOMENT." Why? "MEMO-RIES are TRAITOROUS. They are ephemeral and we instantly remember not the actual thing but the memory of the thing. Imposters." He goes on to reference both *Westworld* and Tom Stoppard's *The Coast of Utopia* before concluding that he sees virtue in both being in the moment and being able to access a memory on demand, "remembered for how it was not how you want it to be. And shared and imprinted in the memories and minds of others."

Dave had alerted me to the tweetstorm from over a year ago and then patiently explained what a tweetstorm is. Wolfe is both in the thick of parenting—he and his wife have three children, ages three, seven, and nine—and professionally imagines the world of the future. He just might be a proto-example of how the next generation will live. I'm skeptical, but I learn that various smart institutions have given him enough money that he now has $2.5 billion under management, which he uses to invest in the future. Like Ted Chiang, he's clearly spent a lot of time thinking about the purpose of photography and documentation, but with a markedly more commercial approach.

Per its website, Lux Capital "invests in emerging science and technology ventures at the outermost edges of what is possible." What this means is: moon shots. Take CTRL-labs, a company developing a device that will translate electrical muscle impulses into digital signals. (As I try to read and understand its mission, I increasingly feel like Scooby Doo, so I'll just leave that description there.) Wolfe spends his days promoting "scientific rebels," he told a *Fortune* reporter. "They are focused on shrinking the gap between sci-fi and 'sci-fact.' In other words, these are things that were once conceived in someone's imagination and are now being crystallized into reality."

For Wolfe, accuracy is paramount, and technology an obvious means by which to ensure it. He and his wife gather together with their kids every few weeks and throw videos and photos up on the television screen. "Since each time you naturally biologically recall a memory you are remembering it imperfectly," he writes me in an introductory email, "having high-fidelity accurate photos + videos creates a universal shared memory amongst our 3 kids and 2 of us . . . and that shared emotion adds salience to the memories, imprinting them more."

It's a particularly pragmatic way to think of maximizing the effect of photos, but I guess it's one way to go about navigating this morass.

When we meet up, he's dressed in a black hoodie and black sneakers, effortlessly fitting into the role of Master of the Universe, bobbing and weaving around topics in a conversation that touches on Daniel Kahneman ("I just saw Danny on Thursday"), Elon Musk ("He's a fraud"), Steven Spielberg ("We have a moral imperative to create technology—imagine a world in which Spielberg exists but the 8 millimeter camera doesn't?") and Zendaya (I couldn't follow).

When the conversation turns to the risks of posting photos of children, he leans back and lets loose a prophecy that echoes Palfrey: "In the future, privacy will be a luxury good," he says. In his house, he employs the Nest camera's video feed to settle disputes. "We use technology as an objective referee," he says. His wife tells him she's asked him five times to do something?

Just pull up the Nest! You claim your little sister was the one who poured out all the Cheerios onto the floor? Just pull up the Nest!

"There's a little of a panopticon effect happening, self-policing," he says, then pauses. "I *think* we're better for it."

This brings to mind Foucault and prisons and Orwell—surely little Bodhi will one day dismantle his Nest camera and rappel down the side of the building to freedom, no?—but Wolfe assures me this isn't harming the kids in any way.

"My kids are digital natives who have no expectation of privacy," he says. "I believe privacy is dead." (When I mention this to Josh Golin, the executive director of the Campaign for Commercial-Free Childhood, he responds, "If you're training kids to live under fascism, I guess that's a good tactic.")

But what about all these fears about lewd pictures circulating online? Surely we need regulation?

"Within half a generation, people will be like, *Who doesn't have naked pictures of themselves online?*" he counters. In the early days of Facebook, he points out, posting a photo of yourself in a bikini, or drinking, or drinking in a bikini was thought too risqué for work. Now no one thinks twice. "And when everybody's doing it, no one cares."

When I met Dave and we moved to San Francisco, he used to tell me that our children wouldn't ever have a driver's license, that they'd be transported around the world in self-driving cars. I, of course, thought Dave was delusional. Now people take videos of other drivers "asleep" at the wheel, as their Tesla automatic driver ferries them down the 101. So even though Wolfe's prophecies rub me the wrong way, I've been put in my place before.

But at least a few experts are as skeptical as I am. When I tell Palfrey about the premise that privacy is dead, or at least on life support, he snorts.

"There's been a myth for a long time that kids don't care about privacy," he says. He's spent fifteen years immersed in the world of online privacy and children, updating *Born Digital* with new research and new interviews with tech-immersed children. "If you've ever been a teacher in high school, or worked with kids in the tween or teen time, there's almost always a conversation kids are having that adults are not having." As the former head of Andover, he's no doubt seen his fair share of kids sneaking around.

The issue is, even if Wolfe's prophecy that privacy is dead is eventually fulfilled, I find the implications of his personal parenting decisions horrifying, and the decisions themselves not necessarily pragmatic. The idea of pulling up live footage of Ella consuming three fistfuls of Teddy Grahams before breakfast to prove to her that she has to eat her eggs seems a questionable strategy, at best.

Thanksgiving is tomorrow. I take just one photo before powering my phone down: of Dave, tired but happy, holding Charlotte, chunky and drooling, as Ella lies on a bed in the background, between my two parents.

* * *

Charlotte turns six months before I get around to reading Daniel Kahneman, the Nobel Prize–winning psychologist Dave mentioned right as I was going into labor with Ella three and a half years prior. Kahneman and his longtime collaborator, Amos Tversky, upended the formerly popular notion that people act rationally when making decisions. (They often don't.) And he's a pioneer in the field of hedonic psychology—the study of what makes life pleasant or unpleasant—and has explored, among other things, how memories affect how people make future decisions. (Often irrationally.)

On the first night Charlotte moves out of the bassinet in our room and joins her sister, I realize, with not an insignificant amount of excitement, that I can now turn my bedside table light on after 6:45 p.m. But instead of picking up a book, I start noodling around on the phone and find myself watching a TED Talk Kahneman gave about the difference between memory and experience and how the concept of happiness relates to both. I'm hopeful that his research can help ground, in a more clinical way, both my photo taking and my photo viewing. If neither makes me happier or my life better, why do it at all? Better I should spend the time organizing my sock drawer with a glass of wine in tow, an activity that unfailingly brings me joy.

The talk focuses on what he calls "the two selves," that concept Dave mentioned way back when on Park Avenue. We are all made up of two selves, Kahneman says. The experiencing self lives in the present. The remembering self—which maintains the story of our lives by revisiting memories of things past—doesn't. When we put our phones away and fully engage with our surroundings, we optimize for the experiencing self. When we take a photo, we optimize for the remembering self. And the remembering self, I learn, can essentially bulldoze an entire moment for you.

For example: how an experience ends is a huge determinant in how fondly you remember it. You've enjoyed a beautiful piece of music for twenty minutes, but the recording is a mess and screeches at the end? It all gets soured. Or: you're undergoing a colonoscopy, a moment we can all agree you'd likely rather neither experience nor remember. Even if your exam is shorter and less painful overall than a longer, more excruciating one, you'll report having had a worse time if your pain level increases toward the end. (This Kahneman concluded after having people report their pain every sixty seconds during the procedure. File under: fun data points you might be asked to record as a psych student of Daniel Kahneman.)

Our memory picks and chooses how to record events and often, in effect, catalogs them improperly. The issue with all of this is that we spend vastly more time experiencing things than we do remembering them. Which leads Kahneman to the million-dollar question: "Why do we put so much weight on memory relative to the weight that we put on experiences?"

Kahneman is so appealing in his talk that later I read *Thinking, Fast and Slow*, in which he explores the two selves in depth. In one passage, he directly addresses photography.

"The frenetic picture taking of many tourists suggests that storing memories is often an important goal, which shapes both the plans for the vacation and the experience of it," he writes. "The photographer does not view the scene as a moment to be savored, but as a future memory to be designed. Pictures may be useful to the remembering self—though we rarely look at them for very long, or as often as we expected, or even at all—but picture taking is not necessarily the best way for the tourists' experiencing self to enjoy a view."

This is the clearest case I've seen for those nebulous concepts of *being mindful* and *living life in the moment*. Pragmatically speaking, why take a photograph in the hopes that it'll prompt a memory when we revisit it later, particularly if we know that, unless we're like Josh Wolfe, we'll most likely *not* revisit it later? Why not just . . . live?

It's a trade-off, of course. And I know I'm not going to banish my paparazzi-ing entirely—babies and kids are evolutionarily designed for cuteness. The random snaps I post of Ella and Charlotte on my family's photo stream bring my parents immeasurable delight. But at least I now have enough information against photo taking, from the psychological to the legal, to encourage me to keep my phone in my pocket a bit more, a tiny rebellion against the dystopian, Ted Chiang–esque future we're hurtling toward. And I'm slightly calmed by a conversation I have with a "Futurist" (his actual LinkedIn-profile title) who assures me that there are ways for programmers to safeguard the sharing of photos, in essence by making them fuzzier, such that pornography and photo-alteration fears will be a thing of the past. I will inevitably keep taking photos, but in the future, I'll be able to keep them more safely than I can now.

When I remember Charlotte's birth, I remember timing contractions on an app a little before daybreak. I remember taking a cab across the park to 96th and Fifth and then opting to get out and walk the two blocks north instead of going to Madison and circling around to the entrance. I remember having to stop every few feet, the pain radiating down my legs causing me to push off the ball of one foot and stand there, *en pointe*, until the contraction subsided. I remember passing a man who was walking his Pekingese. I remember the Orthodox Jewish woman wearing a sheitel who sat next to us in the waiting room alone as her husband parked the car. I remember my doctor examining me and laughing, telling me we were going to have a baby within the hour. And I remember Charlotte, her little fuzzy triceps, the slightly worrying red dot beneath her eye that faded a few weeks later, the tiny plump of fat that was her big toe, and her hair, so much of it, all matted down, as she was put, a breathing warm lump, on my chest for the first time.

Is this accurate? I'll never know—the first photo we have of her was taken an hour after she was born, at which point she was swaddled, behatted, and in Dave's arms. But I kind of like it that way.

4

Buy, Buy, Baby

Are We Strong Enough to Escape E-commerce?

One day when visiting a friend's newest baby, I come across a container of flushable wipes on her sink. Who knew they were a thing? Not I.

Nine times out of ten when responding to nature's call, Ella uses toilet paper. Once in a while, without getting into details, a wipe is helpful. And every time I guiltily flush one down the toilet, I imagine it whooshing toward a fatberg, which my mind's eye paints in *Ghostbuster*-ish overtones: pinkish-beige, pulsing underneath New York City, perhaps smoking a discarded cigarette stub while it waits to rear up through the manhole covers.

Later, when I type in "flushable wipe" on my phone's Amazon search bar, endless options load. Wipes for grownups. Ones for sensitive tushies. Ones in flip-top canisters with Minnie Mouse on the front. Ones with aloe. Ones that partner, somehow, with Hilary Duff. Fifteen minutes later, fully overwhelmed, I give up. I've sworn off overloading my brain with baby-related data, signed out of Facebook and its chattering Mommas, stopped frantically pulling out my phone to photograph moments I'll rarely revisit—and yet here I am, packing in admittedly meaningless information about how best to wipe my child's butt.

I'm certain my mother didn't have to deal with nearly as many options, and the resulting decision fatigue, when raising us in the 1980s. And she confirms as much when I give her a call.

"We just went to that store, you know, the one that had everything around the corner," she tells me. I later confirm the name of that store: The Gap. Putting aside that she most certainly went somewhere else for anything non-clothing related, she encountered limits imposed by real estate when she went to "The Store." There were a finite number of jeans because there were a finite number of shelves. But today, instead of walking two blocks to The Gap, it's second nature for me to head over to gap.com, where I'll inevitably sink an hour into the never-ending scroll of baby jeggings, all perpetually 40 percent off.

It's the excess that's exhausting, but also the relentless advertising, which tells me with very little nuance that if I buy the right thing, my kid will be the right kind of kid and I'll be the right kind of mom. It's a message that has been imparted to mothers for generations, ever since "keeping up with the Joneses" became a basic tenet of the ad market, but it feels more pernicious to me now than ever. Thanks to technology, targeted advertising has combined with the endless options offered by online shopping to form the perfect crucible for anxiety, hysteria, and frittering away one's time when you clearly know better. This is true for any purchase online, of course, but arguably more acute in the parenting realm, when your child's very chances at a successful life apparently hinge on the click of a button. You better not screw up that click. I'm lucky enough to have mom friends in the neighborhood who are a few stages ahead of me, so Ella and Charlotte happily wear hand-me-downs whenever possible. But they're not giving me their BPA-free bottles, their diapers, their baby shampoo. So online I go to click away, read reviews, and form opinions about minutiae I couldn't have cared less about just hours before.

When I ask Dave why he isn't the one making purchases for our children, he doesn't miss a beat: "Because you're too fast! The thing is already purchased!" It's undeniable. Marketers have their crosshairs on me—they know I'm the fastest way past the doorjamb.

But one late summer day, as the weather turns, I ask Dave to help me outfit a rapidly growing Ella with clothes for fall. His instinct, unlike mine, is to go out into the real world. A few hours later, he returns with two heavy, long-sleeved woolen dresses that were on sale at a local store. They're so large that when Ella tries them on, they skim the ground. I give him a look.

"You said to get her something she could grow into!" he protests. "We'll just roll up the sleeves!"

Ella, of course, adores her new conservative options. She spends the fall sweating profusely and gathering up dirt and dust in her trailing skirts, like a pioneer girl on the prairie.

* * *

I become a member of a Buy Nothing Facebook group after Charlotte is born, a "your trash is my treasure" antidote to consumer culture, where people offer up used or unneeded items for free. A friend of mine outfitted her entire nursery from the group. But even in a forum founded, allegedly, to combat the pull of a consumer society, members spend hours searching for just the right item.

"I snagged an Inglesina high chair!" one member gloats to me. It retails for around two hundred dollars. "It was a unicorn, but I like the hunt," she says. And therein lies the issue—that impulsive need to get only the best for your child, even if it's a hand-me-down, is nearly inescapable for parents. Before understanding why, which is likely a mix of economic forces and psychology, I want to understand *how*—how companies begin drumming up that interest, how they begin creating that need at the highest levels.

So I get a press pass to that year's Consumer Electronics Show, branded as CES 2020. (I visit right under the wire—a few months into the pandemic, CES announces it'll be going completely virtual in 2021 for the first time in its history.) The giant of a trade show is celebrating its fifty-third year of giving the world a look at its tech-powered future. It's where entrepreneurs and marketers dream up the next big consumer items, assess interest, then tirelessly shill to their audience. The first-ever home VCR debuted there. So did the Blu-ray Disc. I figure attending will be a bit like the blue sweater scene from *The Devil Wears Prada*, in which Meryl Streep's Anna Wintour–esque fashion magazine editor-in-chief dresses down Anne Hathaway—playing the aspiring writer who's her assistant—for not appreciating that the color of her lumpy J.Crew-type sweater was inspired by Oscar de la Renta. The haute designer, Streep explains, made cerulean the "it" color in one of his shows long before it trickled down to the plebes.

"That blue represents millions of dollars and countless jobs," Streep says, eyes squinted, as Hathaway withers, "and so it's sort of comical how you think that you've made a choice that exempts you from the fashion industry when, in fact, you're wearing the sweater that was selected for you by the people in this room."

I want to be in the room.

So, a few months into Ella's conservative dress phase, I take a plane to Las Vegas, throw a teal press badge around my neck, and join throngs of other teal-badge wearers in the Sands Expo and Convention Center. I'm in search of the baby and family section. Problem is, I can't seem to make it to the right place. I'm at booth number 46128. I need to go vaguely toward the 44000s. I walk, and walk, and walk. I'm clearly looping and backtracking—twice I pass the Capillus booth, where convention-goers sit, Matrix-style, with baseball caps on their heads as low-level lasers secretly stimulate hair growth. But ten minutes later, I'm only in the 45000s. If I were the kind of person to wear a smartwatch, no question I would have hit my step count for the day. I later learn the stats: the 2020 show attracted more than 4,500 exhibitors from around the world who hawked their wares to more than 180,000 attendees over 2.9 million square feet.

The majority of booths I pass offer to solve problems I'm not sure anyone has ever had, or even thought to categorize as a problem. A company called Bzigo alerts your phone when its lasers have pinpointed a mosquito in your home—"The days of unexpected mosquito attacks are over!"—but does not actually do the zapping for you. (That evening, I check their website, which helpfully offers a few ways to kill a laser-located mosquito, including "throw a pillow at it" or "use a vacuum.") I pass not one, not two, but three smart toothbrush booths, one touting a "new augmented reality brushing experience." Putting aside that I'd rather not play a high-energy game through my toothbrush before I'm dressed for the day, let's consider the message: your twice-daily ritual of dental hygiene has languished, undisrupted and chore-like, for decades. Sprinkle in a little tech, and just imagine the possibilities! Truth be told, nearly everything is smart—litter boxes, textiles, sex toys. Convenience and entertainment trump all.

As I wander, periodically checking my CES app to see if I'm anywhere closer to the 44000s (in some sort of permutation of Zeno's paradox, I never am), I inadvertently join a pack of people, led by a chipper man speaking an unidentifiable foreign language rapidly into a microphone. He has a bright-orange pennant sticking out of his backpack, so his group, listening on earphones as he live-narrates the floor, won't lose him in the throngs. En masse, we shuffle around the perimeter of a greenhouse, lush with lettuces, all growing in this climate-controlled convention center plopped in the middle of an arid desert. He gestures wildly and his chirps grow higher pitched. I understand not a word, but his group *oohs* and *aahs* appreciatively. I assume he's saying some version of, *Witness America, in all its grand spectacle.*

Finally, when I'm about to throw in the towel and sit down with a Capillus on my head to give my feet a rest under the guise of stimulating my hair follicles, I see Dr. Harvey Karp. He's at a coveted corner booth, surrounded by SNOOs and a gaggle of Asian businessmen, all listening rapt as Karp says, for the third time in my presence and likely the gazillionth time in his life, "You can rent it, and it's the price of a Starbucks coffee a day, okay?" I've finally arrived in the babytech zone.

The big brands, and lauded up-and-comers, announce themselves with bright, beautiful signage and gorgeous displays. Baby Brezza, which has been in the automatic baby-food prep business since 2011, is showing off its Wi-Fi-enabled FormulaPro to gawking onlookers. It not only automatically prepares baby bottles, but can be programmed to do so from a phone. The Elvie Pump, the first-ever silent wearable breast pump, which received attention after sending a pumping mother down the catwalk at London's 2018 Fashion Week, has an on-site makeshift pumping room (just close the curtain around you) and a fridge for post-pump milk storage. ("One mom is storing her milk in here all week!" a sales rep tells me, proudly.)

Identifiable almost immediately are the wannabe companies. Take Omago, which as far as I can tell implants sensors into diapers. Its banner displays a cryptic tagline that is heavy on exuberance, light on copy editing. "Baby is our future; Elder is our treasure! We care your family!" On the counter in front is a sad cardboard box, pleading, in a charmingly formal translation bungle, "Please grant your business card here."

"Why even pay the money to get the booth?" sighs the assistant of a head babytech honcho I meet the next day, referring to the less-thans. She's attended every year since 2011. "It's like, you're *being. So. Desperate.*"

Well, it's a chance, at least in theory, for recognition, building brand awareness, maybe even funding. And, of course, a highly visible way to introduce people to problems they then become desperate to solve.

I chitchat with various booth reps, one who sells me hard on the potential of a sleeve that can fit over a baby bottle and take the temperature of the liquid inside, another who urges me to hug a round plush blue toy surrounding a tablet that's jammed in its center. I do, reluctantly, and its single eye, projected on the screen, scrunches up in delight. I unexpectedly feel a flash of tenderness, followed immediately by a wave of despair that I've been manipulated so easily by a half-digital, half-synthetic octopus. I'm relieved to remember that I have an actual excuse to leave: I have to get back to my hotel room so I can use my very loud, very clunky pump to trick my body into thinking it's giving Charlotte her evening milk, as Dave, sans Baby Brezza, waits for her bottle to warm up on the stove back east. My feet are pulsing, my brain awash in acronyms and buzzwords, my boobs sending out a tingling warning signal that I better pump, and soon. I find a helpful-looking Sands employee sitting at an information booth and ask him how (the hell) to get out.

"Follow the blue carpet," he tells me. "It's like the yellow brick road." And so off I go, laser-focused on the ground, dodging feet like Frogger. It suddenly dead ends. I look up to find myself in a far-off corner of the Sands where people are sitting on the ground glumly scrolling through their phones and eating Doritos. I start to panic. I retrace my steps on the yellow/blue brick road and join the throngs again. I pass a booth telling me that wearing a biometric headband will quiet any pre-bed thoughts by cooling my frontal cortex, enabling me to sleep "more efficiently." People are lounging around inside, headbands on, perhaps without a single thought in their heads. Nearby is a booth that tells me that if I sleep on a chilled bed, my DNA will repair. I audibly snort before realizing that Dave actually purchased the product after seeing it advertised on Instagram. The "hydro-powered" mattress pad sits under the fitted sheet and chills the bed by running water through a network of small tubes on its surface. Well, in theory. The thing never worked. "I think my kneecap feels slightly cool, maybe?" Dave would say tentatively, after cranking the system to its highest icy setting for hours and diving in.

I start to worry about my DNA, my hair follicles, my racing mind, and that if I ever get to sleep that night in my hot bed, I might get bitten by an unseen mosquito. Finally (finally!) I find an exit sign and a few moments later am spat out onto restaurant row at the Venetian hotel—but not before I pass the Amazon showroom, glowing faintly in blue and complete with an Alexa-equipped Lamborghini (Oscar de la Renta's cerulean blue) and myriad Echo Dots (lumpy blue J.Crew sweater). I wander through room after room, which the Amazon team has outfitted to be Amazon-enabled at every step of the way. *Step right up, folks—our dystopian future, right here on display!* "Alexa, open up Amazon StoryTime," reads one helpful placard in the fake child's bedroom.

"Do you want Samuel L. Jackson to tell you a joke?" a staffer asks me, with a wink. Do I?

"All this advertising, it puts women down," my mother says when I call her from my hotel room across the strip a little while later, jet-lagged and frazzled as I pump. *"Don't watch your baby; we'll have a machine watch your baby. Don't nurse your baby; give it formula.* The message is, *What you're doing isn't good enough.* It destroys nature! You can't buy your way to a better kid!"

I am so eager to get out of Vegas that I head to the airport a full nine hours early and sit there, unsuccessfully trying to fly standby on any earlier flight out. My reporting visit seems to have served as a form of exposure therapy: I went straight into the belly of the beast and shocked my system into recognizing how pointless my hours spent scrolling are, how manipulated I am by marketers, how indistinguishable most products are from each other. It seems more urgent than ever that I amend my mindless behaviors, since I know full well that the vast majority of these high-tech-powered offerings are unnecessary additions to most anyone's nursery. But how?

* * *

"There are certain facts of life so obvious and mundane that one never talks about them. Only the child blurts out: 'Why do people in books never go to the toilet?'" Betty Friedan wrote in *The Feminine Mystique* in 1963. "Why is it never said that the really crucial function, the really important role that women serve as housewives is *to buy more things for the house*? In all the talk of femininity and woman's role, one forgets that the real business of America is business."

Have things changed much? Alas, not really. The advertising industry took off in earnest in the 1880s and boomed in the 1920s, spurred on in part by the reach of mass media. Even in advertising's early days, Carl Naether, a marketing guru who published the influential *Advertising to Women* in 1928, estimated that women bought 80 to 90 percent of all household commodities, and he advised his copy men to deploy "women's own language" accordingly. Startlingly, that percentage has hardly changed at all today. While we don't collect data at the intra-household level—you'll never know who in a household actually pushes "Buy"—if you assume women at least influence all purchases made in their households and cross-reference that with the Consumer Expenditure Survey, you get the data point that women in 2018 controlled or influenced 83.8 percent of aggregate household spending. (Thanks to *American Demographics* magazine and the patient explanations of demographer Cheryl Russell for that. And yes, these studies and statistics are heteronormative and focus on heterosexual couples with one man and one woman, but generations of habit are not easily undone, even in a society that is, ever so slowly, becoming more progressive.)

So, while men and women might both be heading out into the workforce now, it still falls largely with the women to buy the right goods, or to "conspicuously consume," a term coined by philosopher and economist Thorstein Veblen in 1899 in his landmark treatise *The Theory of the Leisure Class*. What you purchase shows your pecuniary strength, so the pressure's on to purchase the right things, then flaunt them—even, apparently, if that's the kind of wipe you use on your child's bottom.

The USDA estimates that middle-income, two-child, married-couple families spend almost $13,000 per year on each child. While the vast majority of that cost lies in housing and food, 13 percent goes to clothing and miscellaneous goods, all well within the reach of the marketer's grasp.

And although, prior to the 1990s, the amount of money spent on children used to peak in high school, by 2007 it was highest when the children were in two age buckets: younger than six and their midtwenties. Some social scientists and economists surmise that this compulsive spending on young children is rooted in economic anxiety. The inequality gap shows no signs of closing, and after several consecutive generations when parents were reasonably certain their children could do better than they, themselves, had done, now the tide has turned and wide swaths of the population fear that their children might fall into a lower social class. One way to combat this is for parents to do everything in their power to set their children up for success, and to do so as early as possible.

Called *intensive parenting*, this new phenomenon—I was expected to amuse myself for long stretches of each summer as a child, and now god forbid your child be alone or bored for more than a few minutes—permeates nearly every part of modern-day parenting, from providing children with enriching after-school activities to ensuring they play with the perfect, developmentally appropriate toy.

While the luxury of stressing about these minutiae is most acute in the upper echelons of society, studies indicate that regardless of income level, education level, and race, parents of all social classes believe the most hands-on and expensive options are preferable for their children. Whether or not you can afford it, the impulse is to spend as much as you can on your children, because if you don't, you might contribute to their future failure. This mindset, of course, completely sidesteps the big issues—that the inequality gap is so big in the first place, that the social safety net in America is so small, that this onus rests on the individual and not society, that the capitalist impulse is to buy your way out of any problem. Operating within a system they cannot change, many parents are easily manipulated by marketers who tell them, in no uncertain language, that the right activity or product might just give their child the edge.

"Advertising has always played on anxieties," professor Susan Strasser tells me when I reach her by phone in Washington, DC. "It's a good way to sell things, guilt-based advertising. Particularly for parents." Her book, *Never Done: A History of American Housework*, traces how housewife duties evolved from hauling water and tending fires in the nineteenth century to outsourcing mealtimes to McDonald's at the end of the twentieth. It neatly lays out the evolution of American mass consumer culture and how it affected wives and mothers, and I was struck at the similarities between the baldly manipulative parenting ads of a century ago and those of today. One baby food ad of yore went so far as to suggest the infant death rate—the implication being that if you didn't feed your child the right food, he or she might be a casualty of bad parenting.

"If we only had the nerve to put a hearse in the ad, you couldn't keep the women away from the food," the advertising agency head said to a copywriter. How different, really, is that from the tagline for that Nanit sleep monitor—"Peaceful Nights. Peace of Mind."?

What is different today, Strasser points out, is the sheer volume of options the modern consumer faces in each product category, which leads to an unspoken, and unfounded, assumption.

"E-commerce gives us the notion that the perfect thing is possible, even when it may not exist," she says. "Part of it is the promise that anything is available—which, in a way, Sears Roebuck and Montgomery Ward offered in the 1890s, but the promise was still bounded within the pages of a catalog. The catalog may have been huge, but it wasn't endless."

In their quest to find the perfect item, mothers I know allow the endless scrolling to seep into every free nook and cranny of their lives. They hop online to purchase bottles while in line for the bus, or diapers when peeing at work, or onesies when drifting off to sleep at night. There is no longer a discrete moment when one goes to "the store." The store is ubiquitous, ever beckoning, and in your pocket.

"Convenience has been conflated with freedom, in a way," Strasser says. "It became a synonym for happiness even, that if something is convenient, then it is by definition good. That's the whole thing of it—you buy this product, it will save you time. Or *how* you buy a product will save you time. Well, will it actually save you time?"

At least in theory, Amazon's Subscribe and Save option, which allows you to schedule regular deliveries of household basics for a discount, should make outfitting Charlotte even more convenient. But then managing the subscriptions becomes yet another task. If executed properly, it would require a complex algorithm that factored in Charlotte's growth curve, our available closet space, and the number of diapers she uses daily, all of which are in constant flux. On the red-eye back from CES 2020, having come off two days of full saturation in the worst of consumer culture, I blearily realized I'd forgotten to order the next-size diaper for Charlotte. A click of a button later, and I'd kick-started an Amazon supply chain that took advantage of the two-hour delivery offered in New York City. They arrived at my door just hours after I did. Surely this kind of convenience trumps dragging Ella to the store, with Charlotte strapped in, to buy diapers.

But at what cost?

* * *

When I snag an interview with Greg Greeley, one of the architects of Amazon Prime, I expect him to unequivocally tell me that Amazon is a net positive for parents. He spent almost two decades helping build Amazon into the e-commerce giant it is today. He refers to the almighty Bezos as Jeff. And he and his wife, a labor and delivery nurse, have three daughters. In the early days, when the kids were young and he was in grad school, he tells me, they had a desperate need for a service like Amazon Prime.

But after a beat, he adds, "I'm not going to weigh in on whether parents *need* all of the things that are available to them, but you're saving people time and money."

It's precisely the issue Strasser brought up with me: the catch-22 of convenience. It's freeing, if only you can allow it to free. And I'm not so sure that any parent hoping to drop in and out of the website like a ninja, just to get what they need, can stand a chance against complex algorithms that ensure eyeballs stay on pages. I surely can't.

Prime launched on February 2, 2005, a date Greeley rattles off with the same assurance others reserve for anniversaries or birthdays. At the time, seventy-nine dollars annually got you free two-day shipping.

"Now we have it down to two hours," he tells me, a proud ex-company man (he's at Airbnb when we speak) who's genial and open and comes across as the kind of person who'd unabashedly write "supply chains" under "Passions" on a dating app. According to the company's annual shareholder letter in 2018, the subscription service—now priced at $119 per year and offering additional benefits like streaming video and music and free two-hour grocery delivery from Whole Foods—boasts over one hundred million members. Analysts estimate that in 2019, more than half of all American households were Prime members. Its appeal is irresistible—I want it, I want it cheap, and I want it now. Walmart has recently launched a competitor to Prime, bringing even more families access to instant gratification.

But before we hang up, Greeley brings up Germany's *Ladenschlussgesetz*, or "shop closing law," a government-mandated shutting of stores on Sundays and holidays that was enacted in 1956 and is still in effect in much of the country today. There's a version of it in Luxembourg, too, where he lived for five and a half years with his family as he worked to expand Amazon's reach around the globe. The country operated under a version of the law, and the ever-so-slightly-slower purchasing cadence gave him a new perspective on commerce.

"At first, it felt like an inconvenience," he says, "But oddly I saw a tendency for Sundays to then become preserved for family time. People would organize their days to get their errands done on Saturday, and go hiking or be outside or with family on Sundays. There's a consumer message in there. About freeing up time. About limits."

Of course, due to his efforts, the Greeleys had access to Amazon on Sundays in Luxembourg, he points out with a chuckle.

* * *

Those amorphous limits. We're horrible at setting them and horrible at keeping them, as anyone can tell you who has fallen down a Netflix binge of *The Great British Bake Off* and surfaced, forty-eight hours later, sleep deprived and mumbling into the void about Victoria sandwich cakes. (It me.)

From a psychological perspective, the ramifications of this are still being worked out, but revolve around the notion of willpower—the ability to resist temptation—and how that is or isn't affected by decision fatigue.

"The more perfectionistic you are—and parenthood promotes perfectionism—the larger the burden on your mind, the more of a detractor decision-making is to your well-being," Roy F. Baumeister tells me when I reach him by phone.

Baumeister, a social psychologist at the University of Queensland, is known for coining the term *ego depletion*—the notion that each of us has a finite store of mental energy. Draw it down, through various activities including making decisions, and it becomes harder and harder to resist temptation. Let's say you forgo eating that cookie on the table. Later, when faced with a difficult puzzle to solve, you'll give up working on it far sooner than if you'd just eaten the cookie earlier. Run through a litany of questions about how you want to outfit your new car, and the further along you go, the less likely you're able to resist a salesman's coaching—something car salesmen of course exploit, posing questions about expensive upgrades toward the end of the process.

Baumeister and another researcher, Wilhelm Hofmann, conducted a massive study in Germany in which participants were pinged on beepers randomly throughout the day and asked to report on whether they were experiencing desire, or had recently experienced it. After collecting more than ten thousand distinct responses, the researchers concluded that individuals spend between three and four hours per day—a quarter of their waking hours—resisting desire. And he posits that we are resisting more desire than ever before.

"That's the 'triumph' of capitalism," he says. "People trying to offer you goods and services—there are more options and more temptations more easily reached."

One of Baumeister's major discoveries involves glucose. The brain runs on it. So an influx of glucose, he found, can help replenish the brain's power stores and, in a sense, fill up your willpower bank. When I ask him if we should all take a hit of a milkshake before diving into the never-ending world of diapers online, he chuckles, then allows that some glucose might help.

So, too, would an appropriate amount of sleep, he points out, which plays a critical role in one's ability to resist temptation. Fish in a barrel, we parents are, what with our lack of sleep and hunt for perfection.

"Look," Baumeister tells me before we hang up, "if you're going to do the serious job of considering *all* the options, and many parents do feel they have to look at them all, that's going to zap your willpower. Particularly because there's not going to be an effective way to make the best choice."

His suggestion?

To *satisfice*.

It's a neologism, coined by Nobel Prize–winning economist Herbert Simon, that refers to settling for what's good enough and not worrying much about the alternatives. The opposite of satisficers are maximizers. They want to make sure every purchase or decision made is the absolute best. Simon argues that, factoring all the costs in, satisficing is actually a maximizing strategy—but that's often incredibly hard for humans to internalize. Particularly when we have seemingly endless options to consider. And particularly if, as Baumeister points out, you're a perfectionist parent.

To wit: The first night my friend's toddler slept in her big-girl bed, she fell out, hit the floor, and woke her mother up sobbing. After snuggling her baby back to bed, my friend tells me, she sunk hours—she estimates four full, whole, actual hours—researching what kind of device would be best suited to prevent middle-of-the-night falls.

"Did I want the solid or the inflatable bumpers? Did I want a little gate that hooked onto the edge of the bed? Did I want the little gate with extenders? Did I want to go old school and put pillows on the ground?" she remembers.

The next morning, she offered up the options, all mapped out with pros and cons, to her husband, who replied, nonplussed, "She probably won't fall out again if she already fell out once." And so it was. But, as a maximizing parent, she couldn't really help herself. (Note to maximizers: marry satisficers.)

So, the multimillion-dollar question is: In a world in which algorithms target our every move and brands march in lockstep behind us around the internet, is there any way to turn our maximizing tendencies into satisficing ones, to force us into becoming the satisficers we know we all should be?

Barry Schwartz has spent much of his career focusing on just how modern society plagues our psyches, and how best to combat it. He's a psychologist, formerly of Swarthmore College and now on faculty at the Haas School of Business at UC Berkeley, a beloved TED speaker (one of his talks has over fifteen million views), and the author of multiple books, including *The Paradox of Choice: Why More Is Less*, which persuasively argues that, contrary to popular opinion, more choice is not always a good thing.

"When people have no choice, life is almost unbearable," Schwartz writes. "As the number of available choices increases, as it has in our consumer culture, the resulting autonomy, control, and liberation is powerful and positive. But as the number of choices keeps growing, negative aspects of having a multitude of options begin to appear. As the number of choices grows further, the negatives escalate until we become overloaded. At this point, choice no longer liberates, but debilitates. It may even be said to tyrannize." (See: *Moscow on the Hudson*, a film in which Robin Williams, playing a defector from the USSR, heads to an American grocery store for the first time to get some coffee. Confronted with an endless aisle when he's used to one sad Soviet option, he becomes undone and falls to the ground, wailing.)

But, like Baumeister, Schwartz is sensitive to why mothers can't resist the call of commerce, however much they'd prefer to—which is concerning to him. In a study he conducted to assess the psychological effects of these two decision-making strategies, he found that "people with high maximization scores experienced less satisfaction with life, were less happy, were less optimistic, and were more depressed than people with low maximization scores."

This becomes a sticking point particularly when we are shopping—or browsing—and not simply buying. When people are hunting down a specific good, Schwartz allows, the internet can be an amazing place. Think of the original Amazon, eons ago, that only provided books.

"Who browses two million books?" he asks me, rhetorically, when I reach him in Berkeley, where he moved to join the Berkeley faculty and be closer to his grandchildren. You don't. But if you know exactly what you're looking for, your preferences can be perfectly matched. The issue, he says, is that "we often have a rough idea of what we want, or we know how much we care about one feature of a product, and then we let the market help us decide. We have half-articulated preferences, and so we get devastated by choice."

There are signs that we might be giving ourselves boundaries. Take millennial parents' extreme brand loyalty. According to the 2018 National Retail Foundation study, 49 percent of us remain brand loyal even in the face of cheaper options. (In another survey, this number rises to 85 percent.)

"That's incredibly adaptive," Schwartz tells me. "It's one way to turn an unmanageable world into a manageable one." But that is likely an unconscious decision.

At the end of his book, Schwartz provides eleven possible steps decision makers can take to mitigate the onslaught of choice. The first: "Choose when to choose." He asks readers to review a few recent decisions, both big and small; itemize the steps, time, research, and anxiety behind them; and reflect on how the decision-making process felt and if it was worth the cost.

"This exercise may help you better appreciate the costs associated with the decisions you make, which may lead you to give up some decisions altogether or at least to establish rules of thumb for yourself about how many options to consider." For example, he says, "you could make it a rule to visit no more than two stores when shopping for clothing."

But, I ask, how am I supposed to "visit no more than two stores" in an e-commerce world? Isn't that a bit of a quaint solution?

Schwartz concedes that while individuals can implement certain safeguards—tailoring various websites to show you only certain goods or making an arbitrary rule that you won't go to Walmart.com more than once a month—it's challenging.

"You need discipline," he says, "because the incremental search costs are so low. And often we don't have that discipline."

But it's imperative that we get it. As a psychologist, Schwartz is acutely aware of the ramifications of minutes spent scrolling through flushable wipes options.

"Sometimes when I give talks about this, I can see smirks among the younger people in the audience," he tells me. "They're hidden judgments that this is a challenge for people like me, but masters of the universe like themselves have it all solved. Every now and then someone will have the chutzpah to say it to me. And I try to tailor the sarcasm in my voice. *You're probably right, because the incidents of clinical depression, anxiety, suicide are all higher for your age group than it's been in history. You're right, my bad.*" When he says this, I think that surely it's not just the limitless choices—there are economic hardships beyond an individual's control, virtually no safety net for those who need it most, the list could go on—but it seems reasonable that it is a contributing factor. He pauses. "People overestimate their ability to handle choice. They see it as an opportunity and not as a liability."

His main tip when you're trying to figure out what to purchase?

"Appreciate that good enough is almost always good enough," he says. "And ask a friend who's made a similar decision. And when I say a friend, I mean it. I don't mean a Facebook friend."

He's just completed writing a paper about large choice sets: the larger the choice set, the more we believe our choices to be statements about our identity.

"When all there was were Lee's and Levi's, your jean choice didn't say much about you," he tells me. "It is hard to feel certain that it doesn't matter what diapers you buy when the world offers you a hundred options."

So, even when we know the decisions are ultimately anodyne, we are psychologically primed to take a vested interest in them. With a million options, each choice takes on outsize importance.

Or as Schwartz puts it, "The diapers you buy become a badge of honor, even if only you know which brand you bought."

Seeing it in writing makes it so stark: Why on earth should I care what animal graces my baby's butt? Perfect is the enemy of the good, and who needs a perfect tush wipe?

*   *   *

As I go about my days, trying to snip my marionette strings off and become a satisficer, it's helpful to remember not just that these decisions are trivial but also that, more to the point, the time I spend participating in our vast consumer system is time away from doing any number of other things with my days. It's similar to an argument I'll go on to hear again and again from professionals when I ask them about the downside of sitting my kid in front of a screen: What is that activity displacing?

Though they were both born in the spring, five days apart, for their first years, Charlotte is at the top of the growth curve while Ella is at the bottom. This means that when she turns three months, Charlotte is comfortably wearing Ella's nine-month hand-me-downs—an issue because Charlotte can't really wear a bear-eared fleece onesie in August. So one hot summer day, I strap Charlotte in, take Ella by the hand, and walk to The Store. There, just two blocks from my house, I encounter the helpful limits imposed by store shelves, just as my mother did a generation ago.

As I'm searching for the right size in the very manageable baby section, Ella marches up to a clerk and announces, proudly, "That's my sister! Her name is Charlotte, but sometimes I call her Bean. Or Bean-Bean."

"Oh, how *lovely*," the clerk responds, continuing to fold tiny shorts into tinier squares.

"And other times, I call her Bubby!"

"Ah, is that so?"

"And then sometimes I just call her Chonk!"

The clerk stops what she's doing and laughs.

"I bet you love being a big sister, right?"

"I do, I do," Ella says. It's the first time she's ever said this aloud. Then she comes over and gives Charlotte's toe, dangling out of the carrier, a little nibble.

As we're rung up, I decide to satisfice on onesies, and maximize on toe nibbling.

Part Two

Babytech

5

Plug and Play

Are Smart Toys Better than Analog Blocks?

One freezing weekend in February 2019, the toy industry's annual Toy Fair took over the Javits Center's 840,000 square feet of exhibition space. Sellers, buyers, and reps staggered from booth to booth—a mastodon-size animal over here, a Fart Ninja over there—in a conference haze, eating salads and chicken fingers at an hour before most of New York had drunk its coffee. Creatures from various games waddled the floor alongside them, sheepishly and silently asking for help navigating the escalators. I watched as an Angry Bird's foot almost got stuck in the moving stair grooves. It took three Good Samaritans to avert an avian disaster.

When I arrived at the basement level, where the panels were held, I found Kate Stone speaking about innovation in the toy world. She was holding up an iPhone.

"I think in a few years, this will be old-fashioned," she said to the audience, turning the very notion of screen time on its head. "Children as young as two pick up a magazine and try to pinch it to zoom," she continued. "They want everyday objects to be able to do something." So, she told us, as a creative scientist at Novalia, a UK-based company with a tagline of "making everything around us interactive," she'd been working on a Touchscape, a digitally responsive piece of paper. Picture a board game. Then imagine that being synced to an Amazon Alexa. Move a piece into a given section of the board, and Alexa might talk to you, or play music, or layer appropriate sound effects onto the experience, seamlessly bridging the gap between game and real life. In the future, the paper itself might just . . . talk! As I listened to her, I pictured the Post-its I kept in the kitchen kibitzing with each other in high-pitched voices about how I'd forgotten to get dishwashing detergent, yet again.

"When we think of the future," she said, "we think of *Minority Report*. But we have a longing for nostalgia. We create things that look old-fashioned. And as technology shrinks, but maintains a connection to the cloud and AI, that becomes magical."

When I later told my mother about talking paper, she was unimpressed. "You can't fool a child!" she snorted. "Won't the kid rip up the piece of paper to see where the quote-unquote magic is?" She had a point.

But that word, *magic*, was being thrown around a lot amongst the toy developers and trend watchers I spoke to in the months leading up to Charlotte's birth, as I began the process of figuring out which toys would be handed down from her older sister and which would be donated. A toy's success, I was told, hinges largely on its magic quality, that indefinable halo that encompasses wonder, delight, and surprise. Surely a piece of paper that responds to touch hits that trifecta. As would any number of the digitally enhanced toys that I saw beeping and pulsing in the convention center, many of which were pushing a neologism that seemed poised to become part and parcel of our future vernacular: *phigital*, or part physical, part digital.

But for the first few months of Ella's life, the wall seemed to hold all the magic in the world. We'd lived in a one-bedroom fourth-floor walk-up with limited space, so as a neat freak adamant that our house not suddenly shift from our adult-only sanctuary into a playroom where we'd constantly be tripping over pointy squeaky things in the middle of the night, I just . . . didn't get her any toys. Zen-like, Dickensian, who's to say? But as a result, Ella was forced to amuse herself by looking around, which she did quite happily for months. Long before she was born, Dave and I, trying to decorate the large, open wall space above our bed with something cheap, had ordered a riddling rack—essentially a wooden board with holes cut out of it, traditionally used in the process of fermenting champagne—from Etsy and hung it on the wall as an ersatz piece of art. As soon as her eyes started to focus, Ella would contentedly look at the thing for hours. The first time she smiled was at the rack. Giggled, too.

And when we moved to a larger apartment with a washing machine, she added laundry to her growing list of activities.

"It's going on a ride!" Ella would say, pointing a dimpled finger at the washer, where her unicorn sock was getting sudsy and starting to spin in circles. "Wheee!" Then she'd take the warm clean laundry from the hamper, dump it out on the floor, and methodically put it back again, piece by piece, a wide grin on her face. As a two-year-old, she had been able to find a sort of magic in an undergarment, in the act of putting things in and out of a container. Did her future sibling really need a piece of paper to strike up a conversation with her?

After I wandered the Toy Fair, it seemed obvious that magic wasn't *just* about wonder and delight. It was about wonder and delight used in service of a goal—to enrich your child in some way.

These days, you'd be hard-pressed to find a toy for the preschool set that comes devoid of claims to teach something—gross motor skills, fine motor skills, basic math, science, resilience, STEM, STEAM. They just started appearing in Ella's room, most gifts from well-meaning friends and family, a few courtesy of my own late-night Amazon binges, fueled by a low thrumming guilt that I needed to make up lost educational ground from her early wall-gazing days. Her Mozart Magic Cube "teaches how sounds combine" and is "recommended for budding young composers of all ages." Her plush Laugh and Learn Puppy, which irritatingly squawks fake-cute phrases when you squeeze its paws—*Tee hee, that tickles!*—comes with a set of CD-ROMs you can switch out of a back panel, depending on the user's age. The toy purportedly not only teaches your child her first hundred words but also boosts fine motor skills. While Ella loved it, I found its chirpy voice so irritating that after a few weeks, I used my fine motor skills to pick it up and my gross motor skills to shove it into the depths of the closet.

To be clear: none of this enrichment stuff is new.

"Beginning in the 1970s, as the number of dual-career families increased and information about child development exploded, parents wanted to be certain they were making every moment with their children count," developmental psychologists Kathy Hirsh-Pasek and Roberta Golinkoff write in *Einstein Never Used*

Flash Cards. Books and toys purporting to make children smarter flooded the market. Childhood, a once protected time, became increasingly academic. This, despite the fact—the authors are emphatic about this—that young children don't need bells and whistles to help enrich their brains. "Unless you are living in extreme isolation or poverty, the natural, everyday environments in which families and children find themselves promote strong development," they write.

But the promise of technology and the anxiety of middle-class parents combined to create a hysterical crucible in which many toys are technologically enhanced and offer curricular benefits—both additions reflexively understood by the public to be positive. More, in our culture, is always equated with better—more personalization, more developmentally appropriate features, more academic learning that can push your child to the top of the pack.

I learned, thankfully well after Charlotte was born, that there are even multiple apps that help track various newborn milestones, encouraging different forms of play with different types of toys. These appear to cause hyperattentive parents an angst commensurate with a mistaken nuclear detonation.

"My friend who has a baby about the same age as mine will call and ask, *Is he grasping yet?*" a friend told me. "*Because the app says she should be, but she isn't, yet.* It's like this weird competition, but then you start paying attention. *Um, no, he isn't grasping yet. What does that mean? Should I spend more time with him on the mat with one of those knobby balls?*"

If doing the laundry exists on one end of the play spectrum, then knobby balls are somewhere in the middle, and Kate Stone's Touchscapes way off on the other. In order to figure out which toys to keep and which to axe, it seemed imperative that I determine what the purpose of play is. Only then would I understand how best to equip my kids to do it—whether that involved folding socks, rolling balls around, or chatting to Post-its.

* * *

A few days into the new year and five months pregnant, I find myself in Rochester, New York, visiting the Strong National Museum of Play, the only collections-based museum in the world devoted solely to play. It was founded in 1969 by collector Margaret Woodbury Strong, an heir to a buggy whip fortune who was bequeathed enough Kodak stock as a wedding gift that she was able to spend her life traveling the world collecting creepy Victorian dolls—to each their own, I suppose. The museum now spans 285,000 square feet and encompasses a year-round, indoor butterfly conservatory; a miniature Wegmans supermarket, where kids can shop for food (including organic soy milk); and a carousel, which is happily making its rounds on the bitterly cold, low-sky day I arrive. I'm here in the hopes that the historians, curators, and general toy experts can help me situate today's next-generation, tech-fueled toys on the historical continuum.

"It used to be easy to make blanket statements about technology and play," sighs Debbie McCoy, the museum's assistant vice president for education, as she adjusts her eyeglasses. We are sitting in a second-floor conference room in the museum's administrative offices, around the corner from an extensive video game arcade. "These days, it all depends. The response to technology has needed to become more and more nuanced." Her demeanor marks her as the kind of person I'd want by my side in the event of a car breakdown or toddler tantrum—pragmatic, smart, unflappable.

She has worked in early childhood education for decades and runs the museum's on-site preschool, which is inspired by the student-centered Reggio Emilia approach—kids, for the most part, drive what is learned in the classroom, and the whole experience is based on collaboration between parents, teachers, and students. When primary school teachers come to her lamenting that students don't know what to do with a box of Legos—they'll throw them all over the place, stomp around, act like wild things— McCoy doesn't point the finger at the teachers or at technology. She points it at the parents or, perhaps, a society that has caused parents to act a certain way.

"Children who respond like that are play deprived and are indicating that they don't have enough time to relax into their play," she tells me. "There's a trend to schedule children up— what it means to be a good parent these days is dance, violin, et cetera. It's good to help adults stand away a bit." Her main criteria for a toy that facilitates good play are (1) the child finds it fun, which she underscores is a very personal thing—just because you like building train sets doesn't mean your kid will; (2) the toy allows the child to interact, whether with a friend or a caregiver; and (3) it encourages the child to be active.

"We do have to think about quality," she warns, "just as we only hand them certain books or magazines." Unless you're a particularly unusual parent, you're not going to give your toddler a single-shooter video game, just as you're not going to give him *Playboy* as bedtime reading material. But she's not so sure that kids need much in the way of physical toys at all, digitally enhanced or not.

"When you see how excited a young kid can be about a cardboard box?" she asks rhetorically, then smiles, which I take to mean, *Why introduce bells and whistles?* Particularly if those bells and whistles will take away from the child's own ability to imagine? A cardboard box can be a car, a fort, a castle. No charging cord required.

I spend the rest of the afternoon wandering the museum, where an exhibit lines the perimeter of one floor, tracing the evolution of toys and play from Victorian times to today. A few paces away from a crude rocking horse is a beeping, blooping room packed with arcade games that sends Dave into hysterics when I text him photos ("NBA Jam? HOLY F!"). In one cabinet I see Lincoln Logs from the early 1900s, which look almost identical to the ones I bought for Ella in the hopes that they might inspire her to become an architect one day. (After they arrived, I'd often come upon Dave studiously working on a log-cabin house addition while Ella sat nearby, barking out orders. "All she's doing is telling me what to build and watching!" he'd complain. "Is this how it's supposed to work?" Maybe we do have an architect on our hands.)

I watch a two-year-old in the center of the floor carefully pack smooth pebbles into the back of a Tonka Truck, dump them out, then begin again as his mother, with the dazed look of someone who just got off a two-week holiday stretch with her sub-three-footer, catches a quick game of Candy Crush on her phone.

So what, precisely, is a toy, and how did we get from physical toys to phigital ones?

Loosely understood to be anything that helps facilitate play, toys have been in existence for just about as long as children have. Stick figures were en vogue in 5000 BC; a stone ball was found in the grave of an Egyptian child who lived a thousand years later; silk and bamboo kites appeared in Chinese stories around 500 BC; and marbles were forever preserved in the volcanic destruction of Pompeii. For those of us who lament that the world is hurtling by too quickly, it's calming to realize that all of these are still available on Amazon. And no matter the era, it's generally understood that since the dawn of man, play has allowed children to imitate the world around them, as practice for becoming grown-ups—just how we believe that baby lion cubs play at fighting so that, one day, they can become good hunters themselves.

In the Strong Museum's library archives, I become immersed in Barbara Kaye Greenleaf's *Children Through the Ages* (1979), which traces how this imitation shifts from culture to culture. "Because the Greeks admired physical prowess," she writes, "many of their toys and games helped develop their youngsters' bodies." In ancient times, there were hoops to roll and teeterboards to balance on, and clothes were either loose fitting or nonexistent, to promote physical activity. In medieval times, kids got "whole armories of weapons" for mock battles; in colonial America, parents, who believed their offspring should be diligent, set their girls up with samplers, bits of cloth on which they could practice sewing letters or the cross-stitch—a valuable pastime because "in addition to improving a girl's skill, it taught her the alphabet and encouraged perseverance and neatness."

But, by and large, toys weren't a critical part of childhood until the modern era.

"At least until recently, adults have valued manufactured toys more than children have—with the exception of a few items that youngsters seem to have cherished, such as dolls, sleds, bicycles, and skates—not a few of those involving being outdoors and running around," writes historian Howard Chudacoff in *Children at Play*.

Mass-manufactured toys really took off at the turn of the twentieth century, due to both a rise in living standards, which freed up children and adults to play instead of work, and myriad industrial innovations that allowed inventors to put out products cheaply. After World War II, with the crackdown on materials used for the war effort lifted and a baby boom flooding America with children, the country entered what many historians refer to as the golden age of toy production. Cheap, plastic toys—Mr. Potato Head, Barbie, Tonka Trucks, Hula Hoops—canted less toward purposeful play and more toward kids being kids. In 1978, there was another seismic shift: Milton Bradley released its Simon Says game (called Simon), one of the first toys controlled by a computer chip, which opened up a new market for battery-operated personal playthings. And here we are.

When I ask Chris Bensch, the museum's chief curator and vice president of collections, how technology has affected the museum over the thirty years he has been there and whether the digital age of play is better or worse than an analog one, he tells me he tries his best not to put a value on the almost half-a-million toys they have in their collection—they're all talismans from the past, which he'll preserve for the future because it's his job. To illustrate the point, he takes me through some of the toy archives, vast rooms with toys filling shelves to the brim, pointing out a doll-size electric chair (fun!) and a 1990s-era Game Boy, as nostalgia inducing for any millennial as Proust's madeleine. Bensch's job is to make sure that in 2320, if someone wants to turn it on and play *Zelda*, it'll work.

But each year, when the museum inducts toys into the Toy Hall of Fame, which honors toys that have "inspired creative play and enjoyed popularity over a sustained period" (past winners: Barbie, Crayola crayons, little green army men), Bensch finds himself forced to place toys on a sort of value spectrum. Recently, Tickle Me Elmo, the Sesame Street doll that laughs and convulses spastically when you squeeze his tummy, was up for consideration.

"It was a real breakthrough in the marketplace," Bensch says, "but it isn't really conducive to open-ended play. A plush Elmo doll would be better, because *you* make him laugh, or cry, or whatever. It comes from you." So, Elmo got the doll-size electric chair.

But Bensch's general outlook tends to be a little less doom and gloom. "Consider technology a tool and a part of our world," he says. "We need to find a way to reach some sort of internal comfort level. As long as a kid's play diet is diverse—a little technology, a little reading, a little outdoor play—it'll be fine."

A few minutes after the museum closes that day, he sends me an email with a link to an American Girl press release announcing the company's latest doll, Blaire Wilson.

"A natural people person, Blaire excels at gathering people around the dinner table but needs help finding balance between the digital world and the real world—like many people today," the release says. "Through Blaire, girls will learn the importance of staying connected to the people they care about and that this means more than clicking and swiping—it means truly being there." At the end of the release: a link to supplemental online Blaire-related activities. Try as they might, even simple dolls can't escape the digital revolution.

* * *

The American Academy of Pediatrics takes an unequivocal stance on all of this. The day it published "Selecting Appropriate

Toys for Young Children in the Digital Era," its statement about digital toys, my Momma's Facebook group exploded, the *New York Times* picked it up, and my mother-in-law sent me the article. It seemed every parent I knew was talking about it. It had gone viral.

"I'm really surprised at how much that took off," Dr. Alan Mendelsohn, one of the study's two authors, tells me at Bellevue Hospital, after he graciously agrees to an in-person interview. His office window looks out not onto the East River but into the hospital's internal atrium—a metaphor, perhaps, for his relative insulation from the mounting hysteria of my parenting orbit. As the associate professor in the department of pediatrics and the department of population health at NYU Langone Health, a member of the AAP Council on Early Childhood, and a coauthor of more than a hundred publications in the space, he is one of the country's foremost experts on how play can benefit children.

The statement synthesizes sixty-nine studies and articles and covers a number of major pain points I need to unpack if I have any chance at figuring out which toys my children should have in their room, including how enrichment has taken over the play space and whether we can qualify play or if, rather, all play is good play.

"The last 20 years have brought a shift in parental and societal perception of toys," the statement begins. What was a toy then isn't necessarily a toy today: "This difference is attributable in part to the proliferation of electronic, sensory-stimulating noise and light toys and digital media–based platforms with child-oriented software and mobile applications that can be perceived by parents as necessary for developmental progress despite the lack of supporting evidence and, perhaps more importantly, with the potential for the disruption of caregiver-child interactions."

"Caregiver-child interactions have been proven through decades and decades of research to be beneficial to early childhood development," Mendelsohn stresses to me, between sheepish apologies for having to plug in his iPhone to charge. Interact with a child, and there are likely to be "serve-and-return conversations" that improve a kid's focus, verbal capacity, cognitive capacity, and gross motor skills.

The issue with a light-up, beeping toy isn't that it is inherently bad, Mendelsohn explains. It's that it displaces and hinders otherwise beneficial activities. Park your kid in front of a toy that does the work for her, and she's less inclined to use her imagination with it, and you, as a parent, are more inclined to tap out—*Phewph, she's occupied, I'll just tiptoe away.* It's just what Debbie McCoy told me at the Strong Museum.

"Pretend and play are what children need—there are lots of data to back that up," he says, "which should remove some of the pressure parents might feel."

* * *

As I start to critically assess the toys in Ella's room, I realize that almost all the ones I like are made by a company named Melissa & Doug. Their toys are mostly wooden, simple, and well-made, and they feel good in your hand. Ella, who often watches me cook from her perch on the high chair, suddenly, thanks to Melissa & Doug, is able to spend the better part of an hour slicing apart velcroed-together cucumbers, tomatoes, and baguettes, making me pepper sandwiches or adding pieces to little metal pots and pans to make "pink soup." She puts together puzzles, just the right size for her chubby hands, and then graduates to a train set, just like the kind I had as a child.

A little research reveals that the literal mom-and-pop company has swum steadily, and pointedly, upstream against the tide of technology since its founding in 1988, growing into a beloved $450 million behemoth. And so, one day, I cold email both Melissa and Doug Bernstein, guessing at their email addresses. A few days later Doug responds and, in a five-sentence email that contains twenty-seven exclamation points, tells me to call their headquarters. After a brief hold (music: "one-eyed, one-horned, flyin' purple people eater"), I'm put on the line directly with Melissa. She quickly invites me up for a visit and takes my breakfast order so she can have something warm waiting for me from the diner down the street. In other words, they both behave exactly how I'd hope two married toy creators would.

"We're in this really horrific crisis," Melissa tells me a few weeks later at the company's headquarters in Wilton, CT, as I adjust a four-foot-long multicolored caterpillar that lays across the office couch's back cushions and take a bite of a superb bacon-egg-and-cheese sandwich on an English muffin. "We're at an inflection point. Forty percent of people in the country are officially addicted to technology. In time, we'll realize that it's as toxic as nicotine." She doesn't mean this metaphorically, and she exhibits very little of the "life is a continuum" and "it's all about balance" attitude I'd seen at the Strong. I take notes as Bernstein rails against the current state of play.

When she and her husband founded the company two decades ago, the technology they were competing against looked like, well, child's play compared to what's on the market now. And she can track its evolution on an intimate level. They have six children, ages ten to twenty-five.

"My first two kids didn't have technology, and it was so much better because there was no competition for time," she remembers. They'd swim together every evening, make paper airplanes and compete for flight distance, tell stories, and sing songs. She could let them run around outside while she headed back inside to dream up new activity creations. Now? Not so much. "I've made a tremendous mistake with the last two," she laments, "and have become central to their play. It's exhausting, but they haven't learned to do it themselves." What does that mean, practically? That as a self-styled "imagination coach," she comes home after a long day at work and, to get them to unglue from whatever device is nearby, coaxes them to play in an old-fashioned way: drawing pictures with their eyes closed, seeing how many times they can throw a ball back and forth before dropping it, or simply pretending. "And it's horrific, because from kindergarten, Google and Microsoft are infused into academics!" she says. "My son's elementary school was all excited that they got Chromebooks for all of the kids last year, and I thought *noooooo*!"

For years, she has tried to saturate the toy market with tools of play that will directly combat Chromebook infiltration. She gestures to a simple wooden clock sitting on the coffee table: Mickey Mouse in the center, movable arms, each of the numbers inset satisfyingly into a color shape—a red star for 12, a blue square for 4.

"If you look at it, you'll see a boring shape-sorting toy," she says. "But it can be a tray where you stack all the blocks on top of each other and carry it across the room. You can turn it on its side and spin it like a wheel." She pauses, assessing a Saint

Bernard–size plush duck who sits on her nearby desk, driving a car. "It can be a steering wheel to the moon. It's a launchpad for every possibility."

Years ago, anxious that shape-sorting parents might not be able to nudge their offspring into spaceship steering–territory, she started enclosing a list of "extension activities" with some of her toys, which describe unseen play possibilities. But over the course of our conversation, it becomes clear that Bernstein has immense faith in the power of children—as long as they're left to their own devices, and not those that plug in. Boredom, for Bernstein, is when the magic starts to happen.

However, in the last few years, frightened in part by the effect screens and overscheduling had on her own kids' lives, she realized that creating new non-tech toys isn't enough. She's become a spokesperson of a campaign she coined Take Back Childhood. Slap a hashtag on it, and you've got yourself a Twitter and Instagram movement. (Later, in an apparent attempt to backtrack on potentially shaming parents who had given childhood away, she partnered with the AAP to promote the essential benefits of play, naming the movement The Power of Play.)

While she is optimistic that people are starting to pay attention, she recently came head-to-head with the very real limitations of her anti-tech vision at a nearby department store where she was asked to speak. Instead of being the keynote at the Greenwich United Way luncheon, her more typical haunt, there she was, facing an audience of mostly lower- and middle-income parents. At the end of her presentation about child-led play and the importance of screen-free time, eighty hands went up. The comments came fast and furious.

"My kid will get shot if I send him outside."

"I spend an hour a week with my kid because I'm holding three jobs."

"When my son is at my estranged husband's house, he only sleeps for four hours because he's playing *Fortnite* the rest of the time, but I can't dictate what his dad lets him do."

"It was sobering," Bernstein told me.

Afterward, her head swimming, Bernstein penned a blog post entitled "Play for All: 20 Ways to Engage with Your Child When You Don't Always Have the Time, Money, or Space." They're sweet ideas, but it's hard to imagine a tired mother coming home from a long day at work and holding a dance party (suggestion #4) or staging a play (#18). On the spectrum of stressful jobs, magazine editor is pretty low, but I still sometimes find myself counting down the minutes until I can put Ella down in her crib for the night and go curl up in the fetal position myself.

But when I relay this exchange to Nancy Carlsson-Paige, professor emerita at Lesley University, who founded Defending the Early Years, a nonprofit organization that advocates for quality early childhood education—that parents, for a variety of reasons, seem to find it hard to give their children a calm, tech-free space to play—she gives me a gentle slap on the wrist.

"I was a single mom from the time my kids were two and five, and did not have money at all through their early childhood years," she tells me. "They had a completely thriving play environment, because it doesn't take much. Kids are amazingly inventive. Put out some aluminum foil, some boxes, some markers."

The two-year-old she's talking about: Matt Damon.

She has devoted her career to trying to ensure that children receive the time and space to play, freely, in their schools and beyond, that their environments aren't structured with "drill and kill"–style instruction, which she believes is far less beneficial to developing minds than open-ended creativity. In 2018, Carlsson-Paige published *Young Children in the Digital Age: A Parent's Guide*, in which she offers six "core ideas from the field of child development" to help parents make decisions about how their children should best spend their time.

First: "Young children use their whole bodies and all of their senses to learn about the world." Brains develop optimally if children are able to move and explore—neurons actively fire when a baby lurches across the carpet to pick something up. Stick them in front of a screen, or a toy that does much of the work for them, and you short-circuit that growth.

Another one: "Young children learn by inventing ideas." What she means by this is less that boredom is a spur for creativity—though it is—and more that rote learning, where children are asked to memorize flash cards and the like, is not as successful as letting children learn a concept through interaction. And interaction is, more often than not, achieved through hands-on, physical play.

Carlsson-Paige thinks there might be something else going on when parents complain that they can't entertain their children without help from technology.

"Parents themselves were raised on screens, often," she says, "and so they actually don't have in their experience a rich play environment. No one has helped them create it."

In 1999, Dr. Mendelsohn, at Bellevue, started a program called the Video Interaction Project (VIP), which aims to specifically address that need. A child comes in for his or her well visit at the pediatrician's, and parents—by and large low-income and high-need—can opt into a free twenty-five-minute visit with a VIP Coach, who talks with them about their child's development while the child plays with a developmentally appropriate toy or book. If needed, the coach can demonstrate appropriate play. The entire thing is recorded, and parents can take their videos home and watch the scene afterward.

At Bellevue one day, as a Spanish-speaking mother and son have a VIP session in the room next door, I watch one of the recordings, of a two-year-old boy named Johannes (Jojo) with a serious head of shoulder-length curly hair. In the video, he and his parents come into the room, and the VIP Coach gives him a Melissa & Doug farm puzzle to do, which he and his father unwrap together as his mother chats with the coach. As Jojo investigates the puzzle, his mom tells the coach that he's getting really good at eating on his own ("That's amazing!" the coach says), and the conversation drifts toward the importance of pretending and playing with other kids. When the coach asks if Jojo ever has tantrums, his mom snorts.

"We tried time-out the other day," she says. "He cried his eyes out, but eventually he stopped."

One huge part of the success of the program is the coaching, of course, the sacred time when parents can be more mindful about their parenting actions, when they can get the support they might not find elsewhere from professionals—but critical, too, is the focal point of the visit, which is the toy, and educating parents in the power of play. Studies show that participating in VIP for children younger than three has myriad benefits, from reduced television exposure to reduced maternal symptoms of depression, reduced use of physical punishment, and enhanced cognitive and language development.

"This is not rocket science, and it's not neuroscience," Mendelsohn later says. "Even a simple toy can act as a prop and keep a conversation going." The more complicated the toy gets, the more it interferes.

* * *

But maybe even the simplest of toys are unnecessarily enhanced. Or so says one particularly beloved parenting philosophy, RIE—pronounced like the bread, and standing for Resources for Infant Educarers.

"We call them *play objects*," Deborah Carlisle Solomon tells me, when we speak a few months after Charlotte's birth. At this age, Charlotte's favorite toy is her own set of toes, but if history is any indication, her arsenal will expand soon. "*Toys* are developed by savvy marketers who are creating something that is sexy to the adult."

Carlisle Solomon, executive director of RIE for eight years, succinctly describes the approach, which is founded on the ideas that independent activity is paramount and that children, however young, should be treated like little individuals, not objects. Your child starts crying? Give her a few beats before scooping her up to try to figure out *why* she's crying. You want to wipe crud off his face? You respect him enough to tell him why you're going to do it before you lunge at him with a wet wipe. The philosophy was developed in post-war Hungary by a pediatrician named Emmi Pikler, who ran an orphanage and believed her approach could set up orphans for life as well as it could set up kids raised in traditional family structures. The method, brought to California in the 1960s by one of her acolytes, Magda Gerber, recently experienced a sort of renaissance, due in part to buy-ins from celebs like Tobey Maguire and Helen Hunt. My friend is such a proponent that she opened up a RIE-based play space for children in Union Square, a cheerful place filled with metal mixing bowls and woven bowls filled with Hacky Sacks. Save for the bright carpeting, you'd be forgiven for thinking you'd wandered into a Berkeley community kitchen.

When Ella, covered with peanut butter and a light dusting of Cheerios, is about to scoot off around the house pretending to be a dinosaur, I'm not necessarily going to ask permission to hose her down. But the one part of the RIE approach that resonates with me is its philosophy on the proper way to utilize toys, which can be boiled down to "Busy babies, passive toys." Hair rollers feature prominently in RIE websites. Kids can put their tongues through them, roll them around, or put a ball on top to make an ice cream cone. What you want is a blank slate, which means that for extreme practitioners, even dress-up clothes are viewed with suspicion. "A doctor kit doesn't become anything else," one RIE adherent tells me. "You want a kid that can think more globally."

For a stint, one of Ella's favorite toys is a doctor's coat, complete with stethoscope and syringe. For weeks, Ella would spend upward of a half hour giving Baby thorough examinations, all prefaced with the sobering words, "Baby, this is going to hurt (*pause*) a LOT." Watching her bop Baby on the head repeatedly with the green plastic reflex hammer after immersing myself in RIE literature, I wonder if I am putting her at a disadvantage—perhaps she should have a hair roller in her hand instead, which could stand in for either a (slightly weird) stethoscope *or* an (even weirder) ice cream cone. But when I bring this up to Carlisle Solomon, she ratchets down my crazy.

"The basic principles are very simple," she says. "In terms of play, it's going back to the way that children have played for millennia."

I mention a company that is starting to make its mark as the go-to subscription toy service, sending parents boxes of toys "specifically designed for each of a child's learning stages"—say, a wooden disc that claims to "build motor skills via hand-to-hand transfer, which promotes cross-body coordination." (Which, let's be honest, sounds more like a CrossFit goal than a goal for a seven-month-old. This is an extreme, particularly ritzy version of mass-marketing slogans that are stamped on most toys—claiming that they'll boost this or that skill at this or that age.) Carlisle Solomon pauses.

"Developmentally appropriate play doesn't come from the outside; it comes internally, from the child," she clarifies. "They will play with the same object in a different way as they develop. When parents understand that, they can relax a little bit. It's not like they have to consult their toy catalogue and say, 'Oh, my child is eight months and now we should introduce something new.'"

The challenge with keeping things simple—opening up your kitchen cabinet and seeing what's in there that might interest your baby, instead of setting them in front of balls and mirrors and stackers and cross-body coordinators—is social pressure. "It's countercultural," she says. You don't want to be the only one on the block whose kid entertains herself with a hair roller, in other words. But the benefits are worth it, she believes, if only because it helps parents gain confidence in raising their children, without the help of commercial interests, and without the hysteria of the digital age.

"It's an antidote," Carlisle Solomon tells me before we hang up. "Children come into the world with enough. They don't need external devices or training to develop. Keep it simple."

* * *

I'm fascinated to discover that one country that seems to have put open-ended play front and center is China.

"I'd imagine that for a lot of people it would be a big surprise that America's intellectual competitor on the global stage feels that the best way for young children to develop is mostly through play," Walter Gilliam tells me. The director of the Edward Zigler Center in Child Development and Social Policy at Yale University and an authority on early childhood education, he does a fair amount of work in China. There, he tells me, the government mandates that preschools—serving children ages two through five—be play-based, without direct instruction.

His colleague sends me the Chinese Ministry of Education's *Teaching Guidelines for Preschool Education*, essentially the state standard for all preschool programs in China. It's startlingly specific, including warnings that all classroom materials should be large enough "to avoid causing foreign matter to enter the trachea" and that teachers should guide their students in self-care, which includes "wash your face, wipe your nose, wipe your butt the right way." (Yes, "wipe your butt the right way" is a phrase in an official Chinese government document.)

It also underscores that preschools should "value games" and encourage open-ended play—just the kid, a few objects, if that, and the time to imagine. Sprinkled throughout are photos of children climbing on tires, kicking balls, drawing, and pretending to make calls on a play phone. "We should forbid education and bootcamp-like trainings that accelerate learnings before the toddlers are ready, like someone who 'pulls up the seedlings to help them grow,'" one section reads, employing a Chinese idiom based on a folktale that describes a "haste makes waste"–like situation. In other words, preschoolers are only preschoolers once. Let them behave as such.

This anti-curricular mandate is so important to the Chinese government that in July 2018, the Ministry of Education issued a policy *specifically* promoting preschool play-based learning. It was in response to a trend of primary schools increasingly trying to prepare their little charges for elementary school education before the government deemed them ready. The upshot? These preschools, the policy reads, had grown "more serious, which not only deprived young children of their happiness, but also dampened their learning interest and affected physical and mental health." It explicitly forbids preschools from teaching Pinyin (the romanized spelling for transliterated Chinese), reading, math, and English. Instead, the policy reads, teachers should "encourage young children to play games and learn independently through personal experience."

As far as I can tell, there's no explicit mandate against using electronic toys or technology, but the message is simple: let the kids play, let the kids explore, and stop trying to push them beyond their developmental stage.

One of the more puzzling aspects of all this, Gilliam notes, is that China is likely pulling their policies from American research. One study conducted here, for example, examined children who attended preschools that were less playful and less child focused than ones where play and children came first. By first grade, the children's intellectual skills were the same, but the children who'd attended a more academic preschool were more anxious.

"We invest a lot of money in research regarding child development," Gilliam tells me. "We don't always invest as much money in actually doing it. Many other countries around the globe don't invest their money in research—they read our research, and then implement it."

And our research says that open-ended creative play is where it's at.

But I wonder, sometimes, if the AAP and Gilliam ever entertained the possibility of talking paper. The logic about toys that do the work for you—those that beep and squawk and sing and move—seems ironclad to me. Toy makers, pediatricians, psychologists—they all agree: if what we're after is creativity and serve-and-return interactions, then the simpler the toy, the better. You'll make it beep and squawk and sing and move, and your mom and dad have a better chance of playing with you.

Thing is, what if our collective understanding of non-analog toys is a little dated?

* * *

Almost a full year after I saw Kate Stone speak at the Toy Fair about paper that can communicate with you, I meet her for breakfast on a rainy weekday morning. Her hand is in a cast ("skiing accident"), a heart brooch is pinned to her bright-red blouse, and her interactive papers, made with touch-sensitive ink, are in a tote bag. Of all the people I saw at the Toy Fair, she had presented a vision—quiet, all about paper and print, very few bells and whistles—that I thought might give us a glimpse of the future of play. There'd be no screens, just beautiful analog objects that somehow respond.

The restaurant is particularly noisy—a rookie mistake for any journalist hoping to make a clean recording, but one that I realize will be particularly debilitating for this interview.

Stone starts to speak over the din, then stops and apologizes.

"I had the, well, you know," she says quietly, gesturing to her throat, where there's a small but visible scar. I'd learned about it the night before, googling around and preparing questions, when I came upon a TED Talk she gave in 2018 called "The press trampled on my privacy. Here's how I took back my story." Watching it, I learned about the horrifying freak accident she endured when coming out of a pub one night in the Scottish Highlands. "I suddenly felt a massive thud, then a second thud, and I fell to the ground," she says to the audience. The cause: a wild stag who shot out of the pitch-black wilderness, collided with her, and punctured her trachea and esophagus with his antlers. She goes on to explain how the press took the already sensational story and sensationalized it even more by pivoting it around gender—Stone is transgender, something she finds completely irrelevant to her work and her stag encounter. After she made a full and miraculous recovery, she decided to take the press on, and as a result of a landmark negotiation with the Press Complaints Commission, a regulatory body in Britain that was founded to uphold ethical standards in journalism (replaced in 2014 by the Independent Press Standards Organization), the papers publicly agreed that their headlines and angle weren't appropriate.

One of the aftereffects: she can't speak too loudly or else her voice gives out.

She's gentle and self-deprecating as she wincingly tends to her wrist and tries, rather unsuccessfully, to eat avocado on toast with her nondominant hand. So I find it rather fitting that she describes her Touchscapes as gentle.

"The child's imagination is incredibly powerful," she says. "We just *gently* add in a little bit of magic."

Stone received her PhD in microelectronics at the University of Cambridge's Cavendish Laboratory, which has produced thirty Nobel Prize winners. When she started working in the field, she found herself a little put off by the attitude of some of her fellow scientists and engineers.

"Technologists have this arrogance," she says. "They want to make everything enhanced and it's all about them. When I started my company, I wanted to make something they'd laugh at, or even look down upon. If I can create something that will delight someone, that's my goal."

At her company, Novalia, she works to create various interactive experiences that can blow your mind, whatever your age. Imagine walking into a mirrored room and being faced with a piece of blank paper on a table (something she's working to install at music festivals). Touch the paper, and flowers bloom on the walls, which then bloom on all of the mirrored walls—your very own psychedelic experience, no LSD required. After our breakfast, in a quieter spot, she shows me some of her cardboard DJ decks, which connect wirelessly to your iPhone—touch one circle on the paper and a beat starts on your phone; tap over there and the beat loops. One of them she describes, matter-of-factly, as "an intergalactic alien music remixing rap battle in a poster." It features neon creatures, one with four eyes, another mop-like one reminiscent of a PAC-MAN character, that battle via sounds. We have so much fun playing with it that a security guard eventually has to come over and tell us to knock it off.

Her Touchscapes, aimed specifically at children, harness the power of that interactive ink to connect what looks like a board game, or a simple book, to the cloud. As she envisions it, you'd receive a bunch of printed tiles in the mail, which you could fit into a puzzle, and as you put them together, you'd be able to press on the tiles, which would activate music, or storytelling, or something from the cloud. It's not like the musical books I sometimes read to the girls, which have spots you can push to hear a snippet of a piece. Those are buttons. In Stone's version, the actual *ink* on the paper is connected.

"If I could create a world I wanted to live in, there'd be no visible technology at all," she tells me. She comes off as a bit spiritual, residing in an orbit of her own making. At one point in the conversation, she tells me how she sometimes envisions herself on the top of a mountain, with little wavy lines flowing into her in different widths, each a different color that corresponds to one of the five senses.

"They look like magnetic field lines, and some go up to the stars, some to the earth," she tells me. "As soon as we get this out"—she picks up her phone—"all of those lines bend into the phone." It's a wacky, but accurate, way to visually capture how technology wrenches us out of the present and into the virtual. Her technology, she hopes, will make people more mindful of their surroundings, something she thinks is critical for all of us, perhaps children most of all. The showy part isn't the tech itself, its wizardry; it's that you don't even know it's there.

"When the inventor becomes the story, that's not right," she says. "The answer might be that we need no technology at all."

When I point out that that line of thinking will put her out of a job, she doesn't miss a beat.

"So fucking what?"

* * *

One weekend afternoon, after building endless Magna-Tile castles and Lego trains, my phone buzzes. It's a group chat I have with some of my girlfriends, and while I'm craving some adult interaction, I know the minute I bring the phone out, Ella will laser into it like a raptor on a mouse. Way back in the depths of the closet, I see a tiny plush puppy foot, which belongs to the Laugh and Learn Puppy I'd successfully shoved in the donate bin months ago but unsuccessfully taken to Goodwill. Knowing it'll buy me ten minutes, I bring it out, power it on, and set it in front of Ella, who happily bangs on its foot and heart like an unhinged EMT, eliciting chirps and half-sung songs, as I chat away.

When I come up for air and Ella has started a tinny "Twinkle, Twinkle, Little Star" for the umpteenth time, I remember something Dr. Mendelsohn told me back at his office in Bellevue.

Having two children in their early twenties, he warned me of the teen years, when, he said, all concept of dictating how your kids spend their time goes out the window.

"For all behavioral issues, parents' capacity to deal with tantrums is a bit like a bank," he explained. "They make investments in their child, and then utilize what they've built when they need it. From birth to five, parents have a real opportunity to do relationship building, so the child can separate, when the time comes, while feeling supported. To the extent that you've engaged in relationship building, you can work together to figure out, for example, screen time limits. It provides you with a foundation." In other words, put the time in now, and it will compound over time. These years are precious—use them wisely.

It's not that he doesn't recognize the immense demands put

on parents these days. They're stressed, overworked, under pressure to be integral to their children's development while constantly being bombarded with conflicting information. The demands escalate rapidly for families in low-income brackets, where making sure food is on the table might be more of a priority than getting on the floor and playing make believe. He assured me that using technology, in moderation, wouldn't harm a child and said that a large part of his job is reassuring parents that they're doing okay and should lay off the self-flagellation. But talking with your kid, playing with your kid, in addition to being enjoyable, also pays dividends down the line.

"'Everything in moderation' is kind of true," he chuckled. "It's really a completely scientifically valid statement."

Which, I assume, applies not just to Ella's Laugh and Learn puppy but to Magna-Tiles that communicate and paper that talks—and my own damn phone. We may, indeed, be inching ever nearer to a world where magic reigns supreme, where a thin layer of technology is pulsing, invisible, under the surface. Perhaps, in a few years, Ella's Magna-Tiles will be able, in some unobtrusive way, to gently suggest how she can better build a taller castle. But until then, it seems best to go back to basics.

So I power down my own toy, power down Ella's, and realize we have a load of laundry to do. We have a blast.

6

Couch Fingerlings

Is Preschool Programming Worse than Ever?

I was thirty-eight weeks pregnant with Charlotte, Dave was running late, Ella had skipped her nap, and I'd just learned that the sporadic shooting pain in my pelvis went by the charming name of "lightning crotch." While I'd done my best to be pretty strict about the "no screens at mealtime" rule—it was verboten in my house growing up, and at one point I so believed in the power of conversation over a good meal that I became a professional cook—Ella could sense weakness in my eyes. She sidled up to the cabinet where we hid away our television and said, as nonchalantly as she could, "Mama, let's just do *one* television. Just. One." Then, more urgently: "The Macaulay Culkin one." Then she proceeded to march around the coffee table chanting Macaulay Culkin's name in rhythm, like a pint-size child-actor stalker.

As far as I knew, she believed the television streamed a single piece of content: the 1993 version of George Balanchine's *Nutcracker* ballet, in which the New York City Ballet corps does its best to shield a young Culkin, playing the Nutcracker Prince, from having to do anything save for run around the stage or flourish his arm as he bows. My mother told her about the *Nutcracker* one afternoon, and I'd found this version for free on YouTube. It was an instant hit. But the prospect of listening to the celesta plink out the opening bars of the Sugar Plum Fairy's dance for the fourteen millionth time made me want to give Pyotr Ilyich a bad case of lightning crotch. So I turned on the television and started scrolling through a few possibilities offered up on Netflix.

There was a full subgenre of princess cartoons, each indicated with glittering pink type, and another of nursery rhymes made more toddler-addictive with chirpy voices and colors so bright they probably rendered my television visible from outer space. I'd half a mind to click on one of the Korean children's shows that, for some reason, the Netflix algorithm thought would resonate with me, and I recognized one of them by name: *Larva*. My editor-in-chief at the magazine watched it with his sons. The cartoon features two curious worms who hang out below a sidewalk grate and speak a high-pitched frenetic language that is neither Korean nor English (presumably, it is Larva). I'd have been more inclined to watch it if I didn't already feel so nauseated. So, instead, I settled on a sweet-looking show, put out by the BBC, called *Sarah & Duck*.

A lot of voices were swirling around in my head as I pressed Play: the friend who told me she equated screens during dinner with Ambien or Adderall ("I know that if I use it, I'll never not want to use it, so why start?"); the children's media professional who said that worrying about screen time is "a really elitist problem to have"; Nicole Kidman, who I read had successfully tricked her kids into thinking the only place iPads worked was on planes; various media sources that hammered home the fact that sitting a child in front of a television was a one-way track to dying alone in front of *Fortnite* while surrounded by packets of Soylent. But the one voice I did not hear was Ella's—the minute I pressed Play, she stopped her Culkin chant and sat down, slack-jawed, like I'd taken her batteries out. I lowered myself, as if by crane, onto the cushion next to her, and as she watched, riveted, I shoveled tortellini into her unsuspecting mouth.

But a few bites in, an odd thing happened: I found myself paying attention as well. The look of the show, the muted, washed-out color palette that had caused me to click on it, reminded me of my childhood *Paddington* books. Sarah, a sweet young girl, and her friend Duck, speak (or, in the latter case, quacks) in a normal cadence and pitch, unlike the Ritalin-fueled characters I'd seen on American cartoons. The only adult in the episode comes in the form of a narrator, whose soothing British voice I later found belongs to Roger Allam, a beloved Royal Shakespearean actor (because: Britain).

While the plot was simple, it was charming. In the first episode, Sarah finds a seed packet that has fallen out of the newspaper, decides to plant it, and then waits, and waits, and waits to see what'll happen. Finally, some shallots—three big ones and one baby—pop out of the ground. With the help of her vegetable book, Sarah comes to realize that they're not onions that will grow bigger, as originally suspected, but rather that her new friends are destined to view the world from a shorter vantage point. At one point, the shallots start jabbering and marching around to triumphant music, which caused me to burst out laughing and Ella to snort into her tortellini. Dave arrived home that evening to find us marching around the apartment, wielding shallots and giggling. "Daddy, it's a shal*lot*!" Ella crowed, putting the emphasis on the second syllable, like a good Eton grad.

The entire episode was less than seven minutes long, so I reasoned that even if screen time was as bad as abusing Ritalin, at least she was getting just a taste.

Then again, as I ran her bath later that night, I thought: *No one wants her child abusing Ritalin, even if it's only a little bit.* Drug use is a binary calculation. Is screen time?

* * *

Every parenting generation has its own flavor of hysteria. In a not-so-subtle knock against fiction, *Madame Bovary*'s heroine, Emma, spends her teenage years reading romance novels, develops a warped sense of the world, marries an imbecile, cheats on him, poisons herself, then dies. In the 1920s, a report from the League of Nations Child Welfare Committee stated that promiscuous behavior in dark cinemas and violence on screens was "one of the principle causes of crime among children." And in the 1930s, the public was aghast to learn that more than twenty-one hours of child-specific programming was aired per week, just as shows with educational content were dropping from the airwaves and being replaced by drivel. As leading media scholar Ellen Wartella writes, new technology is often accompanied by both panic and excitement, which is, in turn, reflected in the press.

My generation's hysteria of choice revolves around a single

trigger: screen time. When I start trying to figure out how much screen time has increased for young kids in the last few years, I find myself adrift in studies that cover children ages zero to two, or zero to six, or zero to eight, but all point to the same conclusion: usage is off the charts. Common Sense Media estimates that children are on screens around two hours and twenty-four minutes per day.

By the time Ella moves on from the gnawing-on-remote-controls phase of her screen-time career and Charlotte arrives in the world, I start seeing articles that differentiate between *types* of screen time—solving calculus problems on a math app is different from zoning out in front of mindless TV, which is different from playing a shoot-'em-up video game. The gist is that the phrase *screen time* is a little like the label *natural*. An apple is natural, but so, too, is arsenic—the implied stamp of approval is hollow. But now that Ella and I so enjoyed *Sarah & Duck*, I am eager to establish a basic household rule on watching children's programming—whether on a big television screen or a smaller iPad—and create a system for evaluating whether screen time can be nutritious or should be avoided entirely.

Within my cohort of millennial parents, personal viewing habits are fraught with guilt, anxiety, and confusion.

Dave attends a Dad's Night Out with fathers from our neighborhood preschool and reports, aghast, that someone there thought it was better to let his child watch *Daniel Tiger* before bed than read him a book. At a gathering in the school's gym, a mom proudly tells us that her three-year-old son used the word *accelerate* the other day when they were driving in the car. He'd learned it from an Amazon television show. "I figure it's okay for him to watch as long as he's learning something!" she quickly backpedals, deflecting judgmental looks by sucking down her paper cup of cheap white wine. Everyone draws their own line in the sand, it seems: One friend allows her toddler to watch the Winnie-the-Pooh cartoon, but with no sound on, and only on long plane flights. Another tells me that for years she felt unduly guilty putting her two young daughters in front of *Sesame Street* because she, herself, had never been plopped in front of the television a day in her life.

"Not watching television was some sort of metric I was measuring my parenting by," she tells me. She remembers her childhood as one in which she listened to audiobooks, or went to the museum and sat on the ground, drawing pictures, or played make believe with her three sisters. Then, a few months after her second child was born, she brought this up with her mother.

"She was like, *I had four kids under the age of six, are you kidding me? You were watching* Sesame Street *from 18 months on— that was the only way I made dinner!* I had this idealized sense that my mother was such a good mom, but she was dealing with the same stuff I am."

The modern iteration of our current hysteria seems slightly more nuanced—the shows themselves feel more frenetic, for one, and many children watch them on iPads or phones, not the big TV in the living room that their parents can watch along with them, should they so choose. It's estimated that about 73 percent of young children's screen time on a mobile device is TV/video viewing, and when I speak to a veteran pediatrician in the field, who often sees parents of toddlers toting in iPads to checkups to keep their kids occupied, he underlines the big issue with this behavior.

"The way the tablet is set up, the relationship is between the child and the screen," he laments. Those sacred serve-and-return interactions I'd learned about from Dr. Mendelsohn, where child and caregiver converse about a block, or the moon, or a song, or whatever—that's rendered basically moot in front of a smaller device whose centripetal force sucks you into its orbit. Whatever is happening on-screen, then, better be good.

Given these changes, is our concern, guilt, and anxiety more warranted today than it was in generations past?

I turn to the American Academy of Pediatrics (AAP) website to find its latest (at the time of this printing) screen-time guidelines:

- Avoid use of screen media, other than video chatting, for children under eighteen months.
- Watch any digital media along with your child aged eighteen to twenty-four months to ensure comprehension, and choose only high-quality programming.
- Limit screen use for kids aged two to five to one hour a day, with continued coviewing.

Pragmatically, the guidelines raise more questions than they answer and, as far as I can tell, leave us parents with marching orders and no shoes. For starters, there's the huge issue that the doctors don't differentiate between types of screen time at all. But beyond that, what happens after the sixty-first minute of screen use, be that programming or apps or reading an e-book? And what on earth constitutes high quality?

Yet another, overarching, issue keeps niggling at me, which my appalled mother helps me articulate.

"That's almost one day a week!" she exclaims when I tell her that, should we so choose, in accordance with our country's national guidelines, we could set Ella up in front of a screen for that long, every single day. "How many hours of childhood do they think these children have?" A few months later, in the thick of quarantine, this seems like a particularly rich way of looking at time, which simultaneously stretches out and folds in on itself, like a Möbius strip, with bedtime somehow farther and farther away as the day progresses. But I take her point—before I know it, Ella will be a teenager. Do I really want her spending a day a week zoned out in front of a device?

As perhaps goes without saying, I grew up in a house with a complicated relationship with the television. One parent preferred it be locked away; the other made a career writing for it. Of course, my mother won out, so we had a single set in the back room, where we'd watch the occasional black-and-white film or, for a few wonderful weeks in the summer, the US Open. The Marx Brothers were on high rotation, as were Hepburn-Tracy comedies. I can't remember ever seeing a single episode of *Sesame Street*—this, despite the fact that my father collaborated with Jim Henson on *The Muppet Show*, creating the character of The Swedish Chef, among others—but by the time I was four, I could recite back a related Brickman-family aphorism: "*Sesame Street* teaches children—it teaches children to watch television." (I have a foggy, traumatic memory of visiting Muppet HQ as a toddler and pulling open a thin drawer to reveal row upon row of googly eyes, all staring back at me. I'm sure that will rear its head in therapy down the road.) The only time we were allowed to binge on Disney cartoons was when we were home sick from school, and even then things sometimes went awry. At age five, feverish and achy, I sat through the first ten minutes of *Dr. Zhivago*, patiently waiting for Thumper to arrive. That VHS cassette had mistakenly been put back in the *Bambi* box. At some point I must have succeeded in wearing my mother down, because I remember coming home from middle school and, under the guise of getting exercise on the NordicTrack (cool!), studying *Beverly Hills, 90210* as if it were the Rosetta Stone. But I've always associated watching television with a sense of shame.

Then I became a parent and discovered what every parent since 1950 had discovered: that the television is the easiest way to buy myself some alone time, whether to do a load of laundry, write this book, or contemplate how much longer we can allow Ella to refer to her vagina as her "front butt."

Seeking permission, I call my mother back and bring up the hypocrisy: Dad wrote for television, but we were rarely allowed to watch it—what was up with that?

"It's not like you were going to be watching Dick Cavett interviewing Antony Tudor!" she replies. "You were going to be watching some dumb bunny hopping around! And those types of programs just talk down to children."

She has a point. Scrolling through the children's options on my television, I find that the vast majority are much closer to bunny hopping than to erudite conversation about ballet choreography. Those neon colors visible from space, the Paw Patrol dogs who whiz around on tiny battleships—a few minutes watching them one afternoon, and I find myself so jangled and wound up, I spend the next hour frantically rearranging the front hall closet. But when I come down enough from my cartoon-fueled high to focus again, I head to the library in an attempt to figure out the effect this kind of television has on not just my fully formed brain cells but the ones developing in Ella's head. One statistic from my stack of books pops out at me from a study published in 2004: "For each additional hour per day of television that children watched during the first three years of their lives, the chance of having a level of attention problems consistent with ADHD was increased by 9 percent."

I come across this startling sentence in *The Elephant in the Living Room*, a book by Drs. Dimitri Christakis and Frederick Zimmerman. The reason for this rise in attention problems, they write, is rooted in a few issues. One is a show's pacing. Some shows get it right—*Sesame Street, Blue's Clues*, and *Mister Rogers' Neighborhood* all get the doctors' blessings.

Why? *Mister Rogers' Neighborhood* is shot in real time. I'd argue it's shot in Boca Raton Retirement Home Time—Fred Rogers talks, and moves, *really* slowly—but the idea is that this slow and steady gentle rhythm, all captured by a single camera, doesn't overstimulate kids' brains. Children can transition back to the real world seamlessly afterward, with no trouble focusing on a given task, unlike their counterparts watching shows with quick cuts. The more cuts in a given scene, the more a show exploits what is known as one's *orienting response*—the brain's reflex to perk up if it sees something new or unexpected. The more rapid pacing becomes the norm for a developing brain, the harder it becomes, down the line, for that brain to recalibrate to the normal slog of life. If your child is used to whizzing and beeping and sound effects, his third-grade teacher might have to spend her class time zip-lining around on a neon-green flashing seat, juggling live farm animals as she recites the times tables in double speed just to keep his attention.

A second issue is that myriad studies show higher-tech environments to be more language impoverished—with the television in the background, kids hear fewer words, which leads to later-in-life setbacks, including obesity, a lower college graduation rate, and a lower overall level of happiness. Not only that—children's play becomes less complex with a TV chattering, seemingly innocuously, in the background. Since I now know how critical play is to the development of children, this information is particularly damning considering that, according to Nielsen, Americans watch an average of almost five hours of television a day.

When I reach Dr. Christakis at his Seattle Children's Hospital office, where he's the director of the Center for Child Health, Behavior and Development, he wants to be clear that television can be beneficial and even enriching, and he brings up a randomized controlled experiment he conducted a few years earlier with preschoolers. It had already been established that watching violent and fast-paced shows resulted in aggressive behaviors and a reduced ability to focus. But could aggressive behavior be reduced simply by changing what children watched? He had parents substitute in educational programming for violent programming while keeping the amount of screen time constant.

"We found that if you change what they watch, you see increases in prosocial behavior and decreases in antisocial behavior," he tells me.

But that 9 percent increase in ADHD is what sticks with me.

I hang up the phone and vow to spend the next couple decades of my children's lives having meaningful serve-and-return interactions—that golden standard of child development—with them. *We'll just talk! How hard can that be? It's cheap, it's efficient, it's effective, and it's intuitive.* I return home a few hours later pumped up to filibuster my way through to their college acceptance letters, and find Ella lying on the floor of the bath-room with Dave standing above her, powerless. Instead of her pajamas, she's wearing a skirt under a dress under her bunny bathrobe, a clear sign that she is calling the shots this evening.

"MAMA, I NEED A SNACK," she wails. "I'M SO HUNGRY." She extends a toe at Dave and pouts. "AND DADDY WON'T LET ME GO DOWNSTAIRS TO GET A SNACK."

"But she had a huge dinner, and I already gave her yogurt and then half the cupcake I took from the office and was going to give to you," Dave whispers quietly to me, eyes wild. "It has rainbow sprinkles on it. She, like, sensed where it was even though I hid it."

"DO YOU WANT ME TO GO TO BED HUNGRY?" Ella wails, missing nothing. "I MIGHT WAKE UP IN THE MIDDLE OF THE NIGHT." She's got a point. Then she slowly sits up and shifts tactics. "Mama, I need to watch something. It will make me feel better." She flops a bunny ear out of her face.

"But sweetie, it's an hour past your bedtime, and—"

Ella flings herself melodramatically across the floor again and lets out the wail of a dying moose.

As I locate a graham cracker in the pantry, I allow that con-versing with Ella for sixteen years might have its challenges. It's incontestable that watching television, and all types of screen time, displaces other activities she could be doing that we all know are beneficial—playing outside, building forts in her room, tinkling away on the piano. As Henry Labalme, founder of an anti-screen movement in the 1990s, told me, "It's not what you're watching, it's that you're watching."

But the realities of my household, with two working parents, means that entirely cutting out television is a tall ask. So I decide to dig deeper on that AAP guideline of watching only quality programming.

Having spent hours and hours with various experts in different disciplines, in person and on the phone, all patiently helping me chip away at an answer to the question—How can various forms of technology help or hurt young children and their parents?—I know even before I get started that a word like *quality* will have myriad permutations. Ultimately, no matter what various authorities go on to tell me, I am going to have to determine what *quality* means for me and my family, what our ultimate value system will be when it comes to the television. (When discussing the very notion of credentials and authority, a historian friend of mine who focuses on Latin America bluntly reminds me, "A lot of Central American politicians have degrees from the Kennedy School at Harvard and then go on to massacre their entire populations.") Just as Ella is growing up, learning how to be independent and make her own decisions, whether that is what color Magna-Tile to put on the top of her castle or what to wear outside during a snowstorm—bathing suits under tutus only in the most particular of circumstances—it is time for me to grow up as well. But I still want to give the shows' creators a chance to explain themselves, if only in the hopes that I'll be able to feel less guilty about putting Ella in front of the television every once in a while.

And as soon as I start poking around, all roads lead to the same place: that sunny street where the air is sweet.

* * *

Arranging an audience with Rosemarie Truglio is harder than getting one with the pope. She moves our meeting three times, four times, five times. (At one point, *Sesame Street*'s comms person asked me if I could meet on Charlotte's due date. I briefly entertained the possibility of Big Bird delivering my child as the Count helped me breathe through contractions, and said yes. I was desperate to speak with her.) She's been with the organization since 1997, and her current title is long and ambiguous: senior vice president, curriculum and content at Sesame Workshop. But what that means is she's the person in charge of making sure Sesame produces quality content for its viewers. And I need her to tell me what quality content is.

In preparation for the meeting, I read through Sesame's whole-child curriculum for the 2016 season, circling and underlining with a pen as I go. Another Sesame staffer refers to this thirty-two-page document, officially titled *Statement of Educational Goals*, as "the Bible." Meant for anyone who'll be creating content for any of Sesame's myriad outlets—the show, the apps, the books—it is a guiding document for what should be emphasized, and how that should be emphasized, in order to support the company's mission: to help children grow smarter, stronger, and kinder.

Parts of it read like they've been written by a very friendly Muppet who's trying his hardest to reduce that vast task into a series of helpful pointers. For example, in a section about making content about vocabulary, *gardens*, *containers*, *building things*, and *stores* are all listed as "recommended child-friendly topics" for creators. (I imagine an overworked thirtysomething in the writer's room, desperately trying to come up with his vocabulary skit for the next day. He bangs his head against the desk. He paces the room. Finally, he flips through the curriculum and a light bulb goes off above his head. "Oh, right! *Stores!*")

But taken as a whole, the curriculum illustrates what the organization views to be important for preschoolers to know in a given year. As a child of the 1980s, I think of *Sesame Street* as the land of Letter of the Day. So I'm surprised to see, ahead of literacy and numeracy, the goal of self-regulation placed front and center.

"In the short term, poor self-regulation/executive function affects school readiness," the curriculum states. "Long term, underdevelopment of self-regulation/executive function skills is linked with aggressive behavior, low academic achievement, delinquency, and higher dropout rates. The encouraging news, however, is that quality preschool education can make a significant and lasting impact."

When Truglio and I finally meet, the meeting having been shoved yet again, she hands me a plush Big Bird for Charlotte, who's now eight weeks old, and we head to the Bert meeting room where Truglio confirms that, yes, for years Sesame had focused largely on what most people think of when they think of preparing a child for school: the letters, the numbers.

"But as time was passing, developmental psychologists were doing all this research on executive function and self-regulation, and they were saying *these* were the most important school readiness skills," she explains. "We were putting a lot of emphasis on learning content, but we weren't putting as much emphasis on the cognitive processing skills that allow us to be learners. So we rethought our whole-child curriculum and put those cognitive processing skills at its core." The Letter of the Day becomes meaningless if little Jane can't sit still long enough to learn it.

To see this shift, which was implemented in season 42 in 2012, look no further than Muppet Land's smash hit "Me Want It (But Me Wait)," a spoof on Icona Pop's "I Love It," sung by Cookie Monster.

"Me get this feeling when me see a cookie on a plate. / Me want to grab it, want to eat it. Oh, me no can wait! / But now me know that self-control is something me must learn. / Me want to grab it, want to eat it, but me wait!" Cookie croaks away in the music video as he does his best to resist eating yet another cookie. (It is undoubtedly the only song in the world to rhyme "straight" with "self-regulate.")

The premise will be familiar to anyone who's ever heard of the Stanford marshmallow experiment, conducted by psychologist Walter Mischel in the 1970s to study the effect of delayed gratification. Young children were offered one marshmallow now, or two if they could wait a few minutes. Those who could successfully delay gobbling up the marshmallow—by sitting on their hands, or singing, or otherwise distracting themselves—not only got two treats but, Mischel also found, went on to have better lives, as assessed by various measures, from SAT scores (higher) and obesity rates (lower) to level of education attained (higher). Later studies reframed the experiment and discovered that income may have been the predictive measure—the wealthier you are, the easier it is for you to delay gratification, a particularly damning finding that speaks to everything that is wrong with America's inequality. But the takeaway, which Sesame ran with, is that if Cookie can restrain himself, he too might get into a top-tier college and lose his love handles.

"When the writers came to me and said they wanted to have Cookie Monster be the role model for executive function skills, I was like, *I am going to lose my job*," Truglio tells me. *"He can't*

do this! He's going to fail. He's going to eat the cookie." She went to
Dr. Mischel, an advisor, in a panic, and he told her to relax. "This
is perfect!" he said. "He's going to fail, just the way we fail. And
then we get to introduce another strategy. And kids learn that
it's okay to fail, but here's another strategy to help." A researcher
at the University of Iowa later determined that kids who watched
clips of Cookie Monster practicing executive functioning skills
were able to wait four minutes longer for a marshmallow than
kids who hadn't seen the video.

Sesame Street first aired in 1969, spurred on by a civil rights
movement to solve socioeconomic inequality. Lloyd Morrisett,
who worked at the Carnegie Corporation and later founded the
Sesame Workshop with Joan Ganz Cooney, noticed that his
three-year-old daughter, Sarah, would wake up early and sit,
quietly, staring at the Indian head test pattern before 7:00 a.m.
programming started. He told Cooney about it over dinner one
evening, and she wondered, Could you harness Sarah's attention,
and television's addictive qualities, for good? Perhaps prepare
children from lower socioeconomic backgrounds for school, so
they arrived on par with their higher socioeconomic class peers?
Armed with that question—and with funding from Carnegie,
the Ford Foundation, and the federal government, among other
places—Sesame Street became the first show to explicitly teach
to a curriculum and test for results. Big Bird is now known in
over 150 countries (though he goes by Shaw Parr in Afghanistan
and Bibo in Germany).

Plenty of people have taken issue with Sesame, concerned
it is imposing American values on the world or masquerading
as a do-gooder organization when in fact it's a commercial be-
hemoth simply teaching children to watch television and buy

related goods, as my parents believe. But even if we accept at face value that Sesame is trying to develop well-rounded, engaged, focused children through its programming, how do we measure the softer qualities outlined in the Sesame Bible? "Being ready for school is about so much more than knowing just the academic basics," it reads. "It's about being smart in every way (e.g., problem solving and creative thinking), being strong (e.g., healthy habits and resiliency), and being kind (e.g., mutual respect and understanding and conflict resolution)." How can Sesame tell me that putting my kid in front of the television will make her a better problem solver, or more creative, or more respectful? I can test, easily, whether Ella retains the ability to identify the letter *T* after watching a few letter-based segments. But other than teleporting her to Camp David in 1978 to participate in Middle East peace talks, how can I be sure she's learning better conflict resolution?

I'm surprised when Truglio quickly concedes the point.

"When you're dealing with the academic skills, there's a right and wrong answer," she says. "This whole idea of imagination, creativity? Real creativity? It's really hard to measure, because then you're getting at the individual."

So, I ask, where does that leave us?

"It goes back to what Einstein says: some things that are important to learn are the most difficult things to measure, but that doesn't mean we shouldn't learn them." Or, as Einstein put it: "Not everything that counts should be counted, and not everything that can be counted counts." (Tell that to the Count!)

In other words, they're trying.

Before we part, I ask her how parents can best harness the power of technology for their own kids.

"I know it's a ludicrous request these days, because it's being used as a babysitter, but I'm constantly asking parents, 'Please watch with your child,'" she tells me. "If you do, you could extend the learning. Talk about, or act out the story you just saw afterwards, and *that's* when they learn. Use it as a springboard."

Those serve-and-return interactions, they're crucial.

* * *

I learn of one program, *Blue's Clues*, that was designed specifically to engage children and teach them even in the absence of a parent—taking Sesame's mandate, perhaps, up to an 11 and asking the children to have meaningful serve-and-return interactions with the television itself. It broke all the molds and, in the world of children's television, was one of the most successful programs ever.

"A good life, to me, is living like a preschooler forever!" Dr. Alice Wilder, who served as the director of research and development and also a producer of the show, tells me over breakfast. "My career started when I watched the movie *Big*. I wanted to be the adult in the room who thought like a kid. When I'm sitting on the floor with kids, I can channel their perspective." She's sweet, a little dreamy, imaginative, thoughtful—she gets so wrapped up in answering my questions, it takes her a full forty minutes to finish a small bowl of berries, which endearingly reminds me of Ella, who can get so absorbed in coloring that she completely forgets about her grilled cheese at lunch. If Dr. Wilder can't communicate toddlers' hopes and dreams to a room full of executives who've forgotten the magic of a life before expense reports and root canals, I don't know who can.

The star of *Blue's Clues*, which debuted in 1996, is a big, two-dimensional blue dog named Blue who is mute, aside from letting loose the occasional yip. Each episode starts with a puzzle that the show's human host, Steve—and then, after six years on the air, when Steve started losing his hair and boyish mannerisms, Joe—presents to his viewers. "What is Blue afraid of?" or "What was Blue's dream about?" Then off Steve/Joe goes, hunting for a paw-printed clue. Each time he finds one, he asks his audience a question. Then he pauses for a Very. Long. Time. Presumably, little kids around the country are offering up answers, which the host then applauds them for (of course, even if they are wrong). When I show an old episode to Ella, she's soon chirping back answers to an inanimate television, a scene that I find too Kubrickian by half. But the breaking of the fourth wall and the encouragement of audience participation is a critical part of *Blues'* success. In 1998, it garnered views from almost five million children and even made its way into Malcolm Gladwell's *The Tipping Point*, where it's described as possibly "one of the stickiest television shows ever made"—meaning it causes its targeted viewers to pay sustained, close attention.

Which is no small feat. Each episode is longer than twenty minutes and follows a single narrative. Both were revolutionary concepts in children's programming when the show first aired.

"They didn't believe in kids' attention spans back then," Wilder tells me. "But I knew you could captivate their attention; you just had to know how to do it."

To confirm that the lessons, whether they revolved around pattern recognition or shape matching, actually landed with their audience, the *Blue's* team field-tested their work multiple times during the development process, bringing scripts to schools and working through them with a classroom full of future consumers. Then they'd go back to the writer's room to tweak the order of the clues or the complexity of the puzzle. Each *Blue's* episode aired every day for a week on Nickelodeon, the thought being that preschoolers could more easily master the show's educational concepts through repetition. Though this was initially met with skepticism from the network execs, the tactic proved to work almost instantaneously. Kids mastered the desired skills.

But the show's very existence underscores, for me, a much larger structural issue, one I keeping coming up against, over and over, when researching supposedly helpful technologies for making parents' lives easier: that so many people rely on *Blue's Clues* to help their kids master skills, that so many families rely on *Sesame Street* to help their children grow smarter, stronger, and kinder. That onus should not fall on Blue the Dog, or on Big Bird, or on their back office teams of researchers and creatives. And it should not fall on America's parents. It should fall on America. There should be universal paid parental leave and universal childcare so that parents don't have to constantly feel like they are adrift in a sea of competing demands and desires—to excel in careers, or simply make ends meet, while raising successful children—and find that their only option is to stick their kids in front of a show so that they can get a few minutes to prepare dinner, or finish up a work report, or simply take a break. It's without question one of the most glaring omissions in the social contract that parents aren't guaranteed free, high-quality caregiving and education for their children. But such is the reality of our individualistic country. So, faced with little support, many parents have no choice but to choose from a series of lesser options, one of which is often a shiny, colorful screen.

And there's an obvious issue with relying on a capitalist society—driven by attracting ever more eyeballs at whatever cost—to provide thoughtful, quality entertainment for children. Josh Golin, the director of the screen-free childhood advocacy organization Campaign for a Commercial-Free Childhood, articulates it for me over coffee: "The educational stuff will be the Trojan horse through which the crap comes through."

(*An important aside:* Another book entirely could be written about the effect on children of YouTube, unregulated at the time of this printing. Innocents are being fed clip after clip after clip on the Kid Channel, many of which advertise, manipulate them, or are simply inappropriate for their age group. In March 2020, Senators Ed Markey and Richard Blumenthal introduced the Kids Internet Design and Safety (KIDS) Act, which, if approved, would limit what and how YouTube is viewed by children under sixteen, covering app design, content, and advertising. It's widely believed that society needs to impose guardrails when it comes to surfing the vast world of children's programming online, so absent those guardrails, I don't let Ella surf YouTube by herself, ever.)

We try *Sesame Street*. We try *Blue's Clues*. We try *Mister Rogers' Neighborhood* and *Reading Rainbow*. The last two leave an impression on Dave, who continues to watch episodes with Ella on weekend mornings long after our family viewings "for Mama's research," the two of them happily sitting side-by-side and learning arcane facts about how bowling balls are made and how toothpaste gets in the tube. Sometimes we let Ella watch *Sofia the First*, a show about a little girl who becomes a princess overnight, which leads Ella to enact elaborate pretend play stories involving amulets and potions and secret spells, and while I can't say it is deeply meaningful programming, she seems to enjoy it. At least she is bringing what she learns on-screen into the real world, which Truglio urges; for one stint, Ella runs around the house bellowing, *"Doppler duplicato!"* and looking irritated when things don't spontaneously duplicate.

As far as viewing things together, the only thing she and I end up watching, other than *Sarah & Duck* and the occasional musical, is the *Muppet Show*'s "Mahna Mahna" skit, in which two pink bovine-esque Muppets sing "do doooo, do do do" as a fuzzy and raffish Muppet with a gravelly voice interrupts them. It's been viewed over 117 million times, and during our obsessive phase, which lasts a few months, we likely contribute a million of those views. It makes me laugh; it makes her laugh. But it is so far on the other end of the spectrum from Cookie Monster teaching self-regulation that I feel that creeping sense of shame again. It is surely not crap—Henson was charming, quirky, eccentric in the best of ways, and so are his creations—but it is arguably closer to silly than enriching on the quality-control spectrum.

On our million-and-ninth viewing, as the little bovine Muppets bops back and forth in unison and Ella bops along too, giggling, I realize that implicit in every conversation I'd had with experts in the space—doctors or creators—was the notion that *quality* generally means *educational*. Preschool kids, when watching television, should be watching quality programming, and that quality programming should impart preschool-readiness skills, whether to identify shapes or strengthen self-control or, simply, be a kind person.

But what about the value of giggling over a bopping bovine?

"It's really taking the piss on everything!" Helle Strandgaard

Jensen cackles to me on the phone when I reach her in Denmark, where she's a children's media historian at Aarhus University. "It's hilarious!"

She's not talking about the Muppets but a Danish show she likes to watch with her seven-year-old, *Onkel Reje*, or Uncle Shrimp, which, on the spectrum from academic to Muppet, is much closer to Muppet. She, for one, is a huge proponent of giggling and silliness when it comes to assessing what her kid should watch.

To understand this refreshing new perspective more intimately, I search for an *Onkel Reje* episode and finally find a translated episode online. It begins with the eponymous character—a bearded, bespectacled man with the eyes of someone who's just downed his fourth double espresso—talking about a "fire glove" he's picked up at the hardware store. The pinky, when raised, throws up a flame like a match, the ring finger one that's like a lighter, the middle like a candle, and the index like a sparkler. And the thumb?

"Il flammekaster!" he crows, nearly singeing off an eyebrow. A flamethrower! I briefly entertain the looks I'll get at the playground if Ella pretends to use a *flammekaster* in the sand pit.

In the next sequence, Shrimp watches a blind man fall off a tightrope down to the concrete below, holding nothing but an umbrella as he sails on down. "What's the lesson you can learn?" he asks his audience. "Be a taxi driver instead!"

The shows her son watches, Jensen tells me, are largely those she also wants to watch with him, and unlike Truglio, she doesn't apologize when she tells me that coviewing is important to her. It strikes me that this is an attitude of someone who lives in a socialist society with a built-in social support system. There's less need to park your kids in front of Nanny Television if you've worked a six-hour-a-day job, biked to a lunch of salted herring with your colleagues, and headed to a fully subsidized doctor visit while your offspring runs around in the forest learning how to be a civilized human under the watch of trained, well-paid professionals. A world to strive toward.

"My son is seven, and he's *just* starting to learn how to read," she tells me. "There's a clear tradition here of having children focus on interacting with other children." I can't very well open the door and let Ella run wild on West 67th Street, but the point is taken: the ABCs will come. While she admits that Scandinavians can get just as caught up in the hysteria of screen time as Americans—"Parents at my school ask me to tell them things like 'twenty-two and a half minutes after the full moon, that's the perfect time for watching,'" she says—she underscores that Scandinavian children's programming plays a very different role in society than it does in the States.

"For starters," she tells me, "it teaches children to stand up to adults."

Take Pippi Longstocking. The nine-year-old Swedish heroine lives in a house not with her parents but with her horse and Mr. Nilsson, a monkey. And she refuses to go to school altogether. She'd likely scoff at Steve/Joe's prompts and tell Cookie Monster to eat as many cookies as he wants.

Jensen has written about *Sesame Street* for various publications. To say that she's not a fan is putting it mildly. When we speak, she's in the midst of writing a book about *Sesame Street* during the 1970s, when it started to expand around the globe.

"My biggest issue is the idea that the needs of American society were universal needs," she says. "Coming out of the civil rights movement, I can see the perspective. It's just a very narrow view, that numbers and letters are something all preschoolers need." She pauses, then mentions another academic who believes *Sesame Street*'s creators are cultural imperialists. She takes a milder view. "I see them as white American do-gooders who are blinded by a mission they felt and believed."

When I posit that preschool programming could go one of two ways—preparing kids either for school, à la Sesame Street, or for a life rich with giggles over silly things with Mom or Dad— Jensen quickly counters me.

"I think you're missing a third way," she says. "You could have a civic, social education. I don't think it's a coincidence that Greta Thunberg"—the teenage environmental activist who was nominated for the Nobel Peace Prize—"is from Scandinavia." Lest I forget I am deep in the world of academia, the conversation quickly moves to *Bildung*, a German philosophical idea that, as I find with many German philosophical ideas, is intimidating, all-encompassing, and impossible to distill into a sentence. The concept has to do with forming intelligence and character and developing a sense of selfhood while being critical about your surroundings. Presumably, one formative factor in Thunberg's life has been her consumption of just this type of *Bildung*.

When I press Jensen to recommend a single academic show for preschoolers, she pauses, then eventually offers up a National Geographic–esque program where you have to identify an animal on the basis of the size, shape, and color of its turd. So there's that.

* * *

When I go into labor with Charlotte in the early morning hours of my due date, we put on an episode of *Sarah and Duck* to keep

Ella calm until her babysitter arrives. This one is about the duo's search for shade on a hot day, which leads them to a "cloud tower" in the park. Up a few flights of stairs, they find a Frenchman in charge of heaving clouds off a platform that looks like a diving board. *"Au revoir!"* he crows as he shoves out a grumpy rain cloud, requested by Sarah. A moment after getting aloft, the cloud opens up and cools down everything below. As I totter toward the elevator, Ella shouts out, "Auf-wah!" and giggles.

After my time spent in the trenches with researchers, developers, creatives, and pediatricians, I've formed a pretty clear set of TV guidelines for my house. We should try to limit watching it as much as possible—it's displacing all sorts of interactions and activities we know are beneficial for our kids. *But*, if I want to turn on the screen, I should try to watch along with Ella, which is made quite a bit easier if that screen is big and not small. And if I can't, I should do my best to ensure she's not being bombarded with high-energy, commercially fueled dreck. It's incredibly straightforward and, I find, incredibly freeing.

During Charlotte's early days, I make sure to carve out solo time for Ella and me. I'm only sleeping in two-hour chunks, so I need our time to involve a low-energy activity, and television fits the bill pretty perfectly. We have books, and bath time, and walks to and from school, but there is also one episode of *Sarah & Duck*, a perfectly bite-size six or seven minutes (on challenging days, we might watch two). Dave often joins us during those heady first few weeks of living with a newborn, and the three of us spend a few minutes snorting together at Duck's pratfalls or the shallots' antics. Is Ella learning preschool readiness skills? Perhaps not directly. But sitting between the two of us on the couch, she's learning that her parents want to spend time with her, that though her world may have changed forever, she's as loved as she was before Charlotte arrived, that there is silliness and magic and eccentricity everywhere you look. She's learning what we, as a family, think is funny. Talking shallots apparently top that list, and Ella is totally on board.

7

Swiped Out

Will Interactive Apps Change the Game?

104.4.

That can't be right, I think. *That's the temperature of a hot tub, isn't it? Not a human.*

And yet somehow that's what the digital thermometer reads when I take it out of Ella's ear. I briefly entertain the idea that the newfangled thermometer is to blame. She's almost three but has been petrified of the rectal thermometer ever since an inexperienced high school babysitter tried to stick it in her mouth a few months ago, so I'd purchased this version in anticipation of her next fever, which arrives with a wallop at bedtime. (Yes, it comes in handy a year later during the months we're living in the COVID Capital.) But I'm pretty sure the readout is right—I can feel the heat radiating off her head like a New York City sidewalk in August. As she wails, I manage to pull Motrin into a syringe, give it to her, and cradle her hot body until she falls asleep. When I reach Dave at a work dinner a mile uptown, I have what my Southern godmother would have called "a good old-fashioned going to pieces," blubbering about frying eggs on our daughter's head, and he teleports home—or so I assume, since he arrives within moments of hanging up—and we spend the rest of the night taking turns checking her temperature and googling things like "how hot toddler head too hot." It's so dark, and I'm so frazzled, that I'm pretty sure I take Bunny's temperature a few times.

The next morning, on the way to the pediatrician, it becomes clear that the bus is never going to come and we're going to have to walk the mile uptown. In her stroller, Ella is shivering so much her teeth are chattering, her body racked with sobs. I am desperate to calm her down. So I pull up some highly rated educational (whatever that means) toddler app on my phone, and within moments, she's deeply engrossed in a game that involves a small dog making smoothies for his cat friend. For the first time in twelve hours, my teeth unclench. Grasping at straws, I reason that it might even be better than setting her in front of the TV—watching TV is passive, interactive apps are . . . interactive. Right? I remember, vaguely, a conversation I had with her preschool teacher earlier that year, who'd told me that one of her students, when faced with a stack of blocks at the start of the year, had absolutely no idea what to do with them.

"Her father came in for the parent-teacher conference, and he said, 'That makes no sense, she plays this game on my phone all day!' and showed me some shape-sorting app. Problem is, none of that translates into the real world," she said. Her student could swipe the blocks into a pile with a finger but couldn't actually place them there with her hands. The story stuck with me—but Ella is quiet for the first time in hours.

A few blocks north, as I massage my jaw, Dave nudges me. "Psst," he says. "Are you catching this?"

He juts his chin up. We get a death stare from a couple of septuagenarians on their way to the farmers market, reusable shopping bags in tow. Then another from a millennial out for a jog. "She has a fever of 104 degrees," I mutter, loudly, when we pull up next to another family at a stoplight. "That's the *upper* limit of a hot tub." The mom flashes me a tight-lipped nod and turns protectively toward her child.

Are they actually judging us? I don't know. But it sure feels like it.

An hour later: Ella has been examined, given medicine, and sent back into the world with the diagnosis of "some sort of toddler virus; there are a million going around." Her fever has plummeted and her demeanor flipped. We stop off in the bookstore to get her a book. On the walk home, she curls up in her stroller, turning the pages to *I Want My Hat Back* while singing the ABCs quietly to herself. And we find ourselves in a different universe, one in which the passersby say "Awwww" and "What a *precious child*!" We beam. Sunlight pours out of our heads.

"Mama," Ella asks softly when I go to the front of the stroller to tuck the blanket in around her, "can I play the map on your phone again?" I mumble something about it being only for special occasions, like when your body's internal temperature reaches that of a teppanyaki grill. "Oh," she says, nodding curtly, before turning back to a book she most certainly cannot read.

If only I could summon the same discipline. A block later, in

Ella's blind spot behind the stroller, Dave starts Slacking his colleagues and, after five seconds of gazing at the street fair on 77th Street, my brain starts to bleat out a furious alarm—*Bored! Bored!* I fish my phone out and mindlessly scroll through Instagram. My self-regulation skills are so rudimentary, if Cookie Monster were here, he'd likely gobble up our phones in protest.

Phones are everywhere, they're attractive and addictive, and I already know I don't have the power to completely remove them from Ella's life. But Ella is getting older. The American Academy of Pediatrics guidelines allow that once children reach twenty-four months, certain types of screen time can be permissible, which goes for apps as well as programming. More to the point, as she heads into her fourth year on earth, she seems able to follow along with apps pretty darn well, even if I'm nowhere near her—before, she'd just randomly swipe and tap with abandon. Perhaps there's an opportunity for Ella to get some enrichment from these tiny screens after all.

Then again, taking a page from my Danish friends and *Onkel Reje*, maybe I should give up on the idea of enrichment altogether. It's not like my hours spent in front of *Mario Kart* as a kid set me up for life success in any tangible way. Dave, of course, protests when I bring this up.

"I can't wait to play *Mario Kart* with her!" he tells me. "It'll teach her all sorts of strategy!"

"Like what?" I press.

He doesn't miss a beat: "When to drop the banana peel!"

* * *

The year 2010 marked the beginning of the screen-time hysteria that has held its steady crescendo to today: Apple released its first-generation iPad, launching us into the world of touch screens for toddlers.

The devices proved so intuitive, and so compelling, that children too young to speak were able to swipe around, pinching and zooming so expertly that it launched a subgenre of YouTube videos garnering millions of views each: babies deftly playing with iPads. The serpent was eating its own tail.

"Programming—whether it was educational or entertainment or violent—the experience was always passive," Dr. Christakis tells me, reflecting on the advancements in tech since the 2006 publication of his book about television and children, *The Elephant in the Living Room*. "There was no contingent response. All of that is made imminently possible by touch screen technologies. That's an enormously powerful thing for many reasons, both good and bad."

I'd flagged one section of *The Elephant in the Living Room* that would need a massive rewrite, should an updated edition ever be published:

Television holds a child's attention through the orienting reflex—through rapid scene changes, fast action, and a dramatic soundtrack. When you read to your child, she is kept engaged by personalized interaction. When your son plays on his own with pots and pans in the kitchen, he is kept engaged through the excitement of self-directed discovery. When your daughter climbs on the jungle gym, she is kept engaged by the joys of physical accomplishment. By contrast, the one feeling that is never expressed (or, for that matter, felt) when a child watches television is, I did it! Yet this simple experience is among the most important in a child's developing sense of self.

"Touch screen technologies offer up an *I did it!*" Christakis says.

That feeling is due to what is known as *contingent response*, which any parent of a small child can understand from the how-many-times-can-I-throw-this-grape-off-my-highchair game. I throw it down, it goes down!

"For infants," Christakis says, "it's intensely gratifying to confirm that something happens as expected. The touch screen technologies provide that kind of gratification ad infinitum." You swipe the virtual grape over there, it'll go over there again, and again, and again, and again.

Another reason children are drawn to interactive screens: the *violation of expectations paradigm*, which is, essentially, the opposite: I was expecting *x* to happen, but *y* happened instead. "Touch screens, in many cases, do this quite deliberately," Christakis says. Every time you log in to your news feed, you see a new set of stories. So, you keep refreshing.

My fully formed adult brain, mature enough to no longer be riveted by the trajectory of a grape, has enough trouble looking away from the phone. No wonder Ella lasers in on my screen whenever it's within view, like a homing pigeon.

Christakis is pretty adamant that "toddlers need laps more than apps." They need to be with another human, not sat in front of a screen alone. While he's far less bothered when he sees caregivers and children hunched over a screen together, talking about what's going on—then, the screen starts to serve much the same function as a toy—the tech is still too new and changing so rapidly, he tells me, that there is no way parents can come to concrete conclusions about how using the touch screen affects children's development. There is fifty years of similar data on television but, he reminds me, at most ten years of comparable data on touch screens. If developers aren't exploitative in their designs, if capitalism doesn't get its dirty motives in the way, the learning potential could be vast. But the rigorous longitudinal studies needed in order to make solid claims about the effects of touch screens on children will take years and lots of money to conduct. We're still five or so years away from that, at which point, for all I know, Ella will be accessing augmented reality games through her cornea.

But I'm impatient, and Ella is three today, not five years from now. So until the jury comes back in, I'm faced with two separate, but related, buckets of questions, each pressing and in need of reasonable—if not longitudinally backed-up—answers:

1. When my children watch me on my phone, is it the modern-day equivalent of secondhand smoke? Is it doing irreparable damage to their soft, fluffy, pliable brain cells?

2. If Ella wakes up at 6:00 a.m. and I'd prefer *not* to immediately hop on a pretend rainbow airplane to Minjakano—the make-believe island located "just twenty hours from Chicago" where it rains all the time and unicorns make pancakes—is putting her in front of an app okay? If I'm going to throw my hands up and lean on technology in some way, is it better or worse than sticking her in front of a television set? And how on earth am I supposed to navigate the Wild West of the App Store, where Montessori Preschool apps that claim to teach toddlers the alphabet are offered up right next to ones that ask the player to

put neon-colored Band-Aids on a cat's open wounds? (Really.) Is there a way to harness the potential of interactive apps for Ella, now firmly in the age of approved screen time, or should I always opt for the book or the analog block?

* * *

Rosemarie Truglio, of *Sesame Street*, tells me of a preschool classroom teacher she knows whose students spend pretend time—instead of playing doctor or toy shop or classroom—sitting on the mat, quietly gazing down at fake phones and not speaking to each other. I find this both horrifying and un-surprising. Kids are born to mimic. If we adults are unable to model good tech behavior, how can we expect them to learn it? Whenever I look up from my phone to find Ella or Charlotte staring at me, it's like they've caught me in flagrante delicto. But the phone's addictive powers are baked into its very design, and nearly impossible to resist. As our children watch us perform our mindless devotion, they not only mimic—they create explana-tions for why we're devoted at all.

"If you use your phone to destress when you need a break, they'll think, 'Oh, it's a calming tool,' and this happens from a very young age," says Dr. Jenny Radesky, one of the lead authors of the 2016 AAP digital media guidelines for young children, who runs a lab at the University of Michigan. Popping out the phone to transfer its Xanax-like qualities onto a tantrumming child is problematic not only because it strips the child of the op-portunity to learn to self-soothe but also because it short-circuits the opportunity that the parent and the child would otherwise have to work their way through a challenge, together.

"When you have a strong emotion that is calmed down through media, it's a missed growth opportunity for parents," Radesky tells me. We're in a café, and one table over is a one-year-old who's about to get fussy. Instead of allowing her to break the quiet hum of ambient noise, her father gives her a phone and she happily begins to tap and swipe away. What Radesky means is that letting that moment build would afford the father a little window into his kid's head, even if it might disrupt my interview: the child gets upset if she's micromanaged, say, or absolutely hates it if you take the straw out of the wrapper without giving her a chance first.

"If you don't work through the moment, and you just quash it by throwing a screen in front of them, you might get an immediate result," she says, "but it's a get-rich-quick scheme. In the long term, it's a bad investment." I later come across a chart that illustrates sensitive periods in early brain growth. The development of skills that regulate emotions peaks around three years of age, then plummets. If you can help your kid learn how to self-regulate early on, in other words, you'll be setting them up for a smoother road ahead.

The irony is that we grown-ups are likely the ones who need to be taught self-regulation even more than our children. In an effort to assuage our guilt over being caught with our devices, many of us have devised elaborate systems to keep our phones out of sight, or at the very least make them less appealing. One friend has an actual lockbox on the front hall table. Another has gone deep into her settings and programmed it to grayscale.

"It just means when I look at it it's dull and boring and I'm less inclined to randomly click on apps or start scrolling," she tells me. Worth a try. I make my way through what seems like a million pages on my phone and select the doomsday button. My phone instantaneously drains of its color, morphing into a black-and-white relic that holds all the appeal of a laser disc. I consider that the path to tackling our lack of impulse control might have been lying here all along, some dystopian escape hatch Jobs threw in at the phone's inception, anticipating that we'd all be reduced to mindless automatons tapping away in silent Morse code, craving another dopamine hit. Facebook's logo is now dull and flat, NPR's clinical and dry. I put it in my pocket and go about my day, feeling virtuous and relieved. Well, that was easy.

A few hours later, it buzzes with a text from our nanny, who's sent along a photo of Ella at the playground. I'm shocked. My little girl has time traveled back to the 1920s, before sparkles and neon-pink shoes. For all I know, there's a breadline snaking its way down the street, just off-screen. Ashamed, I make my way back through the settings to reset my phone. And *pow!* My virtual world transforms back into a comfortingly bright, shiny portal to wonder. Exhale.

So: Assuming we have these little addiction packs tucked in our pockets throughout the day, and assuming we're not entirely inured to their addictive powers, and assuming we're not, um, as intense as the lockboxers amongst us, the question then becomes: Precisely how bad is it for our kids to see us on our phones all the time?

Well, it depends how alarmist you'd like to be.

On one end of the spectrum is Catherine Steiner-Adair, a clinical psychologist and compelling writer who chronicles how family life has evolved in the tech age in *The Big Disconnect*. Using examples of patients she's treated, she unsparingly hammers home the devastation of moments lost and emotional connections dulled the moment tech wedges itself between parent and child. Despite the fact that at one point she uses Magna-Tiles as an example of how the world has gotten too easy for children, because, unlike traditional blocks, they snap together, thus "eliminating the need for more skilled placement" (*Lady, get your scorn off my Magna-Tiles!*), I read it cover to cover. But the experience reminds me of those exercise classes I sometimes pass in the park, run by ex-Marine drill sergeants barking out orders to well-meaning office professionals who clearly don't stand a chance. They'll never get to ten push-ups, let alone one hundred. The bar is too high, the experience demoralizing to all except those who sadistically view burpees as atonement.

Take Ellen, the mother of six-month-old Henry, who feels unceasing waves of guilt whenever she uses the iPad in her son's presence. "Ellen knows she should be attentive when they are together," writes Steiner-Adair, "and respond to his coos and other nonverbal cues, encouraging his attempts to communicate with her. She knows that at six months old, he needs to feel her connection, not the repeated experiences of disconnect in routinely having to wait for her to look up from a screen." Then: "Everything a baby needs from its environment between birth and two years comes from people, from relationships with people and interactions with the environment—physically exploring, playing, crawling, and interacting with others. When we triangulate our relationship with our babies and tech, we compromise that essential connection."

Gulp. Well, um, yes. But the implication is that before screens, we spent our child's every waking moment babbling back to him or her like daffy lunatics in a language known, cringingly, as *motherese*. I'm certain that just as there were mothers in the 1960s who sat their kid in front of the television, there were

Paleolithic-era mothers who caught themselves zoning out in front of a cave painting as their infant lay on a dirt floor, gumming an old mastodon femur.

But her unsettling message is compelling, and perfect for the anxiety-prone millennial parent. I get the book secondhand, and it's furiously underlined and starred. The underlining gets more and more frantic as the book progresses, the stars more frequent. I imagine the reader flipping pages faster and faster, underlining harder and harder, spinning out of control until she finally flings the book down and self-flagellates with her charging cord.

It all seems overwrought. But then I come upon a much older study that leads me, inadvertently, to devise a lockbox-esque solution of my own.

In 1975, Dr. Edward Tronick, a developmental and clinical psychologist who now directs UMass Boston's Child Development Unit, presented his now landmark Still-Face experiment at the Society for Research in Child Development. You can find a video of the experiment online—I watched it while pumping, and at the end, perhaps triggered by hormones, perhaps because it is simply painful to watch on an absolute scale, I found myself in tears. In broad strokes, it illuminates just how emotionally and socially connected children are, starting in infancy, and how withholding contact can have immediate, and then lasting, effects on their behavior.

A young mother is facing her daughter, who's around a year old. The screen is split so you can see both the facial expressions of the child and of the mother. For a while, the mother and child interact normally—the infant coos and babbles, points and claps, and the mother coos and babbles back, follows the child's gaze and looks where she's pointing. Then the mother turns away, and when she turns back, her loving face has been replaced by a dead expression. The baby tries every trick in the book to get her mom back—cooing more frequently, clapping, shrieking. Finally, at her breaking point, she begins to cry (which is when I teared up), and a little while afterward, the mother breaks her still face and comes back to the baby, who's overjoyed.

Tronick established that the child's anxiety is exhibited physiologically—the heart rate increases, the body releases the stress hormone cortisol. When the mother then breaks her still face and returns, the baby's heart rate goes back to normal. But the longer the mother takes to return, the more the child starts to withdraw. Eventually, after getting angry and distressed, after trying to self-soothe by sucking on her hands or thumb, after protesting, the child will give up. Her posture will collapse, and she'll turn away from her grown-up, as if to say, *You're not worth the effort*. If that scenario is repeated often enough, that withdrawn behavior will become entrenched and ultimately shape her outlook on the world. The short video offers a compelling example of how a child responds to neglect, which has obvious implications for children who live with depressive or incommunicative parents. And while I don't think of myself as incommunicative with Ella, she often has to say my name more than once before I look up from an email I'm tapping out. Am I creating the same kind of painful disconnect with my own kids?

Alarmingly, Tronick's work keeps coming up in articles and books I am reading about *technoference*, a new term I learn that captures the act of technology disrupting a moment, like when a cell phone is picked up midconversation. These works equate cell phone usage in front of children with the Still-Face Paradigm: "These days neuroscientists speculate that when parents caring for children turn to their phones, they may 'effectively simulate a still-face paradigm'—in their homes or out in a restaurant—with all of the attendant damage," writes Sherry Turkle, MIT professor and renowned expert on our relationships with technology, in *Reclaiming Conversation: The Power of Talk in a Digital Age*. "It is not surprising if children deprived of words, eye contact, and expressive faces become stiff and unresponsive with others."

Armed jointly with my new vocab word and the terrifying image of Ella being scarred for life and maturing into a withdrawn, embittered adult, I bury our charging dock in our mess of a front-hall closet. But a few days later, slightly irritable that I can't find my phone behind the winter hats, I reconsider. Isn't there a difference between seeing your parent engaged in something else and seeing them look directly at you with a dead expression? In the first scenario, you're being ignored. In the second, your parent is turning into a zombie before your eyes.

So I decide to go to the source. When I speak to Tronick, I'm surprised and relieved when he quickly tells me how baffled he is to see his study being co-opted by technoference researchers.

"In Still-Face, the child is trapped between two messages—one is *yes, it's time to interact*, the other is *I'm not going to interact*," he says. "Your mother disappears in your presence, except she's present. That's very problematic. When a parent is doing something on a phone, children get upset because the parent isn't paying attention to them, and that's really very different. Infants and young children can appreciate that difference."

Then, in an attempt to quickly give me a crash course in child development, Tronick references something a developmental noob like me can understand: peekaboo. True to her birth order, Charlotte is schlepped along to her older sister's activities, often spending afternoons gazing quietly up at the ceiling from her perch in the stroller. But when I remember I'm supposed to actively engage her in the world, I whip out a little peekaboo. At her ripe old age of sixteen weeks, she occasionally smiles. But more often than not, she drools and bobbles her head, as she does in response to basically anything—a rattle, a mobile, her sister pulling her bouncy chair all the way back and threatening to launch her out the window. In a few months, if she's anything like Ella, Charlotte will maybe hold her hand up to her own face. And a few months after that, she'll begin to play along with me.

"To overstate it, all of development is like learning peekaboo," Tronick tells me. "Development is structured by chronic repeated, reiterated events." In other words, it takes a long time for something to stick, both good and bad.

For years, Tronick worked closely with T. Berry Brazelton, the pediatrician and author that many in my parents' generation turned to for calm and guidance, so it's no surprise that he offers up a measured take on technoference hysteria.

"Watch the baby and trust your feelings and instincts," Tronick tells me, echoing Brazelton's main message. "So, your baby is getting really upset when you're on the phone. How do you feel about that? How upset is the baby? How often are you doing it? If it's problematic, it's probably not what you want to be doing. The idea that you can't be on your phone when you're with your child, though—that's Mary and Jesus. That's the romantic view of what parenting is about."

A few hours after we speak, an email from him pops up in my inbox, following up on one strand of our conversation. I'd been relieved that, in the Still-Face video, when the mother returned, the baby quickly offered up a huge gummy smile. There was no real resentment, no *How dare you*, just relief.

"For me, that's very much the critical feature," he writes. "I think repairs of discord are what drive development. The SF [Still Face] is a mismatch that we create but they occur all the time. They are stressful and negative but when they are repaired to a match good things happen. The child learns they can trust, their emotions can be changed, they can be effective and have mastery, they gain resilience and hope, and more, including growing brain cells."

But a few weeks later, deep in one of those cell-phone-as-Still-Face studies, I find a wrinkle: the children of mothers who reported heavier phone usage during their typical day took longer to reconnect during the experiment. They'd picked up their phone in the middle of playing with their child, as instructed, but when they put it away again and tried to reengage, it didn't go as smoothly as it did for those who didn't use their phones as much. It suggests that repeated exposure to parental distraction can, in a sense, condition children to withdraw.

When I send Tronick the study and ask him where it might fall short in ways that I can't see, he replies that there are a bunch of possible red flags: a wide age spread, no breakdown of reaction by age, and the knowledge that most people do not accurately self-report on how much they use their own devices.

But before throwing out the study entirely, I give the lead researchers a chance to defend themselves.

Again, I'm surprised when Dr. Tracy Dennis-Tiwary, the professor of psychology at CUNY who conducted the study, readily admits that equating distraction with Still-Face is extreme (yet another sign that the media is at fault for wildly ratcheting up the import of one-off studies). Still, she says, when she and her colleagues "did the tummy test"—a cute way for an academic researcher to say "gut check"—they kept circling around this idea that technoference is more than just distraction, because it's so constant and so all-consuming. It's led her down a new line of research.

"The real problem with devices might be that they're disrupting our extremely human need to have eye contact," she says. Some scientists, like Michael Tomasello, director emeritus of the Max Planck Institute for Evolutionary Anthropology in Leipzig, have argued that the whites of human eyes are considerably bigger than those of primates simply because that seemingly aesthetic feature enables you to track eye gaze, an evolutionary adaptation.

"If we have this advantage, if eye contact is the earliest way we make sense of the world, and now we're continually disrupting it because our eyes are drawn down to these screens?" asks Dennis-Tiwary. "Now, that's interesting to me." Chronic and persistent interruptions in attention, she believes, weaken this fundamental channel of human communication.

I'm not an evolutionary biologist and I'm not a psychiatrist. But, with a few parenting years under my belt, I'm more confident that I'm an expert on all things Ella-related. Plus I know how irritating I find it when I'm midconversation with someone and they glance down at their phone "just to check something." So however high this distraction rates on the level of Horrible Things My Child Could Be Witnessing, however much the whites of my eyes are no longer connecting with my children's, I figure that at a basic level it must be annoying to Ella and Charlotte when I disappear into my phone, even if just for a minute. And as Tronick tells me, that may be reason enough for me to take it out of the picture. So I decide to keep our cell phone charging station in the closet, and after a few days, it becomes habit to plug it in before I've even taken my shoes off. One day, Ella pretends to put her "phone" in the closet. That mimicking, I can handle.

* * *

Now, on to perhaps the more pressing question: the promise of apps.

If, as Christakis said, the power of interactivity can theoretically be harnessed for good, it sure would be nice to find out where, in the App Store, that's being offered.

It strikes me that what might be irksome about all this is that playing with apps is such a solitary activity. It's so dissonant, the image of a bright-eyed little kid hypnotized by the beguiling screen and not the world around her. It might be more palatable if I could be there with Ella, playing the app alongside her—plus, I'd then have a shot at those valuable serve-and-return interactions. But whenever I give a touch screen to Ella, she hunches up over it like a squirrel with a forbidden nut.

"Kids create a walled-off space," Dr. Radesky confirms for me when I call her to see if Ella is unique. (Sigh, she is not.) It echoes what the pediatrician told me about the child forming a one-to-one relationship with a device. Radesky refers me to a study she conducted at her lab to determine how tablets affect parent-child interactions. She and her researchers watched as, time and time again, parents were forced to lie melodramatically over the back pillows of a couch, necks craned at unnatural angles as their little ones elbowed them out and tapped away. "Kids are simply not as open to social interaction when a tablet is involved," she says.

Furthermore, most app games aren't designed for more than one player—perhaps because designing them for two is such a challenge, even if you have a whole team of well-meaning designers behind it. A few years back, Sesame developed a dual-player driving game that required the child to use the keyboard while the adult or older sibling used the mouse, as they collaborated to unscramble words. And it worked, but in the course of research, they discovered something else.

Miles Ludwig, Sesame's head of digital media development, tells me that kids and parents playing together can often be messy. "Kids get super frustrated very quickly. Maybe mom is super goal-oriented and is just trying to get to the end of the level; meanwhile the kid's in some sort of emergent exploratory mode," he says. The result: aggravation, game over. "I think in the end that comes down to good design," he says—build a game that works for both parents and kids. In the early iterations of preschool appdom, though, co-engagement is the exception, not the rule.

So, one evening, I pour myself a generous glass of wine, tap open the App Store, and type in "Toddler Apps." I'm curious whether, with a concerted effort, I might be able to triangulate a handful of apps that are, if not enriching, at least fine for a preschooler to play solo.

Two seconds in, and my world has devolved into a maelstrom of pulsing neon colors, glittery prizes, popping bubbles, and chirpy avatars that sound like a slightly maniacal Jennifer Tilly, fresh off her third espresso. Oh, I think, how far we've come from *Pong*.

All modern-day interactive games hail *Pong* as their ancestor, the video game that hit the market in 1972 and is essentially 2D table tennis. Its analog ancestor can be traced back even farther, to the time of Louis XVI when, in 1777, a new table game called Bagatelle made its debut at a party thrown for the king at Chateau de Bagatelle. It was played on a billiard table set at an angle, away from the player, who used a cue to strike a ball and avoid wooden pegs along the way. Add some electricity and paddles, and you've got yourself a pinball machine, or a proto-*Pong*. By the 1960s, labs were innovating on the concept of interactivity. When Stewart Brand, the founder of *The Whole Earth Catalog*, came upon some Stanford students playing an early video game called *Spacewar!*, which involved two spaceships fighting each other, he uttered something that could have been lifted out of an article about *Fortnite*: "They were absolutely out of their bodies," he remarked, "like they were in another world. Once you experienced this, nothing else would do. This was beyond psychedelics."

Today's App Store is just the logical extension of this historical trajectory. One of the first I see on my tour is *Baby Games'*, which garners a 4.3 rating from 12,200 people. Despite the oddly placed possessive apostrophe, it catches my eye because it looks a little like the old Mario Bros. of my youth, which I adored. A chicken runs along a green landscape, bouncing around and scooping up coins.

"In this game the chicken collects various decorations on the run and receives prizes and bonuses for it," the description reads, creatively sidestepping proper English grammar. At the end of each level, completely unrelatedly as far as I can tell, the kids are taught a new word. The description concludes, "This is one of the best first apps for kids." Methinks the fowl doth protest too much. Next.

I dismiss out of hand all apps that have in-app purchases, like one in which the character starts crying if you don't buy him a prize—manipulative, much?—and the myriad beauty salon apps, not only because I want to delay Ella's awareness of fashion but also because being asked to trim a dog's nails for entertainment seems like something out of Dante. Same for the dry heave–inducing dentist-related apps, unquestionably created by sadistic programmers who survived orthodontia.

"Here you can blast all the germs away, remove any holes that may be cracked, suck all the gum from the teeth, as well as remove and pull any rotten or cracked teeth!" one description crows. I switch to bourbon.

At the end of my hour perusing the toddler app offerings, I feel a little like Tom after Jerry repeatedly smashes him in the face with a frying pan. I explore a number of innocuous-seeming sorting apps—put these same-colored objects over here, these same-shaped objects over there—and ABC identification apps, but I think back to what Ella's preschool teacher told me—how one student who played with block apps somehow couldn't connect them to the real world. Furthermore, when I try a few of these apps with Ella later, she keeps inadvertently dragging up my phone's control panel. For pudgy toddler hands, the designs are a mess. And while I know there must be thoughtful material out there somewhere, I can't find it.

So I put out a clarion call to the small cohort of educators, developmental psychologists, pediatricians, and researchers I now speak to more often than I do my own parents, and I settle on two apps that receive rave reviews for executing two very different visions.

Sago Mini, up north in Toronto, is one of the App Store's most popular creators of toddler apps, run by a CEO who believes that open-ended free play is the only thing young children should be doing, whether outside or online. Save the letter identification and sorting for later. Across the country, in the belly of the tech beast, is Khan Academy Kids, a preschool-readiness app aligned with national Common Core Standards. It's borne of Khan Academy, the beloved brainchild of Sal Khan, who made his name posting academic videos on YouTube, acting as a virtual tutor to anyone who wanted to listen, and creating what he calls a "one-world schoolhouse."

I had run into a similar split when refining my thoughts about television programs—Did I want to enrich Ella with curricular content, or did I find value in silly entertainment? Now my questions about Ella's app usage hinge on the passive/active dichotomy. Can thoughtfully constructed applications enrich her life, as Christakis hinted might be possible, even if I'm not there to play alongside her? And why couldn't that kid transfer what she'd done with blocks on-screen to blocks in the real world?

* * *

On a rainy day in March 2019, I watch as Clark, wearing a bright rainbow-star tank top almost hidden underneath a black hoodie, comes into the offices of Sago Mini, retrieves an iPad, settles into a couch in the main room, and loads up an app that features a car running along a road. For a solid four minutes, he quietly and seriously uses his index finger to run the car back and forth, until, with a little *what-the-hell* grunt, he flicks his finger up, causing the car to shoot off the road and high into the air. He yips, quietly, and then sends it soaring into the air again, and again, and again, crowing each time and pausing only to use the back of his hand to wipe some accumulated snot from his nose.

Clark, three-and-a-half, has come to the preschool app developer's offices with his mother, Robyn. "I also have a six-year-old daughter, and with her, I was very hesitant around screens," she tells me, offering up a tissue that Clark vigorously and silently shoots down. "If there was one in the room, I'd physically turn her away from it." She pauses as Clark, realizing he can also fling loose boulders into the sky, lets loose another one of his quiet crows. "This is not the case with my son." The shift? Robyn snorts. "Fatigue." How quickly the tables turn from restricting screens to offering up your second as a guinea pig for an app developer.

Sago Mini's apps have consistently received sterling ratings from Common Sense Media and other researchers and pediatricians I've interviewed. The games are open-ended, with few bells and whistles, no prizes or gamification—which, researchers posit, mistakenly teach children that winning is the point—and a friendly but slightly muted color palette. The company's philosophy, as told to me by the CEO, is simple: "Play is paramount. Play and education are completely the same thing." It's an outlook shared by my Scandinavian *Onkel Reje* fan, which isn't surprising, since Sago Mini and Toca Boca, a Swedish app developer that is consistently the App Store's number one most downloaded developer for the preschool set, are owned by the same company.

When I reach Toca Boca's founder, Emil Ovemar, in Stockholm, he tells me his job is essentially to translate the creative potential of a Lego set to a touch screen.

"We looked back on when we grew up, mostly in the eighties, and no one was supervising the way we played," he says. "We could play freely and we did dangerous stuff." Like what? "We'd go into the forest! But play is how you learn about the world, how you learn to take risks and be creative, and a lot of those skills are going to be very important in the workplace of the future." The notion of teaching little children to be good workers would normally set off my alarm bells, but the implication is that, with more and more automation, workplaces of the future will hinge on one's ability to be creative and nimble, to think outside the box.

Clark is taking part in one of Sago Mini's weekly Thursday playtesting sessions, where apps and toys in various stages of development are presented to children ages two to five to see how they run in the wild. Flinging cars off a road might be a completely fine feature for one app, but what if you built an app in which a train with multiple connected cars ran along a track? If a toddler wants to fling one train car soaring into the air, should that even be allowed? And if it were, should that particular car detach, or should it bring all the others along with it? And if it *did* detach, should the other cars spontaneously reconnect? Such are the concerns of developers when your target demographic's favorite color is rainbow. Clark plays, quiet and engrossed, for a full hour and ten minutes before, flushed with the work he's done, he takes off his sweatshirt, rubs his star-shirted belly, and asks for a snack of goldfish and clementine sections on an orange plate. ("He's into orange," Robyn explains.)

Compared to other highly downloaded preschooler apps, the Sago Mini suite offers up incredibly simple games. You run a car along a looping track, with large swaths of quiet space where not much is going on. A bunny and a dog wash dishes together, and you get to hose off the suds. A baby bird takes a bath and you get to hose off *her* suds (what a clean people the Canadians are!). These are little tasks, but satisfying. When I let Ella play with the app for a few minutes, she delights in pressing a button that makes a little blender whir and mix up purple juice. "Just like with smoothies in the morning!" she says, beaming. "But less loud." A clear stamp of approval.

Richard Hilmer, the brand's senior developer, who used to design apps for, as he put it, "testosterone-fueled teenage boys," tells me that he can't count the number of times he's thought, "I could totally add some cool feature onto the app," before realizing that his audience won't really care. And he runs into design issues all the time that he'd never face if his primary audience could use a soup spoon.

"You realize quickly that little kids sometimes don't know where their hands are," he tells me. This means they'll often keep one hand on the screen while they try to manipulate something with the index finger of the other, rendering the controls moot. While he admits that "there are moments where you're like, *Wow, we know it's not coming from a bad place, but why can't they make it work?!*" his mandate is to make an app experience that responds *exactly* the way a toddler would want it to respond. The design is paramount, and the toddler rules. If, when visiting the farm, the child wants to fling all the horses way up into the heavens until they disappear, that is totally fine. Off the horses go, without even a slight eyebrow raise, and land back on earth a little farther down the loop.

"There are so many kids' apps that are developed by well-intentioned people that kids can't even use," Jason Krogh, the CEO, tells me at lunch, over a plate of shrimp pasta at a nearby Italian restaurant. "It's important for us that the child is in the driver's seat, that he feels ownership over what he's doing, so we do playtesting sessions every week. It's hard to remember what it was like to be three."

He likens his apps to a playground. Some kids follow the rules and sit in the swing properly. Others (like Ella), prefer to swing on their bellies or (like Charlotte) side to side. The lesson: there is no right way to swing. The more you steer the kid, the less they feel ownership, the less they get from the experience. And the whole point of swinging is to have fun, however you want to do it.

Early on during the development process, Krogh experienced an *aha* moment. He was working on an app in which a bird flew around, with narration following the bird as the child moved her—"She's flying over here!" "She's sleeping now." When they took the narration out in one test, the kids started doing their own voiceovers. All of a sudden, the app became a tool for storytelling. *Aha!*

They have educational advisers, two with PhDs in child development, but Krough tells me he uses them more as a safety net—for example, they'll tell him if patterning (an activity that asks the user to find circle, circle, square over and over again, say) is too advanced for three- or four-year-olds. But the advisers are not integral to the design of the apps.

"So what is little Clark really getting out of flinging cars up into the heavens?" I ask, betraying my American enrichment-focused neuroses. He sighs.

"If you give the kids the building blocks, they'll *find* the education," he says.

Well, maybe, but I didn't witness Ella narrate once, likely because she was so enamored of the movement on the screen. And repeatedly flinging virtual horses will never mimic repeatedly flinging toy horses, because real flinging takes more work—both physical and cognitive. When Ella throws her toy unicorn around the room, she's more often than not engrossed in elaborate make-believe stories about flying horses. Not once does Ella attempt to do something on Sago's app that doesn't work—the thoughtfulness behind the design is critical. So it's not that Ella playing Sago Mini seems to be the nutritional equivalent of mindlessly eating fistfuls of candy corn. It's more like eating those baby puffs, which dissolve on the tongue and seem to be made of nothing but air.

* * *

Across North America sits Khan Academy, which defines itself as a "nonprofit with the mission to provide a free, world-class education for anyone, anywhere." If dentist-related apps are on one side of the nutrition spectrum, next to candy corn, and Sago Mini is in the middle, then Khan Academy would be much closer to broccoli—but maybe the kind you really like to eat, like tempura broccoli slathered in a sweet soy sauce. In 2004 Sal Khan, an MIT graduate working as a hedge fund analyst in Boston, started making videos to help his cousin back in New Orleans with math. A few more cousins started paying attention. Then more relatives. Five years later, his videos, posted on YouTube, were so popular he decided to leave his job and pursue his dream of building out a global, virtual schoolhouse, where you could find tutoring videos on any number of subjects, from kidney function to polynomials, disrupting the traditional classroom and harnessing the power of technology for good.

"If Isaac Newton had done YouTube videos on calculus, I wouldn't have to!" he says in his TED Talk, viewed more than five million times. A Bengali raised in Metairie, LA, he uses "y'all" not infrequently and exudes trustworthiness. In 2012, Khan was named one of *TIME* magazine's 100 Most Influential People, and today millions of students all over the world watch Khan Academy videos, which are available in more than thirty languages. (As I write during the COVID pandemic, the site's offerings are providing critical stopgap measures for parents at home with their school-age children, who are navigating an educational system that was never built for remote learning.)

In 2016, Khan Academy bought Duck Duck Moose, a preschool app developer, and launched *Khan Academy Kids*, an educational app aimed at two- through six-year-olds. Pre-acquisition, Duck Duck Moose was best known for its interactive *Wheels on the Bus* app, in which you can not only listen to the song in Italian or German (*Dei Räder vom Bus drehen sich rundherum!*) but also slide the doors open and shut, make the people go up and down, and, of course, turn the wheels round and round. Unless you want your child to know how to sing the song in Italian, I'm not sure how much education there is in the app—at one point, you can literally pop bubbles coming out of a fish's mouth, which numerous cognitive psychologists have used as an example of the quintessential mindless activity—but even though Ella loses interest after a few *rundherum*s, it's kind of fun. Now the Duck Duck Moose team is tackling the curricular world.

I download the *Khan Academy Kids* app early one morning, in the spirit of research but mostly hoping it'll entertain Ella from a supine position. Within minutes, she's lying on the bed next to me, chugging along through the app, picking out letters and making Kodi the Bear bounce around. The characters are sweet and the music isn't annoying, and even though Dr. Radesky told me that what most of these apps are teaching aren't the things we really want to instill in our kids—"You want kids to learn critical thinking, frustration management, grit, all the things that will set them up to do better later on in life"—on the spectrum of preschool media I've seen, this seems pretty benign. Early on, I spot a few missed opportunities. During a section that asks her about her feelings, Ella clicks on the sad face to indicate she's sad—which I find hard to believe, as she literally jumps out of bed every morning and triumphantly rips off her diaper with an accompanying yip. Instead of pausing to say, "I'm so sorry to hear that!" or otherwise acknowledge the sadness, a string of stars spews out of the sad character's head, and the app keeps right on going. Which, by any measure, is a weird response. But I figure that, unless I spectacularly fail at parenting, she won't grow up thinking stars shoot out of people's heads when you tell them you're sad.

"We've seen a big change in our kid testing over the years, and this is not a happy story," Caroline Hu Flexer, a Duck Duck Moose co-founder, tells me when I visit her at Khan Academy's Mountain View HQ. Dogs wander around the open–floor plan office as employees enjoy free Spindrifts and snacks. "It used to be that it wasn't until kids were five that we'd see a foray into adult gaming. Now, children as young as three come into the office, conditioned to playing adult-level apps." She pauses. "When you get a kid that's used to that level of auditory and visual stimulation, it's really hard for them to focus on something that's designed *for* them."

A former Ideo employee, Hu Flexer, like the Sago Mini team,

is particularly attuned to the design of her app and goes through many iterations to make sure little hands can navigate it well. She also takes pains to make sure it's paced correctly—it's a relatively quiet app, with the occasional piece of cheerful music in the background, often played by a single cello.

Khan Kids works closely with Renee Scott, an early childhood development specialist at Stanford University who directs Preschool Counts, part of the school's Education Partnerships program at the Haas Center for Public Service.

"The most important thing at this age is giving kids just enough," she tells me. In the education industry, this is known as the *zone of proximal development*, a phrase coined by psychologist Lev Vygotsky in the early 1900s. "They need just enough help to be able to do it independently, and then move on to the next thing."

As such, much of Khan Kids' content is scaffolded—Sandy the Dingo takes you through a room and points out all the things that have words on them, then directs you to an activity where *you* have to tap every sign that has a word on it—but there are also large sections of the app that are open-ended, holding to the Sago Mini philosophy. One day, Ella taps a button and my screen transforms into a bug terrarium. As she drags a fly into the terrarium from the screen's border, it starts to move around. If she taps it with her finger and drags, it goes along with her. "What's the purpose of that?" I ask Scott.

"They can be working on their fine motor skills," she allows. "And the other piece is that kids naturally group things. It's our brain's way of understanding things, to look or order things by color or size, so this gives them a similar experience."

Okay, fine, but why not just let them do that in the real world?

"Of course using their hands and their body and having a physical conversation with someone is preferable for sure, because we learn in social settings," she says. I think I detect a sigh. "But the reality is that a lot of times, kids are on screens. They just are. So if they're going to be on a screen, this mirrors the way our brains tend to learn, and gives them a chance to do something worthwhile."

But Scott's answer doesn't address the larger issue: that at least until the age of four or five, there's a very real question of whether kids can transfer knowledge from the screen to real life at all—what Ella's preschool teacher had related in that anecdote about the blocks. This is the sticking point for *all* apps targeted to younger audiences, calling into question whether any app for children under five can *ever* be considered enriching.

"There's this miscommunication that you have to interact around a book but that around newer media, children will just pick it up, it will just come naturally," Dr. Rachel Barr tells me. "But joint engagement is needed for all media."

Barr, the director of the Early Learning Project lab at Georgetown University, studies knowledge transfer from various media to the real world and surfaces two explanations for why a child can't learn something on a screen and then take that knowledge into the real world, which is known as *transfer deficit*. First, the child's memory and learning systems are still developing. Transferring information from a 2D world into the 3D world requires *minds-on thinking*—a psychological term of art that means, essentially, being engaged—which is challenging for developing brains. Second, while trying to learn a given skill, the child must simultaneously master how the different gadgets work, even if it's a book that requires pages to be turned. The result? Having a human being help them translate 2D information into 3D is critical. This happens seamlessly with a book—you'd rarely hand a toddler a book and expect her to figure it out on her own. Your engagement is integral to the book-reading experience and, Barr tells me, it should be integral to most any media experience involving young children.

"With books, TV, tablet, we find a pretty consistent result from six months to four or five years: kids find it hard to learn from *any* of these forms of media," Barr says. "If you show them a game face-to-face, they'll learn about 50 percent more."

* * *

Given the ubiquity of screens, the inevitability that children will be exposed to them, and the lack of co-engagement built into the medium, I consider one final school of thought on preschool apps before fully giving up on the power of interactivity to beneficially engage Ella solo: that successful apps should strive to redirect the child's focus outward, into the real world.

"It's a split I call 'prompting-versus-partnering,'" Dr. Kathy Hirsh-Pasek tells me during a visit I make to the Infant & Child Laboratory she co-runs at Temple University (tagline: Where Children Teach Adults). If the app is prompting you to do something in the real world, excellent. Big Bird wants you to find words, so you use your app to take pictures of the words you find as you go about your grocery shopping expedition? Great. It's when the app is designed such that you partner not with the outside world but with the device itself that you start running into trouble.

"As humans, we are social more than anything," she tells me. "The challenge is figuring out how to keep that social connection in a virtual world."

A senior fellow at the Brookings Institution, Hirsh-Pasek has, among many other delightful and important contributions to the world, transformed multiple low-income parts of Philadelphia into a playful learning mecca of sorts—putting enriching puzzles on the backs of bus stop shelters, adding sidewalk hopscotch games to certain stretches of concrete to promote various educational goals. But for people outside the field, the biggest marker that she is on the right track with her research seems to be that her son, lyricist Benj Pasek, won an Oscar in 2017. (Between her and Nancy Carlsson-Paige, who spoke to me about the importance of play, there appears to be a surefire way to prepare your child for an Academy Award: become a developmental psychologist and hyphenate your last name.) "Son's Oscar win affirms professor's parenting strategy," one press release blared after he won Best Original Song for "City of Stars" from *La La Land*. In his acceptance speech, Benj thanked his mother, whom he'd brought along as his date, saying, "She let me quit the JCC soccer league to be in a musical. This is dedicated to all the kids who sing in the rain and all the moms who let them."

I find it hard to imagine that she let Benj quit soccer as some sort of strategy. Seconds after I knock on her door in the suburbs of Philly, she envelopes me in a huge hug, and moments afterward, I'm semi-naked in her library pumping as I take in her bookshelf—Nietzsche, Spinoza, and Shakespeare next to Woodward (Bob) and Potter (Harry). It takes only a few minutes in her presence to realize that she exhibits all the best qualities of her subjects: an openness, an inquisitiveness, a wide-eyed friendliness that makes my need to pump preinterview wildly less awkward than it might have been. This is not the kind of woman who'd force her son into shin guards if all he wanted to do was watch Gene Kelly films.

"I'm really good at becoming a three-year-old," she says as we pass her downstairs bathroom, decorated with carnival masks and a butterfly the size of a toddler, and head to her car for a day at the lab.

The cornerstone of her philosophy is something called *playful learning*—a little bit of learning, a little bit of play. It's her North Star. "Playful learning is a pedagogical approach that bridges the divide between play and instruction," she tells me.

At the lab, she and a gaggle of intense graduate students puzzle over questions such as "If a cell phone call interrupts an interaction between a parent and a child who's trying to learn a new word, will that affect the child's ability to retain the word?" (Yes.) "Do parents use more varied language when playing with traditional toys than electronic ones?" (Yes.) "Are apps that are labeled 'educational' actually educational?" (Generally, no.)

Hirsh-Pasek likes to say that while in certain circles "play can be a four-letter word," her studies have shown that it's a critical way for children to learn. "Free play"—running around in the forest alone, say, or building a fort in the living room—is important, but if an adult wants to teach a child something specific, anything from a new word to how to solve a problem, the most successful strategy is to link play with guided instruction. So instead of running around in the forest by yourself, add a grown-up huffing and puffing behind you, pointing out shadows or a bug or a leaf, and you're bound to have a more enriching experience. The grown-up is integral to the child's experience, and how this philosophy translates to the virtual world is a topic she believes to be of the upmost importance.

"Children are in the midst of a vast, unplanned experiment, surrounded by digital technologies that were not available but five years ago," she writes in "Putting Education in 'Educational' Apps: Lessons from the Science of Learning." The paper is both an attempt to guide developers on how to create quality content and a takedown of the unregulated App Store, where so many apps are listed as "educational" that the word is essentially rendered meaningless. Though published in 2015, it rings even more true today. Consider Toca Boca's *Hair Salon*, one of the more downloaded apps in the educational vertical, which involves shaving and giving a blow-dry to a lion, among other barbershop tasks. While Hirsh-Pasek allows that some ancillary learning can happen when lion shaving—you're learning cause and effect; you're learning that razors are part of the barbershop category—to me, *Hair Salon* is educational only if you're prepping for a job at a particularly trendy zoo, likely one in Bushwick. But as she tells me on a later call, "That Toca Boca? That's a dang fun app!" For her, the fun and the play are still essential.

While her paper tries to be optimistic and discuss how one *might* harness the potential of apps—those "designed to promote active, engaged, meaningful, and socially interactive learning"—I can't help but sense that, like me, Hirsh-Pasek would much rather these devices not exist, however much she says otherwise.

During our car ride, she tells me in no uncertain terms that "the most important thing for kids in the zero-to-three range is interactions with real people. You don't want to disrupt that!"

But she's realistic. She gestures to the phone in her cup holder and the one in my front pocket. Phones are inescapable. So if you're going to try to use them mindfully with your kids, she suggests, use her partnering-versus-prompting framework.

She cites *Pokémon GO*, the augmented-reality app that bridged the virtual and real worlds and resulted in lots of people bumping into each other on street corners as they tried to capture cute, tiny robot creatures on their screens. That was fun, sure. But what if you turned the concept on its side, ever so slightly?

"Imagine you're on a family vacation," she tells me, pressing on the gas as she gets more animated. "Wouldn't it be fun if you guys could all meet the historical figures that made that city what it is? What if you could interact with the monuments?" Her eyes gleam and we accelerate. "That would bring things alive."

She's planning a trip to Italy with her grandchildren later in the year. "What if I could help the hills of Rome come alive when we're there?" she asks me. "Just imagine!"

Well, perhaps. But as I take the local train back to Philadelphia's 30th Street Station, I think about her trip (which I later learn was canceled due to COVID) and find myself remembering a book I read in grade school that told the story of Romulus and Remus. The illustration on one page (the left-hand side, I can still remember, black-and-white) was of two little boys nestled against the belly of a wolf. I have the same reaction I did then— imagining that the wolf's taut belly must have been warm, and a little scratchy, and wondering whether or not that would have been comfortable for the twins, who were depicted naked. If I'd seen an augmented-reality version of the twins next to a wolf, would the image be seared in my brain the same way, decades later? Would the sensations, the memory, be as strong?

A few weeks later, Ella is having a full-on bedtime meltdown. I remember an app a doctor had recommended to me, a *Sesame Street* one called *Breathe, Think, Do*, which involves calming down a little monster, so at my wit's end, I pull out my phone. We help the monster take deep breaths, and Ella takes deep breaths, too. Crisis averted. There are use cases when an app, like any other form of media, can make a challenging moment a little less challenging. And there are those that are designed thoughtfully by developers who do their best to make sure chubby toddler hands can navigate successfully. But I've relinquished hope that Ella will get more out of interactive virtual play on her own than I got out of *Mario Kart*, which, banana strategy aside, served as a mostly mindless release.

As for bringing the hills of Rome alive with an app—sure, it might seem like magic, but if you have to augment reality for a three-year-old, what does that teach him about reality itself? The wonder, the magic—it's already there, in the way the setting sun hits the hills, in the smell of pizza from that little trattoria around the corner, in the sound of the choir practicing on the steps of a nearby church. You just have to look up from your screen, and take it all in.

8

See Spot Sprint

Can E-books Improve Upon Print Ones?

The day we brought Ella home from the hospital, I straightjacketed her in a swaddle, propped her up on the bed like a demibaguette, and started reading her *Goodnight Moon*. I'd have picked up a book or magazine of my own to kill time before the next nursing session, but it seemed kind of antisocial to read the *New Yorker* next to my new roommate, this silent, wide-eyed creature I barely knew. Plus, I could already surmise that she was genetically programmed not to want to read an article about Henry James's amanuensis, even on more than three hours' sleep. *Goodnight Moon* seemed about all we could manage. Even though I admittedly felt a little silly reading aloud to someone who could only see a few inches in front of her nose and who forty-eight hours earlier was literally living in my stomach, I turned the page and began.

Seconds later, Dave came in to find Ella silently gazing about four feet into the middle distance and listing to one side, like the Leaning Tower of Pisa, and me loudly weeping.

"What's wrong?" he asked, bolting over as I wiped snot away with the back of my hand. "Is she okay?"

She was fine. I was the wreck. It was the hormones, sure, but something much deeper. That fluffy bunny, the orange and green color palette, that little bowl of mush—I hadn't seen the book for at least thirty years, but all of it was so deeply woven into my earliest consciousness that I was struck by a powerful, moving certainty. My own mother must have done the same thing: taken me home from the hospital, tucked me into bed next to her just as she'd done with my older sister, and started reading the comforting, repetitive, understated book to me. Even though I wouldn't have really been able to see, I would have heard her voice, smelled her, felt that cocoon of comfort that slowed my breathing down and communicated, wordlessly, that everything was going to be okay, now and for always.

And then, three years later, I give birth to Charlotte and realize: nope. As the second child, Charlotte spends so much time lying on her back the first few weeks while we tend to her whirling dervish of a sister that she develops a bald spot. She's nearly four months old before I so much as hold a book in her vicinity. She fixates on it with so much intensity, I realize she likely thought the world was made up solely of ceilings and large floating heads. As a second child myself, I empathize.

But everything I've read tells me it's never too early to start the bedtime ritual—the American Academy of Pediatrics (AAP) recommends people start reading aloud to their children as soon as they're born—so I start bringing her into Ella's room each

night. In between attempting to answer the unanswerable queries Ella babbles out, rapid-fire—"Do the Gruffalo and his child
brush their teeth? Do they use a normal toothbrush or a special
Gruffalo one?"—I sneak glances at Charlotte, who sits there silently, riveted by the images, the words, her older sister, and
wonder what on earth is going on in her brain.

Quite a lot, I later learn—although I am warned off even imagining that she's picking up phonemes or letter recognition by one
developmental psychologist, who alerts me to a now-defunct scam
of a program called "Your Baby Can Read." ("Um, no, she can't,"
she tells me.) Charlotte is firmly in the literature-as-teething-tool
phase of her life, but she seems to be content, and I start to count
down the minutes until the three of us can pile into Ella's daybed, snuggle up, and read together, completely protected from
the interruptions of my phone. Ella turns the pages, Charlotte
drools on them, and I feel one with a long line of parents who
have helped their children fall asleep to stories each night. (When
I look at the copyright page of some of the classics—*Babar* was
published in 1931, *Madeline* in 1939, *Curious George* in 1941—I
realize that children have been falling asleep to the *same* soothing
stories about colonialism and appendicitis for a century.)

Thing is, even with my phone safely plugged in downstairs, I
can sense the tentacles of tech slowly inching under the door, coming for us. Everywhere I look, the book is being disrupted: in app
form, on e-readers, with augmented reality that its creators claim
can bring static pages alive in ways that I, as a sleep-deprived
parent, cannot. Even some of our beloved Sandra Boynton books
are available on app form, full of fun hotspots where you can do
things like make a cow moo as many times as you'd like. I'm no
stranger to the promise of disruption. At least once a week, Dave,

now working as a venture capitalist after more than a decade as a tech entrepreneur, comes home from a meeting, exhilarated, and declares something like, "Baby, we're going to disrupt the *dentist*!" Or "It's about time we disrupt the hell out of parking garages!" I mean, maybe?

But . . . the book? That seems like sacred territory, doesn't it? And if nothing is sacred anymore, then how, precisely, can technology make a print book better?

* * *

To break down that vast question into component parts, I spend one morning delineating the discrete reasons I read to my kids, and land on two main ones.

The first: Stories, and storytelling, are a critical part of the human experience. The more you read, the more you learn, the more empathetic you become, the wider your world grows. The shape of a story, with its beginning, middle, and end, is inherently comforting. It brings order to an uncontrollable world. And is a life bereft of Pooh really one worth living?

My hope is that, however nuanced, all the stories we read together are not only entertaining Ella but also teaching her something about the world, her potential, how to handle situations, and on and on. This objective, to entertain while educating, existed even before John Locke famously articulated it in *Some Thoughts Concerning Education* (1693). If you go back far enough, to the grim days when childhood death was part and parcel of life, you'll find that the lessons on children's book pages were really dark. When poking around one day, I learn of a Dr. A. S. W. Rosenbach, who archived early childhood publications between 1682 to 1836.

He found that during those years, "the literature provided for [children] was with the definite purpose of teaching them how they should die in a befitting manner." (Take that, *Moo, Baa, La La La!*) One story I come across from 1736, Thomas Fleet's *The Prodigal Daughter*, features a spoiled child making a deal with the devil to kill her parents. When an angel tells on her, the girl falls into a deathlike trance, comes back from the dead a while later, takes the sacrament, and repents. Fleet advertised his story in the *Boston Evening-Post* as "very suitable for Children." Sure, I guess, if you're Wednesday Addams. At least it's written in cute rhyming couplets: "So close the Reverend Divine did lay / This charge, that many wept that there did stay."

Macabre aside, if we assume that the act of reading aloud to young children is the first step on a journey toward independent reading, then cultivating bookworms at an early age becomes even more crucial for a simple reason: a child's third-grade reading ability is one of the most important predictors of lifetime success.

In 1995, the researchers Betty Hart and Todd Risley published *Meaningful Differences in the Everyday Experience of Young American Children*, a book that came out of a study about parent-child interactions, in which they tape-recorded the conversations of forty-two households. The conclusion: low-income parents spoke less to their children than wealthier parents. As a result, by age four, each low-income child heard thirty million fewer words. This socioeconomic verbal inequality became known as "the word gap," and Hart and Risley's work continues to be the foundation of more recent studies that underscore the importance of saturating children with words and reading as early as possible.

For example, in 2010, the Annie E. Casey Foundation—a private philanthropy founded in 1948 that grants money to federal agencies, states, cities, and neighborhoods to help roll back the negative effects of poverty on children and families—published *Early Warning! Why Reading by the End of Third Grade Matters*. The report launched the national Campaign for Grade-Level Reading, a coordinated effort to promote early literacy throughout America. If you cannot read proficiently at the end of third grade, the report stated, you will have a harder time in school, likely won't graduate from high school on time, and will be at a severe disadvantage when it comes time to hit the job market. The implications are particularly concerning for low-income families: 50 percent of low-income students were below basic fourth-grade reading as of 2009, compared with 20 percent of moderate- and high-income students.

Their 2013 follow-up report, *Early Warning Confirmed*, underscores that, much like income inequality, the word gap expands over time—and once opened, it is hard to close. But the earlier you start encouraging reading and the earlier a child loves curling up with a book, the more likely you are to close that gap. Other studies point to *dialogic reading*—the parents' ability to use the book as a jumping off point for conversation, a variant on those serve-and-return interactions Dr. Mendelsohn told me about—as having more influence on a child's vocabulary and brain development than simply the absolute number of words heard. You don't read *to* the child; you read *with* him, prompting him with questions, helping him articulate his takeaways. But a word-rich environment is key to language development, and language development is key to greater life success.

So that's the first big, important bucket.

The second, though slightly smaller, is equally important: it's nice to have a warm, sleepy toddler or baby body nestled into yours. Full stop.

When I start digging into the question of whether there's anything specific about a print book that makes it uniquely more suited to achieving these two goals, I find myself in the crosshairs of two camps.

The first camp views the book as an object. Replace it with another object that functionally serves the same purpose, but with added enhancements, and you might be able to create a more beneficial experience on all measures.

"I really think technology is a savior!" Dr. Anne Cunningham tells me when I reach her at her office at UC Berkeley, where she is a professor in the Graduate School of Education. She used to serve on the board of LeapFrog and is the coauthor of *Book Smart: How to Develop and Support Successful, Motivated Readers*. "It doesn't matter if it's a cardboard book or if it's an iPad. What matters for the one- or two- or three-year-old is that they get to sit in Dad's lap." Then, she says, when the kid gets older, you can load up the iPad with e-enhanced books, and if they click on a word, the program might define it for them, or read the whole book aloud to them. All added bonuses, in her view.

The second camp asserts two things: the tablet's design is inherently problematic, and enhancing a story in any way—be that through music, animations, or words that light up—distracts and is, ultimately, detrimental to a child's comprehension and deep engagement.

I already have an opinion on the snugglability of a device, cemented when I was researching how engaged Ella can be on an iPad or iPhone, either watching a show or playing a game. Whenever I give Ella a tablet or smartphone, she tends to form a little solo cocoon around the device. More than once I've gotten an elbow nudge to back off.

"There are design affordances of a print book that let you know that this is a shared object," Dr. Jenny Radesky, one of the lead authors of the American Academy of Pediatrics' 2016 screen-time guidelines, confirms for me. She's conducted studies to see how open children are to sharing iPad games and the like with caregivers (like that one involving parents lying dramatically over couches to inch their way into their child's virtual world). The upshot: not very much. "With a tablet it's more, *this is just for me.*"

Admittedly, that dynamic might change over time, as programmers and product designers build affordances into their products to encourage snuggling while reading. If we're both looking at a large holographic screen that pops up in the middle of Ella's bedroom, say, instead of trying to crowd around an iPad, there might be hope. Though, to be honest, I can't quite wrap my head around what that future would look like. So until then, when it comes to the snuggle factor: Analog 1, Tech 0.

What about the biggie, the ability to convey the nuances and excitement of a story? Can tech make that better?

Most toddler e-books offer three main attributes, either built on already published print books or created particularly for the new medium: a "Read to me" feature; word highlighting as the story progresses; and interactive hot spots, which launch animations or games or quizzes or sound effects and the like. Particularly when dealing with younger kids, the research shows that the benefits of these elements, as compared to a real live person who's sitting there reading the book, are questionable at best.

For starters, that "Read to me" feature mostly incinerates the potential of using the book for serve-and-return interactions. One Harvard pediatrician who's been practicing for over thirty years tells me that immigrant parents come into his practice relieved that even if they can't read English themselves, their children will be able to hear English stories anyway, at the click of a button.

"But that isn't the point!" he says. "Just make up a story that vaguely has to do with the pictures on the page, and the children will benefit immensely." For young children, the book should be seen as a vehicle for connection, not a vehicle for word consumption.

As for highlighting the words on the page?

"Three- and four-year-olds can't read, right? So it's kind of precious to be lighting words up for them," Georgene Troseth tells me when I reach her. "When they're starting to do things like, *My name starts with an S*, then they're ready to start to pay attention to letters and words. But not before. Then it's just a distraction."

Troseth is an associate professor of psychology at Vanderbilt and the head of the university's Early Development Lab, where she studies what toddlers learn from touch screens, videos, video chat, and more. When we speak, she's in the midst of developing an e-book that specifically encourages dialogic reading. Multiple folks in the field tell me this project is a bright spot—perhaps the lone one—in which the science of learning undergirds the tech (as opposed to the tech undergirding the race for eyes on screen and, thus, dollars at whatever cost). Troseth is hoping that this innovation teaches not only the child directly but also the parent, by modeling how dialogic reading can work in the best of circumstances. At the start of the book she shares with me, built on PBS Kids' *Peg + Cat*, an animated series that embeds mathematical and spatial concepts into each page, a little character named Ramone pops up in the corner.

"Did you know that when parents and children talk about what they're reading, that's when the learning happens?" he asks. On one page, when Peg tells us that her mother asked her to put five letters in the mailbox, Ramone pops up and asks, "Can you tap the letters?" After Peg and Cat come upon a big dog sitting in front of the mailbox and Peg exclaims that she's afraid, Ramone pops up again and asks, "Why are Peg and Cat afraid?"

"Open-ended questions, questions that make connections between the book and life, defining words—the idea here was that it could be a training tool, where if parents used this, it might give them ideas they could apply to other books," Troseth tells me. She and her team found that by using the enhanced e-book, not only did parents of lower socioeconomic children talk three times as much with their children and use more words, but the children also talked much more and with more varied language. It's massively promising. But Troseth in no way wants Ramone to be an evergreen crutch.

"I view this as temporary, as giving people an idea of how to treat a book," she tells me. "It could be *part* of the literacy landscape for parents. But take the place of print? That would cut my heart, frankly."

Of course, if you come from a background where there aren't many—or any—print books available to you, e-books offer a remarkable solution. One oft-cited study from 2001 reported that there are approximately thirteen books per child in middle-income neighborhoods, compared to one book for every three hundred low-income children. Compare that with the stat, from

Common Sense Media, that 95 percent of families with children ages zero to eight have a smartphone, and thus access to a scientifically grounded program like Troseth's, and the upside of e-books for underserved populations is obvious, as long as they're used correctly.

Now, for the third bucket: interactive hot spots. The Joan Ganz Cooney Center found that when it comes to enhanced e-books, parents spend more time telling their children what button to press than chatting about the story itself; these hot-spots, however well intentioned, tend to distract.

"If you break off to do a game you think is related to the story but it breaks the narrative, that's where you run into problems," developmental psychologist Dr. Kathy Hirsh-Pasek tells me when I reach her for one of our many phone conversations after my visit to her lab at Temple University. "Some of the clearest examples of this are when you're reading a book about animals at the zoo, and all of a sudden it goes *Da ding! Which animals start with the letter A?* That's like, *Oh my god, you're crushin' the narrative!* And there are other narrative crushers. When you watch parents reading those books with children it looks like what one of my students called induced ADHD."

I witness this one day when I download an innocuous-seeming, and quite highly rated—both on the App Store and the Children's Technology Review—Dr. Seuss e-book, *Green Eggs and Ham.* Every single part of the page seems to be a hot spot; for nearly anything Ella touches, a word balloons up as the narrator identifies what she's touching. "Wuh-wuh-wuh-wall!" the app says as Ella touches the wall behind Sam again, and again, and again, and again. "Sam's friend! Sam's friend! Sam's friend!" it chirps at another page. The app, to be fair, is marketed at children ages four and up, and after a little bit of hunting around, I learn I can turn off the picture-tapping effects. But I still find the implication concerning—that you can improve upon Theodor Seuss Geisel's witty drawings by having word bubbles float up out of Sam-I-Am's head. It sure seems satisfying to Ella that she can effect word bloops, but any real educational benefit of the feature is lost on me.

And when I reach Heather Kirkorian, director of the Cognitive Development and Media Lab at the University of Wisconsin-Madison, who studies the impact of screen media on attention, learning, and play in infants and young children, she confirms as much, in a very simple way.

"When we think about best practices with reading, we wouldn't encourage a parent to point at an element on the page and say the same word over and over again," she says.

Well, yeah.

* * *

I figure if anyone can weigh in on the power and drawbacks of tech in the storytelling realm, it's Sandra Boynton, someone for whom the hippo is a muse, pigs fly, and chickens square-dance— both on the printed page and on a handful of award-winning apps.

So one fall day, I hop in my car and drive two hours northeast from New York City into the Connecticut Berkshires in search of this most beloved, and successful, children's author.

But I plug the wrong address into my phone, so find myself driving back and forth along a quiet country road searching for a house number that doesn't exist. I have no service, and as I double, then triple back, I'm struck with the real fear that I've made this trip for naught. I'm about to ask a cow for directions.

Then I see the chickens.

They're perched on either side of a white gate, high up on columns like sentries, bright orange feet stuck straight ahead, eyes fixed on the middle distance, doing their best Buckingham Palace Guard impersonation. Either this corner of Connecticut has an unduly high saturation of cartoon chicken fans, or I've arrived at the right place.

"Come to the barn in the back," Boynton says as she buzzes me in. Down a short drive, past a pond on the right and a covered pool on the left, I come to the little two-story red barn where Boynton has drawn her hippos, chickens, and rabbits for thirty-some-odd years. Fittingly, there's a hippo weather vane on top.

Boynton started out making greeting cards in the 1970s while still at Yale, and the company estimates that she's created somewhere between four thousand and six thousand, a few of which are displayed on a stand in the barn. Her most well-known, a quizzical hippo standing next to a flying bird next to two dancing sheep, with the caption "Hippo Birdie Two Ewes" (get it?) says a lot about her unique way of looking at the world—slightly off-center, big on charm. There is no Boynton team; there is just Boynton, here in her barn cluttered with books and memorabilia and surrounded by farmland. Which is remarkable, considering that in addition to those cards, there are her six music albums (one of which, *Philadelphia Chickens*, was nominated for a Grammy), her calendars, her desk diaries, her plush toys, her interactive book apps, and more. But she's best known for her fifty-odd books, which have collectively sold over seventy million copies. Millions of children go to bed with her words in their heads, something made possible by the simple reason that grown-ups like her characters and stories, too.

Many a besotted parent has done a deep reading of Boynton's books in an attempt to uncover their appeal. (Take Ian Bogost's "The Hidden Depths of Sandra Boynton's Board Books" in *The New Yorker*, which offers an antediluvian reading on why the animals in *The Going to Bed Book* head upstairs to exercise—gasp—*after* brushing their teeth.) But the simple reason they've remained on the bookshelves in my house for years is because they make us laugh. Dave, a college a cappella baritone with little opportunity to let it rip except for in the shower, gravitates toward her singing books, particularly *The Bunny Rabbit Show!*, which features high-kicking hares. I particularly like *Belly Button Book!*, a tight, twenty-page story that features Ella's nickname, Boon. It is because of Boynton that Ella first started to participate in story time. One evening when making our way through the gazillionth reading of *What's Wrong, Little Pookie?*, about a young pig who's not quite sure why he's upset, eighteen-month-old Ella started piping up as Pookie. Her intonation was flat and robotic, like Wall-E, but we captured it on video. The day she starts reading Shakespeare in high school, I'll be able to show her the video and say, "Your love of reading started *right there*."

A few years ago, Boynton turned five of her books into interactive apps. Like many e-books available on the App Store, they feature the "Read to me" button, which activates narration, and hot spots. If you want to actually make the bunny bounce, the duck strut, and the chickens spin in *Barnyard Dance!*, Boynton gives you the opportunity. And I want to know, essentially, why—why someone who so clearly believes in the power of print decided to wade into the wide world of the App Store.

"You may find me zombie-like," she warned in an email before our interview—she's coming off a night helping out with her daughter's seven-week-old baby boy. But when she meets me at the door—work boots, jeans, white cardigan, long blond hair shoved into a hair tie—she looks less zombie and more gardener. Within minutes we're set up in the barn's cheery kitchen, made to resemble a 1950s diner, complete with vinyl stools and a hanging sign advertising ice cream. She sets out some French press coffee to accompany the chocolate babka I brought, and when she opens the fridge to get out the half-and-half, I spy, Saran-wrapped on a plate, a single pancake with ears.

"I'm proud of the work we did," she tells me about her apps, "but I have doubts about creating for the medium at all."

When apps started becoming all the rage, she found herself intrigued by the clever and creative work of a Canadian interactive app developer called Loud Crow Interactive. Out of the blue, she reached out, and together with Calvin Wang, the founder and president, began the process of translating five of her books to the screen.

"I am trained in theater"—she was originally on a career path toward being a stage director—"so I looked at the device as a stage," she tells me. Still, she is acutely aware of the shortfalls of the e-book. For one, she tells me, "the book implies more movement than the screen animation can deliver," making the e-book, essentially, "just a nifty spin-off, and perhaps more toy than book." That being said, she put her characteristic attention to detail to the app development process, laboring not just over the music and sound, which she made in her small recording studio, but also over exactly what the animations should be—Should this animal jump up and down or shimmy? Should this pothole be openable or not?

I share that it took Ella and me a few beats to figure out what we were supposed to do on one page of *The Going to Bed Book*—the one where the animals head up to exercise. We poked them. We tried to make them jump. We tried to drag them up the stairs. Nothing. Then Ella pulled a moose back, like a slingshot, and as she let go, he whizzed up the stairs, exiting stage right, which left us both in hysterics. Coming off a few months of researching how screens can or cannot educate children, it struck me that humor might be a particularly good North Star to follow when creating kids' digital content. That, and keeping the pacing nice and measured.

"I'm glad it took you a moment," Boynton says. "You should slow down." Her books are an antidote to today's fast-paced children's programming. Ideally, she wants her interactive books to accomplish the same thing. (After a lot of discussion with Wang about nomenclature—whether they were e-books or apps or what—they settled on *interactive books*.)

Of course, her drawings are whimsical at heart, and Wang's job was to help translate that whimsy to the screen.

"We were all sitting around a table and we thought, Wouldn't it be cool in the scene where the animals brush their teeth if you could turn on the spigot?" he remembers when I reach him in Vancouver. "If they turn on the hot water spigot, wouldn't it be cool if we could steam up the book? And then on top of that, if you could take your finger and erase that steam and have it make that little squeaky sound? There's no scientific method in terms of figuring these things out," he continues, "but we'd keep asking, 'Wouldn't that be neat?'" And yes, it is super neat.

But Wang is healthily wary about the work he does. He remembers showing his son, then two years old, one of the Boynton interactive books he'd created.

"When we sat him down to read the actual board book, he'd touch the characters and expect them to react to his touch," Wang tells me. "It was a bit of an epiphany for me, because it showed just how much we were molding how kids see the world. It reinforced that we really have to strive to make sure what we're making is quality, and not too gimmicky just to try to get the kid's attention." He exhaled, audibly. "It's always easier said than done."

His son is now a gamer.

"I'm terrified as a parent, thinking, *What if my ten-year-old is really addicted to* Fortnite, *or another app?* Play is good, but like everything else you have to have limits." This was a kind of honesty I hadn't encountered in other app developers, who, driven by the realities of the market, are always striving for more eyes on screen.

Boynton shares Wang's caution. She only reads real books ("Their physical being is a great part of the pleasure of reading"), and the Boyntons never had a working television at the house in Connecticut. They just never installed an antennae after doing a big renovation. But over a second cup of coffee, she tells me about an "inadvertent, interesting experiment" she undertook in 1991 that informs her outlook on tech in the lives of her target audience. Her husband, an Olympic slalom canoeist (you read that right), had been asked to train with the French team for the Barcelona Olympics, so on short notice, they uprooted their four children—the oldest was thirteen, the youngest seventeen months—to go live in the French Pyrenees. For the first time in their lives, she sat them in front of the television, thinking that saturating them with French would help them learn the language. It helped with the older ones. With the littlest, something else happened.

"She learned the language, but she really grew to *love* the television," Boynton says, "more than any of my other children. It was something about her age. And now with her own kid? No screens at all."

She recognizes the magic potential of her e-books—after our visit, she writes to me that "discovery and delight are usually worthwhile things, and creating the sense of the iPad as a theater stage rather than a TV screen or computer screen appeals to me"—but she's horrified when she sees little kids staring dumbly at screens in restaurants, their parents pointedly ignoring them.

"You really don't want to spend time with them?" she asks, incredulous. She fears that devices seem "to shanghai a young child's brain. . . . It's not normal for a young child to be undistractible." She takes solace in knowing that with her books, at least, the parent is built into the experience.

"The children are so young, you *have* to read it to them," she says. Unless they're being employed exclusively as a teething toy, they demand interaction.

But even for the teething tool crowd, her books strike a chord. Over her many years of book touring, she's had numerous parents approach her with a tiny kid in their arms, or in a sling, just a few weeks old, and they'll tell her, gushing, "Oh, this book is his absolute favorite!" and Boynton will think, *Um, that child can barely see in front of his face.*

"But then they'll bring out the book and the child will just light up," she says, with wonder. "Even my daughter, she sent me a video of her son—and he's just a few weeks old—responding to one of my books. It's wonderful."

What is the baby responding to? I can't say. Likely not the pictures themselves, or the story, but more that his parent is so engaged and enamored with the text and so badly wants to translate that enjoyment, that all he feels is love.

Before I leave, I ask her about something Ella clicked her way to on one e-book app. Recognizing the cover of *Harold and the Purple Crayon*, she'd tapped on it, which kickstarted a cartoon of the book (which dates, I later learned, to 1959). It's a sweet little film, but presented on an e-book app, where allegedly you're supposed to be reading, not watching, it seems jarringly out of place. Boynton has long referred to its illustrator, Crockett Johnson, as an inspiration, so I ask her what she thinks about a cartoon of *Harold*.

"The irony of that is extraordinary!" she says immediately. "That is the exact opposite of the point of the story, of the creativity, of . . ." She trails off, gobsmacked, then after a beat says, "I'm referring to zero studies, but if you animate it, you're taking away from the experience. If it's static, the child fills in actively around it, and what one child sees could be very different from what another child sees. That's the beauty of a book."

* * *

She may be referring to zero studies, but there are a few out there that illustrate, on a biological level, just how differently children process e-books from print books.

John Hutton, a researcher and the director of the Reading and Literacy Discovery Center at Cincinnati Children's Hospital, was one of the first to put preschoolers through an fMRI to determine what happens in their brains when they're exposed to different forms of books. In one study, he told twenty-seven children ages four and five a story in one of three ways: via a traditional illustrated print book, via audio only, or via an animated e-book. The aim was to determine which format provided the best setup for preschoolers' comprehension, as indicated by optimal integration within and between different networks in the brain—attention, vision, and language. The higher the connectivity, the better the comprehension, the better the brain development.

I can muddle my way through some of it, but most of it reads like it was written by R2D2's Ivy League–educated cousin. To wit: "For animation relative to illustration, FC was lower between DAN-L, VAN-VP, VAN-VI, L-VI, and L-VP, suggesting less focus on narrative, reorienting to imagery and visual-language integration."

When I reach Hutton, who also used to run a children's bookstore with his wife, he patiently, and extremely clearly, breaks down his work for me.

"The layman's term we used was 'the Goldilocks effect,'" he tells me. His study illustrated, on a neurological level, that animation was too hot, audio was too cold, and illustrated print books were just right. In an ideal reading situation, a preschooler will be able to easily shift his attention from the pictures to the words to his own imagination, calling on different neural networks to help him understand what's going on. "There's only so much capacity in the brain to process anything at a given time," he says, "and the illustrated storybook appeared to be the most optimal and balanced way for these different brain networks to work."

The root of understanding what's going on at a neurological

level involves the brain's two attention networks: the Dorsal Attention Network (DAN) and the Ventral Attention Network (VAN).

Hutton likens the DAN to a spotlight: it's whatever you're paying attention to at a given moment—in your case right now, I hope it's the words on this page. The higher the functional connectivity within the DAN, the deeper your focus, the higher your language comprehension, and the better your visual processing abilities. Your DAN capacity is finite—you only have so much focus to give at a given moment, so if you're completely taken with a Monet in the museum, for example, really leaning on your visual network, you might not be able to hear someone calling your name the first few times, which relies on your auditory network.

The VAN acts as the DAN's gatekeeper, determining whether unexpected or distracting stimuli are worth paying attention to or should be ignored. It's what happens when a shiny object flashes at you, or a rabbit tears across a field. The VAN, in effect, directs the DAN to switch, to start paying attention to something else. (If the phone in your pocket has been buzzing about news alerts over the course of the last two paragraphs, you likely have, at best, a fuzzy idea of what you just read, since your VAN keeps redirecting your DAN to pay attention to your pocket.) When it comes to reading, it is the dynamic relationship within and between the VAN, the DAN, and other functional networks—including language, visual imagery, and visual perception—that affects a child's comprehension and, in turn, how well that story helps their brain develop. In an ideal situation, the VAN hands things off to the DAN at just the right time.

What Hutton found clearly demonstrates the Goldilocks effect.

With animation, the VAN got stuck on the visuals. "If the visual stimulus is moving so fast," Hutton says, "and if there's too much going on that's taking up the child's attention, it's hard for them to redirect and focus on the words. There's evidence that this happens when working memory capacity is strained." Too hot.

Audiobooks, lacking pictorial prompts, don't provide enough scaffolding for the kids' brains. Ella likely hadn't known what a mole rat looked like the first few times we read *Naked Mole Rat Gets Dressed*, since naked (or clothed) mole rats don't frequent the Upper West Side of Manhattan. But Mo Willems helpfully illustrated one for her right there on the page. Instead of straining to figure out who the main character was, Ella's brain connected the visuals with the word she heard, and now she understands that mole rats are cute rodents that occasionally wear seersucker suits. Without the illustration, the format is too cold. This explains why it takes until Ella is almost three for her to focus on the stories we make up for her at bedtime, with the lights off. We try when she's two or so, and she simply can't stay engrossed long enough for us to get past the first few sentences—she needs a physical object, an illustration, to ground her. She gets there, eventually, but in the younger years, a picture is critical. Those static pictures allow the brain to fire on all circuits, calling on each network at just the right speed, like a little choreographed ballet.

"During a story, there's a lot of dynamic switching that goes on," Hutton says. "There's *I'm listening to Grandma say these words*, and then *I look at the picture because she just said 'rabbit,'* and *I'm looking at the rabbit and starting to think, 'Okay, the rabbit could hop across the field; let's imagine that,'* then I *think 'Wow, I like rabbits!'* Picture books are slow enough that they allow the child to process all of this in a cohesive way."

Hutton points to a single, stark indicator of how far downhill we've come when talking about children's ability to focus: picture books from the 1970s. "They were really long," he tells me with a sigh. "Now they're not." Just look at the unabridged *Babar* books—they're hefty.

The issue with e-books, even without animation, is the occasional bell or whistle—"If a child keeps seeing bells and whistles, they're going to have that much less time to think, *Wow, I like dogs*"—and the format itself. E-books are often read on tablets, which, in addition to offering limited snuggle affordances, are little portable pads of distraction, with emails and news alerts popping up at frequent intervals. "We, as humans, aren't very good at staying on task in general—grown-ups, too," he says.

So for Hutton, the physical book remains a tool that's hard to improve on.

"If in the first two years the most important thing for a child to learn is, *My grown-up loves me and I'm valued and safe and connected*, then an analog book that brings them together in a really focused way is pretty perfect," he says. "If preschoolers are supposed to be developing their imaginations, and bringing their own cognitive resources to imagining what's going on in a story, then it's pretty perfect." He pauses. "In the first year, you can likely read anything—*War and Peace*, the phone book, *Goodnight Moon*. It's about showing up and spending time with your child."

When he says this, I remember one of Ella's favorite board books for a couple-month stretch: *Eating the Alphabet*, an illustrated alphabet book that starts with *apple* and ends with *zucchini*. There's no narrative, just illustrations and labeling. Every time we'd reach *X*, with its single illustration—of a *xigua*, which I now know, after googling, is a watermelon cousin—I'd gaze at Ella and wonder, *Why on earth do you want to read about xiguas before bed? Why not a story with a beginning, middle, and end, that preferably ends in someone going to sleep?* If androids dream of electric sheep, did Ella dream of xigua, and if so, was that a good thing? Now it seems I was asking the wrong questions.

* * *

I hop off my call with Hutton and spend the next month casually dropping into conversation tidbits about my DAN and VAN. My smug-o-meter measures in the high thousands.

But after speaking with Dr. Barry Zuckerman, who contextualizes all the DAN and VAN excitement for me, I'm brought down a few pegs. He's a professor of pediatrics at Boston University School of Medicine and a founder of Reach Out and Read, a program in which pediatricians give children a book at each pediatric visit and encourage their parents to read to them. Started with a single site at Boston City Hospital in 1989, it now boasts over six thousand programs in the United States, having distributed an estimated seven million books to 4.8 million children. It's a simple, high-touch way to reach families, since in the early years, parents and children find themselves at the pediatrician's office quite a bit.

It's not that Zuckerman doesn't see the value in Hutton's work; he allows that the work is "theoretically sound." But he cautions me not to put *too* much stock in it: not only were Hutton's sample and magnitude of difference small, but what he did was, in effect, illustrate that there are differences in brain wave functionality when you show a child a book on different mediums. How much you can extrapolate from that is an open question. Changes in the brain indicate . . . changes in the brain, Zuckerman tells me. Many factors go into those changes, so all you can for sure take away from Hutton's work is that the brain is affected in some way.

The extrapolation I've done seems to be part and parcel of my status as a layperson who views biologic changes—especially those occurring in the brain—as gospel.

"Who wants to read a study of *Oh, I made an observation*?" Zuckerman asks. "But if you show the brain is different, it's, *Oh my gosh!*"

Then Zuckerman echoes something Rosemarie Truglio told me back at Sesame: "It doesn't matter if you can't measure it. It still may be there." In other words, even though you can document a biologic change in the brain with hard numbers and graphs, that doesn't necessarily make it more powerful data than simply observing how a child responds to a print book. It's yet another indication that I should continue to approach the blaring headlines I keep reading with a healthy dose of skepticism, however much they're rooted in science.

As someone who's testified before state legislatures and uses his work to drive public policy, Zuckerman recognizes the potential, however misguided, of pushing the biologic message over the observational.

"They want to do things for a child's brain," he says, wearily, of legislatures and society, writ large. "Biology drives public attention. God forbid you do something because we know it's important."

Take fetal alcohol syndrome.

"It's pretty rare, even among alcoholics," he tells me. "You have to really drink heavily for many, many years. What about mothers who start drinking after the pregnancy, and the child who has to live in a house with an alcoholic mother? But that never gets attention. It was the biologic impact on the baby in utero that made a public impact."

How this relates to reading, for Zuckerman, is simple. He's spent decades seeing, firsthand, the effect of giving a child a print book.

"If I was going to approach some cutting-edge tech people and say, *Create an app that is going to stimulate a young child's cognitive development, fine motor skills, and emotional development,* they'd make me a book," he tells me. Studies indicate not only that parents in the Reach Out and Read network are 2.5 times more likely to read to their children but that doing so improves their children's language development by three to six months.

He reminds me that for the first few years, the term *reading* can be understood flexibly. But he assures me that even if the book's appeal is more oral than aural, Baby Charlotte's interest in literature is important. It's her way of interacting with it, showing her interest, and, above all, learning to associate reading with warm, comforting moments spent squirming and drooling on my lap.

"Reading with an adult is a shared experience, and that's what makes it powerful," Zuckerman says. "It's a matter of joint attention—both the mother and baby can pay attention to it at the same time. The book is nothing more than a tool to create enjoyable interactions. And the way the tablet is set up, the relationship is between the child and the screen. The next generation will figure out how to include the parent, but we haven't yet."

Before he signs off, he points out another benefit to reading a print book. "It's probably the only unhurried time during the day. It's hard to speed-read a book with a child—the child is just not going to be engaged." Put that experience on a tablet, which is used for so many other hurried moments, and you just about destroy that opportunity.

* * *

One winter evening before Sunday dinner when Ella is three years old, I am lying on her bed reading a cookbook, the longest prose greater than a tweet I can manage at the time. After an elaborate flurry of packing for an imaginary trip to Chicago, where she's never been—in her luggage: two swim suits, four changes of clothes for her baby doll, and a kazoo—she pulls out Monopoly and asks me to play, by which she means roll the dice and move the wheelbarrow ahead as many spaces as she wants.

"I'm reading, sweetie; in a little bit," I tell her.

"You're not *really* reading," she counters, looking up.

Oh?

"You're just *looking*," she continues, "like I do with books when you and Daddy aren't here. When you're *reading* you say the words. Out loud."

"Just 'cause I'm not speaking out loud doesn't mean I'm not reading," I tell her. "When you learn to read yourself, you'll hear the words in your head, so you won't have to say them out loud."

"Oh, *sure*," she says, like I've just informed her that affixing an aluminum foil hat to your head will ward off alien beams.

Ella is just starting to recognize letters, her name, a few words here or there. We're still firmly in the learning-to-love-reading phase but are inching ever nearer to the learning-to-read phase.

So, the next morning, replenished after a 9:00 p.m. bedtime, I pick up *Proust and the Squid*, a book that is part biology, part philosophy, part call to arms. Written by Maryanne Wolf, a professor of child development at Tufts University and the director of the school's Center for Reading and Language Research, the book chronicles the history and mechanics of reading. In one fascinating section set off in italics, Wolf details the technical processes that allow you to read, process, and understand a sentence, from millisecond to millisecond.

Okay.

Read this sentence.

No, this one.

Okay, so what you just did—and what you are doing *right now*—is nothing short of astonishing.

The first thing to understand about the miracle of reading is that while things like vision and spoken language are preprogrammed in the brain's circuitry—you don't have to work to learn how to babble or see; it's just in your genes—the ability to read is not. Every kid who ever picks up a book has to start from scratch, using his or her innate abilities to create a new skill. It's arguably one of the hardest things they'll do in their first few years of life.

As Wolf writes, "Reading depends on the brain's ability to connect and integrate various sources of information—specifically, visual with auditory, linguistic and conceptual areas. This integration depends on the maturation of each of the individual regions, their association areas, and the speed with which these regions can be connected and integrated." Generally, by about age five, all of that should be working up to speed, at which point readers can begin their journey of haltingly stringing words together and reading to themselves. But it all starts on a loved one's lap, in moments that forge the interest in figuring out this hard task.

At the level of the alphabet, before enough practice yields automatic recognition, neurons that deal with visual cues need to develop into "specialists," so they can detect every unique stroke and curve of a letter—the difference between an *I* and a *T* is minuscule unless you've been trained to see it. At the level of a word, consider this: every time you read one, your brain cycles through every possible meaning of that word in an instant. Wolf uses the example of *bug*. Out of context, what did you think of? A bug that was crawling around on a leaf? A bug in your computer? A virus that your kid just picked up at school? A cute little VW beetle with a Grateful Dead banner hanging in the back window? The thing is, your brain activated every one of those, even if you didn't realize it. Which, when you think about it, is amazing: you read *bug* in a sentence and your brain is able to use context clues to pick the correct meaning.

And while you may think that your eye is moving seamlessly along this sentence, from left to right, what's actually happening is far more complex. It's worth including Wolf's description in its entirety here:

> *Our eyes continually make small movements called saccades, followed by very brief moments when the eyes are almost stopped, called fixations, while we gather information from our central (foveal) vision. At least 10 percent of the time, our eyes dart back ever so slightly in regressions to pick up past*

information. When adults read, the typical saccade covers about eight letters; for children it is less. One brilliant design feature of our eyes allows us to see "ahead" in a parafoveal region and still farther along the line of text into the peripheral region. We now know that when we read in English, we actually see about fourteen or fifteen letters to the right of our fixed focus. . . . Because we use foveal and parafoveal information, we always have a preview of what lies ahead. The preview then becomes, milliseconds later, easier to recognize, contributing further to our automaticity.

Understanding how many discrete mechanisms are needed to connect in just the right way, such that the sentence "I squashed a bug under my foot" elicits the image of a shoe stepping on an ant and not a giant boot stepping on a Volkswagen, makes clear to me, even at this very basic level, that any additional information must be sprinkled into the reading process *very* carefully, if at all—particularly as children are nearing the age when they're starting to develop the tools to read solo. The act of reading requires an enormous amount of concentration. Why would you ever risk distracting a novice reader with highlighted words or animations?

I email Wolf to ask her about Ella's tendency to fill in words from her favorite books, which is clearly a result of memorization, not actually sounding out words. "It can become a scaffolding," she allows, "but always best later on to give systematic explicit teaching about how letters and sounds work together." In other words, having memorized a passage of a favorite book may help children as they stumble through the first few stages of learning to read, but the work of explicit teaching is still necessary.

Wolf's book was published in 2007, but even then she was concerned with how technology might affect our capacity not to decode sentences but to access the deeper, more sophisticated knowledge activated by the deliberate, often all-consuming act of getting absorbed in a book. Will learning to read snippets on a screen somehow wire the brain differently and, the implication is, more poorly? She peppers the book with questions, often grouped together in a relentless rat-tat-tat of fears and premonitions: "Will modern curiosity be sated by the flood of pat, often superficial information on a screen, or will it lead to a desire for more in-depth knowledge? Can a deep examination of words, thoughts, reality, and virtue flourish in learning characterized by continuous partial attention and multitasking? Can the sense of a word, a thing, or a concept retain importance when so much learning occurs in thirty-second segments on a moving screen? Will children inured by ever more realistic images of the world around them have a less practiced imagination?"

Instinctively, I'd answer those last three with a no, no, yes, and jury's out on the first. In her latest book, *Reader, Come Home*, published in 2018, which grapples with the effect of technology on reading, she posits a fascinating hypothesis (which my own behavior seems to play out) regarding the question of why, as studies have shown, children remember fewer details about stories when they read them on-screen and more when they read them in print.

"There may be an incremental diminishment of the use of working memory for children due to what they perceive as the impossibility of trying to remember all the information typically presented on a screen that often moves on," she writes. "Because children so often associate screens with TV and movies, the question emerges whether their perception of what is presented on a tablet or computer screen is being processed unconsciously like film, thus making the many details and different stimuli on the screen appear impossible to remember."

There's just something about reading on a screen that *feels* different to me, that causes me to skim for information and occasionally break to check my email.

This lack of ability to focus, says Sean Palfrey, one Harvard pediatrician I consult, is visible even in the books children do read today, in whatever form.

"It's quite clear to me that even *Harry Potter*, which is a good, well-written story, uses about a third of the vocabulary of *Treasure Island*," he says. The ramifications? "You can get along and be very smart and technically innovative without having a complex vocabulary or knowledge. But what is lost there is the ability to think critically. You need vocabulary in order to express yourself and you need to understand complex vocabulary in order to understand more complex thinking."

I speak to some people—scientists and psychologists and historians—who warn me that we're so early on in this experiment, we might be wildly off. Maybe my brain's circuitry is screwed, but Ella, who will grow up immersed in technology, is in fact forming ever new circuitry that will help her think more deeply and faster than I could ever imagine. Brains are plastic. But that doesn't feel quite right to me. I come across one stat that indicates that kids, perhaps, are naturally inclined toward a physical book over a digital one. Scholastic conducted a survey in 2018 and found that 69 percent of children ages six to seventeen reportedly preferred print books to e-books, and 59 percent of those who had read e-books in the previous year reported preferring print books. Maybe they're responding to the fact that e-books have not yet reached their technological potential. Perhaps they're responding to the fact that all the hot spots and doodads are making their brains feel like Doc Brown's in the clock-tower scene of *Back to the Future*.

What I do know is that years and years of research show that reading a print book to a child is certainly not a *bad* way to spend one's time. In order to give Ella the proven benefits of reading, in order to set her up to be successful in life, all I have to do is something that happens to already be particularly pleasurable for me. Parents will do most anything to help their children excel, including but not limited to enduring years of sleeplessness; having dramatically fewer social engagements with people who are old enough to tie their shoes on their own; and pausing their own careers. All I have to do is crack open a book, snuggle in, and read.

Conclusion

The room is still dark when I feel Baby, the Nutcracker, and Ella's favorite pillow sail in quick succession onto the bed, announcing her arrival and the end to whatever semblance of uninterrupted rest our family of four is getting tonight. I've been going to bed earlier and earlier to combat this new reality, which I keep telling myself is a phase (though when do phases end?). What used to be 10:30 p.m. inched to 10:00 p.m., then 9:30 p.m., then 9:00 p.m., and one night, 8:30 p.m.—a bedtime I haven't kept since velcroed shoes were an un-hipster fashion choice. It doesn't do much for my social life, but it keeps me relatively sane.

As I swim up out of a dream, the bed shudders. Ella has hooked a foot on the frame. After a moment of intense, audible exertion, like a free soloist during the last heave over the mountaintop, she's flat on her back next to me, breathing hotly in my ear.

"Mama, is it morning yet?" she stage whispers. Baby Charlotte, now almost a year old, starts up a slow moan from the depths of her Pack 'n Play, where she's been sleeping on the same elevation as the dust bunnies for months. We valiantly tried to get them into the same room, Charlotte in the crib and Ella in her daybed, but then Charlotte started teething, and Ella started her middle-of-the-night pilgrimages, and this solution somehow seemed best. Of course, it isn't. I haven't been able to turn on my bedside table lamp after 6:30 p.m. for months. Dave and I spend our nights whispering through dinner, ears piqued for a yelp from upstairs. I put on my pajamas in the dark. And any hope at intimacy has to withstand the occasional pterodactyl squawk from the right side of the bed. But the American Academy of Pediatrics advises sleeping in the same room with your infant until she's a year old, so as Charlotte inches past her eleven-month birthday, I guess I can chalk this up to being a safety measure and not a result of general disorganization and minimal square footage.

I nudge Dave, who squints at the glow of his Apple Watch.

"Five fifty," he says, then sharply inhales and curls into a ball as Ella bounds over him to hang off the bed and dangle her head into the Pack 'n Play.

"Hi, chicken noodle!" she crows to her biggest fan, who's now fully awake, wildly grinning and clapping in her honor. A beat later, Dave exhales and wheezes out, "Right in the balls."

The OK to Wake! clock is sitting on Ella's windowsill, a useless relic from a lost time. At CES 2020, I had come across a newfangled iteration—this one with a secret treat drawer that opens only at a prespecified time, turning our children into Pavlov's puppies—but never purchased it, having given up on the idea that a clock or any device might impose order on the condition of living with two children under the age of four. Although one venture capitalist I interviewed, who invested in the SNOO early on, lauded the potential of data collection to ease these predawn wake-ups with two kiddos—"If you have two children in one room, and one is crying and waking the other up, and it's a clusterfuck? *That's* where baby tech needs to go!"—in this particular moment, I'm not sure how Dr. Karp can help us, short of buying me a third, soundproof, bedroom.

* * *

A few weeks prior to that morning, Governor Andrew Cuomo had shut down New York in an attempt to quell the voracious spread of the COVID-19 pandemic. The world heaved on its axis. Holed up in our apartment, muddling through as best we could, I wondered if technology—which, with the help of the experts I'd interviewed, I'd come to regard with a wary acceptance—would rise from the ashes of the pandemic as a savior for children. In the first few days of quarantine, with people going stir-crazy and trying to impose order on the madness of their new lives, I received countless links to preschool enrichment classes—livestreamed and virtual ballet, story times, arts and crafts step-by-steps, kids' cooking hours, *Moana* yoga, and on and on. Like everyone, I was so overwhelmed I could barely manage to get my work done and all of us washed and fed before falling face-first into bed, where I clutched my phone and read increasingly panicky news stories about how I was living in the center of the storm. Coming up with a schedule for Ella and sticking with it—*kids thrive on routine!*, all the advice shouted at me—seemed almost as impossible as squaring the world outside with the world I'd known.

My concerns of the year before—Was I taking too many photos of her? Relying too much on social media? Buying too much online?—receded. My parents, now quarantined in their apartment eight blocks away and unable to see the girls, delighted in the photos I shared to our stream each day—I couldn't take enough. Starved for social connection, I restarted my daily visits to Instagram. And I couldn't go to the store anymore, so I unabashedly started to rely on e-commerce to feed and clothe my family. There seemed no other option than to buy into Parentech hook, line, and sinker.

As for Ella, technology became a daily requirement. A few weeks into our new normal, Ella's preschool started conducting Zoom meetings each morning, a little half-hour dose of dystopian reality to kickstart our days. I found myself, more than once, willing the little squares of far-flung friends to cohere into one large friendly face, like a Magic Eye puzzle. Ella spent most of the first session in my lap, turned away from the camera and whimpering that she didn't want to "do school." One classmate called in from what appeared to be an all-white, all-leather dungeon with no natural light and fancy stairs leading up to somewhere, no parents to be seen. Caroline, Ella's best friend, left for quite some time and then reappeared with something (or, rather, someone) in her lap. Two ears popped up at the bottom of her screen. I asked Ella who it was, and she peeked quickly and then turned back to me, burying her head in my neck and whispering, matter-of-factly, "Lamby." Will occasionally dropped out of the screen entirely, presumably because he'd fallen off the couch. I knew, after delving into the science, that none of this was particularly bad for Ella—the American Academy of Pediatrics allows that FaceTime is fine even for very young children, and what is Zoom except for one vast group FaceTime?—but the notion that Ella was really learning what she needed to learn at her age, via a screen, was laughable. What she needed more than ever was physical activity and social interaction—with kids her own age, fine, but with a human more importantly. And that wasn't going to happen through a screen.

Did she watch more movies than usual? Pack in more cartoons before weekend breakfasts? Of course. My husband and I were still working full-time from home and had another full human to tend to. We FaceTimed with friends. We baked cookies. We read and drew a lot. We did outdoor scooting, steering clear of playgrounds and other people. We watched musicals together, and for a stretch, I came across Ella singing, under her breath, *"I'm just a girl who cain't say 'No.'"* We managed, and technology helped us manage.

As the months stretch on in self-quarantine, I am grateful for, among so many other things, the researchers who've hammered home that for young children, particularly the preschool set, free play and imagination and even boredom are the best activities to fill the day. Maurice Sendak, I learn in a Terry Gross interview, was often sick as child, so he spent his days staring out a window. And in that window, stories bloomed. Ella idly coloring or pretending to be Baby's mother in a magic fort, I now know, is key to helping her grow into the resilient, creative, smart kid I want her to be. Sitting her in front of an online class surely is a welcome distraction whenever I get my act together, but, armed with my year-plus of research, I now no longer feel worried that if I don't constantly and actively enrich her, she'll fail at life. Leaving her to her own devices for hours is, actually, a beneficial thing. (How lucky I am to have a child young enough that this remains true. I look, in awe, at full-time working parents of school-age kids who've had to become teachers overnight.)

And as we bake, and color, and play pretend, and muddle through, it dawns on me that, after all this time spent washed in nostalgia for a purer, more analog time of child-rearing, here I am, inching ever closer to the role of Ma on the prairie. The only thing missing is the gophers.

* * *

As Charlotte's squawks get more urgent, Dave gingerly steps out of bed and lifts her up, kissing under her cheek rolls until she giggles, a sound that's a balm to an ungodly early hour made exclusively for parents like us, bakers, and Diane Sawyer. And then there are four of us in bed, Ella's feet up by my chin, Charlotte courageously navigating the mountainous terrain of pillows and limbs to find her way to breakfast. I'm pretty certain I've been in some state of semi-awakeness since the previous day at 3:00 a.m., due to a spinning brain and a cough I worryingly can't kick, but I try to remind myself that, one day, my children will be embarrassed by my very existence and I should do my best to embrace this moment, if I can.

It's a mindset shift that has been hard won, developed painstakingly and slowly over the past year of research. And it's likely due to the women I interviewed—Ellen Langer, Kathy Hirsh-Pasek, Jenny Radesky, Nancy Carlsson-Paige, Deborah Carlisle Solomon, among others—all of whom said, in various permutations, that friction is not only part of parenting but also important and beneficial to both parties. Embrace the middle-of-the-night wake-ups, the tantrums, the fourteen minutes it takes to choose a sock, and you'll become the kind of parent who really knows your child, who can help prepare her to thrive in a brave new technology-fueled world we are only beginning to understand. While I thought I'd been writing about how to navigate the technology-bombarded world of parenting, in fact, I'd been exploring what it means to be a parent and how to raise a human I actually want to hang out with. Friction and discomfort are all part of that process.

A friend who is not a parent read over an early version of this manuscript. In the margins of one page, where I was wrestling with putting Ella in front of a television in the predawn hours, she wrote, "Does anyone get up at 6:00 a.m. and hand their kid a block? Or is that an oppressive expectation?" The answer is, people don't get up at 6:00 a.m. and hand their kid a block because it's harder. It takes more work. The kid has to learn how to engage with the block. Placing them in front of a screen that sucks them in means that I, as a parent, can have time back for myself—it makes things easier for *me*. One of the biggest revelations I've had, poring over history books and chatting with experts, is that when I'd been obsessing over whether various technologies help Ella actively learn and grow, I'd missed a huge part: I, the parent, also have to actively learn and actively grow. Perhaps I have to do that even more than Ella does. Children by and large just . . . grow up. Parents are the ones who have to recalibrate their mindset, have to internalize that their needs no longer come first, have to recognize that, even though sitting on the floor in the early morning hours with a block and a toddler might be tedious and draining, it also might be the most important way to spend that moment. Growing up, for me, means finding beauty in playing with a block on Ella's floor when I am so tired I'd rather curl up in a ball and suck my thumb. I might not always be able to find that beauty, but I need to strive to find it.

As Charlotte locates my boob and, with a razor-sharp set of fingernails, pulls down my tank top, I blearily remember something David Rose told me during a conversation months before. He's a "Futurist" (his actual LinkedIn title) who worked for years at the MIT Media Lab and has spent his career envisioning and creating the world of the future, wondering what it would be like if your living room lights responded to a gesture (bring your hand up, make them brighter) and building smart gadgets like an umbrella that can nudge you to take it along on a rainy day (connected to a weather app, his Ambient Umbrella glows whenever rain is in the forecast).

"There's a role in Japanese culture of someone who is more senior but takes a back seat, a circumscribed role that lets the person-in-training take the lead," he said. He likes to exercise on a Peloton-esque rowing machine—a coach sits on the water in a screen in front of him, guiding him through his workout. He asked me to imagine a world in which everyone has "a constellation of coaches"—one to help you stay fit, one to help you get dressed in the morning, and so on. He likened this model of service to *Downton Abbey*—specific helpers for specific tasks. Combine that with the trend of putting ever cheaper and smaller cameras into everything, from your oven to your doorbell to your fridge, and the subsequent ability to analyze millions upon millions of hours of footage, and you've got the makings of a team of personal, virtual parenting coaches.

"Maybe there would be an app that has rules that help you look at how you're disciplining your child," Rose wondered aloud during our phone call, then changed into a slightly cooler, calmer, robotic voice. *"Maybe what would be better here is a point-based reward system. I've seen where the kid escalates and the parent escalates and that's not a great parenting pattern.* The idea of people watching and coaching seems incredibly intrusive, but maybe it's useful. You'll get actionable tips that are distilled for just the right amount of attention." Later, he admitted, "You may want to turn them down, say *I'd rather not have any parenting assistance for this year*, and I think good coaches will get out of the way. But other people really want guidance."

I posited that a supersmart virtual parenting coach might take a back-seat role *most* of the time, maybe even *all* of the time. Rose thought for a moment, long enough that I wasn't sure he was still on the line. Finally, he said, "One of the problems I have with a lot of these start-ups I see that are hoping to make our lives seamless and utopian is that they don't acknowledge that that's what's interesting in life sometimes—that friction, that drama, that dramatic tension. It's why we travel, why we seek out adventure and nature, why we climb mountains." He paused again, during which I thought, *and have kids.* "It brings us closer."

Would I want a virtual assistant that could coach me through keeping my kids in bed for another hour? Maybe. But at the expense of closeness? Likely not.

As Charlotte noisily finishes up one side and switches over to the other, Ella snuggles in next to her, making a sort of Charlotte sandwich, then sweetly reaches around for my hand. For a brief, blissful moment, I feel like Gaea, mother of the earth, cocooning and nurturing my young in a warm, cozy, protected womb. All is quiet, all is soft, all is warm, my pose ancient and vaguely animalistic, a doe curled around her fawns. Technology has no place in this moment; of that I am certain.

Then Ella sneezes loudly and a startled Charlotte pops off, sputtering milk and jolting me back to reality. I look to my bedside table in search of a baby wipe, but the container is empty. Thank god a shipment is en route, to be delivered later that day.

* * *

While I get the heebie-jeebies envisioning a world where virtual assistants are the norm and the lack of everyday privacy a foregone conclusion, I am no longer as anxious about how technology is transforming my role as a mother or my girls' experience as children. I owe that largely to Alison Gopnik, the developmental psychologist who wrote *The Gardener and the Carpenter.* Her calming peripheral presence in the first few years of my parenting journey, as I reread her books and relistened to her podcasts, prompts me to reach out once I've gotten into the semi-swing of being a mother of two. She invites me to her lab in Berkeley before the pandemic—a hop, skip, and a jump away from where much of the technology that is my focal point is being conceived of and rolled out to an innocent world.

Before getting on the plane, I seriously consider brushing up on my Hume. Gopnik is such a fierce intellect and her books so thoughtful and deep, but all my brain cells have been rerouted to figuring out a single problem, a maternal variant on the fox, chicken, and egg riddle: How many pump parts are the fewest needed for a thirty-six-hour trip involving a three-hour time difference, access to two washing stations in between pumping sessions, and one freezer bag that only holds six 8 oz. milk bags comfortably? So, I wing it.

As a developmental psychologist who deals with big timelines—

like, human evolution–grade timelines—Gopnik comes across as decidedly unimpressed with my generation's techno hysteria, if only because she's lived long enough to have seen her own generation's come full circle.

"I was listening to Tristan Harris the other day"—an ex-Google employee who's now a vocal critic of the unregulated power of Big Tech—"and he was saying, 'Look, you know how terrible this is? Kids aren't even sitting on Saturday morning and watching cartoons anymore!'" she says, sucking on a Ricola outside her office. "And I'm thinking, *My God, I spent years of my parenting worrying about my children sitting and watching Saturday morning cartoons!*"

While she posits that this hysteria might be rooted in economics—parents are panicked they'll drop out of the middle class, so, using childhood and parenting as a proxy for that anxiety, they obsess over educational attainment—she succinctly places it on the evolutionary spectrum: "There's nothing about this round that is unique or disruptive or dangerous in some deep, profound way that makes it different from all other rounds." Our job, as has been the job of each generation, is to figure out how to handle it.

After a rollicking discussion that pings from the French Revolution to carpentry to her grandson, Augie, we land on the topic of circuit breakers. Without them, electrified houses burn down at a more frequent rate. So years ago, insurance companies, eager to protect themselves from having to shell out cash, started mandating that homeowners install or update them. Now standard in all insured houses, they're a nice metaphor for our current predicament.

"The people in the insurance company said, *Wait a minute, this is a disaster; we're losing all this money with the incredibly dangerous technology!"* she says, meaning electricity. *"We're going to have a code that says you need circuit breakers.* When cars started, there weren't any traffic laws. It's the regulation that makes the technology work in the world at large. And we're at a state now where for a lot of these technologies, we have to work out what the code is going to be."

There's no regulatory framework for the App Store, so parents find themselves adrift in stamps of quality that might as well be meaningless, adrift in a consumer culture that promotes buying but does not regulate products' claims. As of this printing, there's no perfect way to monitor what children can view on YouTube. There's no real understanding about how children's data can or should be used. We're at an inflection point.

"It's not going to appear from the regulation fairy," Gopnik says. "It's going to have to happen at a broad societal level and also at the individual level of a particular family. That's one of the things families do: write code for their kids."

She brings up a Bay Area filmmaker and founder of the Webby Awards, Tiffany Shlain, who institutes a "technology shabbat" in her house—no devices for twenty-four hours, from sundown Friday to sundown Saturday. That's a norm Gopnik likes. As another example, she offers up the norm of her childhood dinners: no books at the table.

"I grew up in a family of writers and readers," she reminds me, "and if we'd been able to just bring all of our books to the dining table, everyone would have sat by themselves reading." I briefly consider that if I ban books from our dining room table, Ella and Charlotte will also grow up to be preeminent members of the intelligentsia, then remember how much easier it is to feed

Ella dinner with *The Naked Mole Rat Gets Dressed* nearby to ward off broccoli refusals. Our norms will have to be different, but I'm on board with Gopnik: figure out your values and do your best to instill them at a family level, as you wait for the world to catch up.

Toward the end of our interview, Gopnik brings up a concept she speaks and writes about frequently, the explore-exploit trade-off. Childhood is meant for exploration, for opening up one's mind to all the details of a given situation (trying on all the socks in the drawer). It's a period during with our brains grow enormously, and a period unique to humans in its length—other mammals don't have nearly as long a time to romp around and play. When we grow up, we exploit the information we have in order to accomplish a task as efficiently as possible (pick the unicorn socks because they're awesome). Our lives are lived in the constant tension of exploring and exploiting.

"But I think there's actually a tripartite description of the things you have to do to be effective—you have to explore and you have to exploit and you have to *care*," she says. "And caring is, *My role is to serve somebody else who's exploring and exploiting, and to design a framework in which it's possible for them to be able to do that.* From an evolutionary perspective, it's really central to being able to exist." If you can't care, you aren't, in a sense, a full person.

This irks Gopnik, this dismissal of the importance of caregiving. It seems even more clear to her now that she is a grandmother herself.

"When a baby is born, you have no idea of what their characteristics are, but suddenly it's the most important, interesting, amazing thing in the world," she says. "And the way we typically interpret that is, *Well, it's an illusion. It's your hormones or something.* And I think it's just the opposite. That's the only time when you actually really appreciate human beings the way that you should appreciate human beings. It's the only time when you really are recognizing what is in fact true, which is that every single one of those human beings is just that valuable intrinsically no matter what their features and characteristics are. And the only time you see that is when you care." She pauses. "It isn't just about, *Well, if I care for this person, then I can make them come out to be a productive individual.* There's something much deeper about it. It's intrinsically important to care."

My conversation with Gopnik helps me find what I have been seeking for so long—a unifying theory of technology and how it might be used in child-rearing: Does the tech help you care? Soothe a child who is fussy? Buy yourself some much-needed time? Impose some sort of order to the data you think you should be tracking, the memories you want to file away, the minutiae of keeping a household running as you raise the youngest members of our society to thrive? Or does it act as a Band-Aid, an easy fix to a single moment—instead of using those moments to build a deep foundation of love and trust (convenience be damned)?

Some of us really do find calm and joy in tracking our children's height and weight, memorializing their every moment, equipping them with the latest and greatest gadgetry, giving them curricular education before they are old enough to know what a curriculum is. Can the Nanit help you get a few more hours of sleep per night? Perhaps. Can watching Cookie Monster refrain from cookie eating help our kids learn self-regulation skills? Perhaps. But the gadgetry, the enrichment, the enhancements layered upon our everyday, they've started to remind me a bit of running. My dad, not the most willing exerciser, used to joke that the amount of time you spend running extends your life for precisely that long. In the minutes we spend obsessing over that child-related data, we're not actually spending time with our children. We're focusing on the noise of it all, the anxiety of how we're supposed to optimize caring for them, and not the signal, which is simply the act of caring. Parents have been caring since the dawn of humanity. Deep down, surely we know how to do it just fine, without Silicon Valley disrupting it for us.

As for the minutes we throw them in front of a screen so we can take a break? Sure, take the break. Calm them down if they're in a bad spot. (Ella got a particularly bad case of the flu, piggybacked on a non-flu virus. The poor kid was sick for ten straight days, with fevers that spiked to 103.5 each afternoon and evening. Did she watch *Frozen* once, sometimes twice, a day? Yes.) But let's not do it in the name of enrichment. Know that if we can teach them that more magic exists in their imagination than on a screen, that's where the secret sauce gets made.

Will the technology change rapidly over the course of the next few years? No doubt. Will new and improved devices hit the market that take into account the concerns raised by the experts I interviewed, ranging from the inability to co-engage with your child on a small screen to the distractions of added doodads to e-books? For sure. Will those ever do more for your child than a few analog blocks and your love and attention? Likely, no. And that, I hope, can be a source of immense calm for parents as they continue to navigate the new products, the screaming headlines, the guilt, the drumbeat that they can improve their child if they only buy the right gadget or toy. The gold standard—spending time with your children and playing and reading and talking with them—may be tedious on some days, and near impossible on others, but it sure is a straightforward directive. Sprinkle in technology as needed, but aim for it to be just that: a sprinkle.

As for the promise of technology to level the playing field, the jury is still out. I speak to Susan Neuman, the former US assistant secretary of education and a professor at NYU, about an app she studied called *Homer*, which bills itself as "the proven learn-to-read program powered by your child's passions." I'm curious to understand whether the word *proven* is backed up by data or just slick marketing jargon. She tells me that after conducting a randomized controlled trial with three- to five-year-olds—the ideal age group for academic trials—she saw real positive changes in the children's print knowledge, phonological awareness, and letter sounds.

She has spent lots of time in Head Start classrooms observing teachers and sees the app as a way to help children who might not be getting proper instruction.

"You can do professional development until the cows come home," she says, "but if your articulation is not clear, you've got problems. In other words, if *pin* and *pen* sound the same to you, you're not easily going to be able to convey that difference to kids." Put the kids in front of a scripted, controlled app, and *pin* and *pen* will always be pronounced perfectly.

But that is, at best, a stopgap measure, a Band-Aid over the gushing wound that is our public education system. What we need are teachers who are supported and equipped with enough tools to help our youngest people learn and thrive. Employ technology where it can help, but don't let the smoke and mirrors distract from the much bigger problem: society needs to help parents and children more, show them more empathy, deploy more resources in their direction. Just as Gopnik told me that it's intrinsically important for one person to care for another, it's imperative that society care for the youngest among us and those most closely connected to their upbringing: their parents. Until society catches up, it falls to us parents to bumble along alone, find our villages wherever we can, make do with what we've got, and hope that our individual decisions, however small they may feel—turning off the television during dinner, shutting the phone away in a closet, not downloading a baby-related app— are the right ones for our families. Our choices, however futile they may seem, can influence Big Tech. Perhaps by the time our children become the next generation of parents, American society and technology will have evolved to genuinely help them parent and provide every child with an opportunity to succeed. Here's to hopin'.

* * *

Milk pooled in her neck crease, Charlotte finishes her second course and pops up, a little prairie dog waiting for her post-prandial activity.

I nudge Dave.

"Six twenty-six," he croaks.

Oy. There's a moment of silence, and then Ella, sensing that the day is finally beginning, pipes up, "Mama, let's build a fort!"

I could give her my phone, set her in front of the television, buy myself another few minutes. But I think about a date far off in the future, when she's eight or nine or thirteen or fourteen, when I'm home alone with a room full of Magna-Tiles and no one to build with, and she's off zipping around the city on her personal jet-pack, communicating to friends via hologram projections and leaning on virtual coaches to help her navigate social hiccups at school. I am exhausted, but I can sleep in my empty house full of Magna-Tiles in a few years, I figure.

So I hand Charlotte off to Dave, heave my legs over the side of the bed, take Ella's hand, and stagger off. As we turn in to her room, there, glowing green on the windowsill to greet us, is the OK to Wake! clock.

"Look, Mama!" Ella crows. "It's morning!"

And so it is.

Acknowledgments

The common understanding is that writing is a lonely profession, and writing a book a particularly lonely process. While I did spend hours looking at a blinking cursor, second-guessing sentences the moment I'd written them, and wondering just how I'd ever get to the finish line, I never, ever felt lonely. And for this, I know exactly whom to thank.

Yaran Noti: should every writer be so lucky to have a friend like you. The germ for this book began as a series of low-stakes writing exchanges between the two of us, and without your whip-smart editing, endless patience, and relentless encouragement—in the form of walks in the park, nonstop text messages, myriad email chains, and a constant willingness to read yet another draft of the same damn chapter—this book quite simply would not have happened. I'm so happy to have you in my life, so grateful for your friendship, and forever thankful that you were such a gracious, and sharp, first reader.

To the close friends who provided emotional support, and

then got their hands dirty reading chapters, thank you, thank you, thank you. Talia Kaden, you read this while eight months pregnant with your third child—and during the early days of a worldwide pandemic, no less. You were, and remain, an inspiration. Leticia Landa, Rachel Nolan, and Heidi Orley, your thoughtful notes turned my manuscript into an actual book. Sandra DiCapua, Sarah Gronningsater, Isobel Morton, Rebecca Ritter, Leila Zegna—thank you for responding to my myriad emails and texts asking random questions about your lives as mothers and being a steady source of support and encouragement throughout. Anna Moody, Julia Siemon, and Rachel aka #Peppoli: our WhatsApp chain is my lifeline. Thank you for being my joint therapists, cheerleaders, and forever safe space.

To all the experts who took time out of their busy days to patiently explain rudimentary science, medicine, and psychology to me, bless you.

To Mike Steele, for not only happily reading multiple drafts but giving me the time and support to get this work done—you are a mensch. To Jake Bittle, for your excellent research skills—thank you for helping me ensure that what I wrote is as truthful as possible.

To Shannon Welch, Gideon Weil, and the rest of the wonderful team at HarperOne, thanks for taking a chance on me.

To my agents, Molly Atlas and Kari Stuart, who function not just as champions but line editors, psychiatrists, and career coaches, I feel lucky and honored to have you in my corner.

To Jess, thank you for your thoughtful notes and endless encouragement.

To Mom and Dad, I strive to be as good of a parent as you each are to me. It's a hard example to live up to, but know that it's my North Star.

And finally, to Dave, Ella, and Charlotte. Without you, I'm not me. I'm certain that together, we'll be able to weather whatever the world throws at us next, even if that's a virtual parenting coach that kicks data back to our corneas. I love you.

Index

AAP Council on Early Childhood, 168

abuse groups, 78

ADHD, relationship between screen time and, 196, 197

advertising: decision fatigue and relentless, 132–33; female consumers targeted by, 140–41; guilt-based, 142–44

Advertising to Women (Naether), 140

Airbnb, 145

Alexa device, 139

Allam, Roger, 189

Allo app, 81–85

alloparenting, 82

Amazon: Alexa, 139, 158; ancient toys still available on, 165; convenience of Subscribe and Save option of, 144; Echo Dot, 139; Prime, 144–45. *See also* e-commerce

Ambient Umbrella, 294

American Academy of Pediatrics (AAP): AAP Council on Early Childhood, 168; breastfeeding recommendations by, 33, 67; *Bright Futures Guidelines* by, 42; digital media guidelines (2016) of, 222; first six months sleeping recommendation by, 45, 288; The Power of Play movement, role of, 172; on reading aloud to children from birth, 254–55; screen-time guidelines by, 193, 199, 260; "Selecting Appropriate Toys for Young Children in the Digital Era" statement by, 167–69; SIDS task force of, 15, 50. *See also* pediatrics profession

American College of Obstetricians and Gynecologists, 88

American Demographics magazine, 140–41

Index

American Girl's Blaire Wilson doll, 167

American Museum of Natural History, 100

Ammari, Tawfiq, 77–80

Angry Birds, 157

Annie E. Casey Foundation, 257–58

anthropometry, 40–41

anti-vaccination movement, 78–79

Apple Watch, tracking sleep with, 6

apps: addictive powers of phones and, 222; considering educational potential of, 236–51; contingent response to using, 220; examining promise of, 232–36; impact of the iPad release (2010), 218–19; impact on parent-child relationship, 224–32; real-world experience vs., 216–17, 235; self-reflection questions on using, 221–22; study on parent–child interactions impacted by, 232–33; used to distract child, 216, 217–18, 222–23. *See also* iPads/tablets; iPhones

App Store: efforts to regulate quality of content, 249, 298; *Green Eggs and Ham* e-book app, 263–64; historical trajectory of, 234; "Read to me" button on e-books, 266; Sago Mini apps on, 235–37, 238–39, 241; Toca Boca apps on, 237, 249; toddler apps on, 233, 235–36

Arrival (film), 111

attention: the brain's Dorsal Attention Network (DAN) and Ventral Attention Network (VAN) and, 273–74; children's declining ability to focus, 275; consequences of constant disruptions on, 231–32; Levitin's proposals for facilitating, 54; state of flow and, 53–54; studies on television viewing and problems with, 196

attentional filter, 53–54

audiobooks, 274–75

autobiographical (or episodic) memory, 113–14

Babar (de Brunhoff), 255

Baby Brezza, 137, 138

Baby Games' app, 234

baby photographs. *See* photographs

babytech. *See* technology

Back to the Future (film), 105, 285

Bagatelle table game, 234

Bamba (peanut snack), 112–13

Barcelona Olympics, 269–70

Barnyard Dance! (Boynton), 266

the Beatles, 28

Beers, Ethel Lynn, 41

Bellevue Hospital, 168, 174–75, 175, 185

Belly Button Book! (Boynton), 266

Bensch, Chris, 166–67

Bentley, Amy, 35–36

Berkman Klein Center for Internet and Society (Harvard University), 121

Bernstein, Doug, 170

Bernstein, Melissa, 170–74

Index

Index

Index